Heidegger and Theology

D1564381

PHILOSOPHY AND THEOLOGY SERIES

Other titles in the Philosophy and Theology series include:

Heidegger and Theology

Judith Wolfe

B L O O M S B U R Y
LONDON • NEW DELHI • NEW YORK • SYDNEY

Bloomsbury T&T Clark

An imprint of Bloomsbury Publishing Plc

50 Bedford Square
London
WC1B 3DP
UK

1385 Broadway
New York
NY 10018
USA

www.bloomsbury.com

Bloomsbury is a registered trade mark of Bloomsbury Publishing Plc

First published 2014

British Library Cataloguing-in-Publication Data
A catalogue record for this book is available from the British Library.

ISBN: HB: 978-0-567-03375-8
PB: 978-0-567-03376-5
ePDF: 978-0-567-65623-0
epub: 978-0-567-65622-3

Library of Congress Cataloging-in-Publication Data
Wolfe, J. E. (Judith Elisabeth), 1979–
Heidegger and Theology/Judith Wolfe p.cm
Includes bibliographical references and index.
ISBN 978-0-567-03375-8 (hardcover) – ISBN 978-0-567-03376-5 (pbk.)

Typeset by Deanta Global Publishing Services, Chennai, India
Printed and bound in Great Britain

CONTENTS

NOTE ON THE TEXT

All translations are my own unless otherwise indicated, and endnote references are to original-language editions. Where English translations exist, they appear in the Bibliography immediately beneath the main, original-language entry.

All biblical quotations are from the *New Revised Standard Version* unless otherwise noted.

I am grateful to the Wingate Foundation for a grant facilitating the research of Chapters 4–6, and to Oxford University Press for permitting the use of some material previously presented in my monograph *Heidegger's Eschatology: Theological Horizons in Martin Heidegger's Early Thought* (Oxford University Press, 2013).

ABBREVIATIONS

Books & Editions

ESGA   Edith Stein Gesamtausgabe [Collected Works]

GA   Martin Heidegger Gesamtausgabe [Collected Works]

HJB   *Heidegger-Jahrbuch*

WA   Martin Luther Weimar Ausgabe [Weimar Edition]

Abbreviations are followed by volume number.

Correspondences

Arendt/Heidegger   H. Arendt/M. Heidegger: *Briefe 1925–1975*

Barth/Bultmann   K. Barth/R. Bultmann: *Briefwechsel 1911–1966*

Barth/Brunner   K. Barth/E. Brunner: *Briefwechsel 1911–1966*

Barth/Thurneysen   K. Barth/E. Thurneysen: *Briefwechsel 1913–1935* (**3 vols**)

Bultmann/Gogarten   R. Bultmann/F. Gogarten: *Briefwechsel 1921–1967*

Bultmann/Heidegger   R. Bultmann/M. Heidegger: *Briefwechsel 1925–1975*

Heidegger/Blochmann   M. Heidegger/E. Blochmann: *Briefwechsel 1918–1969*

Heidegger/Elfride Heidegger	*Mein liebes Seelchen!': Briefe Martin Heideggers an seine Frau Elfride, 1915–1970*
Heidegger/Jaspers	M. Heidegger/K. Jaspers: *Briefwechsel 1920–1963*
'Heidegger/Löwith'	'Drei Briefe Martin Heideggers an Karl Löwith'
Heidegger/Müller	M. Heidegger/M. Müller: *Briefe und andere Dokumente*
Heidegger/Rickert	M. Heidegger/H. Rickert: *Briefe 1912–1933*
Heidegger/Welte	M. Heidegger/B. Welte: *Briefe und Begegnungen*

Other abbreviations

KNS   Kriegsnotsemester (War Emergency Semester)

WS   Winter Semester

SS   Summer Semester

Introduction

Heidegger's relationship to theology is both complex and wide-ranging. A cradle Catholic originally intended for the priesthood, Heidegger's studies in philosophy led him to turn first to Protestantism and then to a resolutely a-theistic philosophical method, before returning, in later life, to a renewed engagement with his Catholic origins, guided by the conviction that 'one's origin always remains one's future'. Throughout his career, Heidegger's writings remained deeply indebted to theological themes and sources, and the question whether he has 'overcome' traditional theology or remains inadequate to it has been a subject of contention ever since his own day.

This book offers theologians and philosophers alike a clear and nuanced account of the sources, directions and interdisciplinary potential of this debate. It recounts Heidegger's own theological-philosophical path (often with reference to manuscripts only recently made available in German) and analyses the role of theology in his major writings, including his lectures during the Nazi era. It reviews the reception of Heidegger's thought both by theologians of his own day and by those of recent times, offering suggestions for theology's possible future engagement with Heidegger's work throughout.

The first six chapters of the book chart and analyse Heidegger's life-long engagement with theology, theorizing from a position of empirical strength established by the use of newly available German texts both of Heidegger's own writings and of other archival material, contextualized within the church-political and theological debates of his university career. In the years 1909–15, Heidegger, originally immersed in an anti-Modernist Roman Catholic milieu, gradually dissociated himself from post-Vatican I Catholicism against the background of his growing sense of the importance

of philosophical questions '*as questions*'. By this he chiefly meant
two things: one, the epistemological questions about metaphysics
posed first by Kant and now by Husserlian phenomenology;
and two, the problem of 'historicity' for an understanding both
of individual human existence (as inherently temporal) and of
Christianity (as a historically situated and developing religion).
Searching for a theological method capable of doing justice to
lived experience rather than remaining entrenched in a statically
conceived *philosophia perennis*, Heidegger, after 1915, began to
develop a synthesis of Schleiermacher's and the medieval mystics'
'proto-phenomenology' with an emphasis on the basic religious
experience of affliction – suffering our own finitude – which he
found in the early Luther, Friedrich Hölderlin, Fyodor Dostoevsky,
Søren Kierkegaard and Franz Overbeck.

These concerns converged on a re-appropriation of early
Christian eschatology in Heidegger's thought of the early 1920s,
within the context of similar but competing appropriations by
other theological thinkers of the time, especially Karl Barth
and Eduard Thurneysen. Following a dominant interpretation in
early-twentieth-century Protestant scholarship, Heidegger posited, in
the early 1920s, a profound irreconcilability of earliest ('authentic')
Christian experience – centrally characterized by eschatological
expectation – on the one hand, and the subsequent development –
when this expectation failed to materialize – of a Christian 'philosophy' on the other. Building on his phenomenological analysis of
affliction with our own finitude as the basic religious experience,
Heidegger now found in early Christian eschatological expectation
an instantiation *par excellence* of authentic religious existence. His
description of this expectant restlessness, however, is fundamentally
at odds with its original Christian context, for Heidegger's commitment to a phenomenological description of the human situation –
that is, a description of that situation solely from within – leads
him to divorce the 'existential' experience of expectation from
its (from this perspective merely 'existentiell' or derivatively
postulated) object, the 'blessed hope' of the coming Kingdom of
God. As a consequence, that hope no longer appears as constitutive
of, but rather as fundamentally inimical to 'eschatological' unrest as
Heidegger understands it, because it projects an end to that unrest,
and so a cancellation of the nexus of authentic existence.

Against the Christian vision, Heidegger thus developed, in the mid-1920s, an eschatology without eschaton that found paradigmatic expression in his account of being-unto-death, and underlay both his critique of theology ('Phenomenology and Theology', 1927) and his re-conception of metaphysics ('What is Metaphysics?', 1929). On this account, one's own being is, at the deepest level, a *question* for each person. This question cannot be answered or resolved in any traditional sense, because the consummation of human existence – death – is at the same time its negation. Authentic existence is the resolute anticipation of this perpetual, inavertible and inescapably personal possibility – it is being-unto-death.

The years following the composition of *Being and Time* and Heidegger's return to Freiburg as Chair in Philosophy and, briefly, university rector, are notoriously difficult for an interpretation of Heidegger's path as a whole: His brief but enthusiastic embrace of Nazism and adulation for Hitler threaten to compromise both his preceding and his subsequent philosophical thought. I propose a reading of Heidegger's year-long participation in the Nazis' programme of university reform as a serious misstep motivated by a vision for spiritual reform which he briefly believed to be shared by the National Socialist movement, but soon discovered to be fundamentally incompatible with their 'blood and soil' ideology. This spiritual reform was to be rooted in a Hölderlinian vision of the 'god to come' answering to Heidegger's aspiration (already signalled in the final paragraphs of *Being and Time*) to formulate a collective or national counterpart to the individual 'eschatology without eschaton' of his early work. In the late 1930s and 1940s, this collective eschatology became increasingly resolutely a-political, and Hölderlin not a harbinger of Hitler but a prophet of the unknown 'last god'.

The 1930s also marked, for Heidegger, a period of institutional strife with the Catholic Church (which had imposed a church-controlled Chair on the Philosophy Faculty) and personal struggle with the faith of his youth. He emerged from these conflicts with a new appreciation for the value of alienation from one's own inalienable roots: only through such personal experience, Heidegger thought, could the uprootedness or 'godforsakenness' of the present age be adequately felt and thus expressed. Heidegger's late work is, among other things, an attempt to valorize this 'godforsakenness' philosophically, rejecting the damaging, falsely claimed god's-eye-view of a world-enframing metaphysics in favour of an attitude of a calm receptivity to the world and to the potential inbreaking of a yet-unknown 'god'.

The last two chapters of this book turn to theological engagements with Heidegger, first among those who knew him and then by readers of his work to the present day. Heidegger maintained a close and life-long friendship with Rudolf Bultmann, but had strained interactions, both direct and indirect, with the other members of 'dialectical theology', which acted as catalysts for some of the most acute theological disagreements within that movement. Later in life, he also developed friendships with some of his younger Catholic colleagues, especially Max Müller and Bernhard Welte – friendships which modelled some of the approaches Heidegger himself regarded as most constructive in a theological engagement with his work.

If the penultimate chapter charts these personal interactions, the final chapter aims to provide an intellectual genealogy and map of the subsequent theological reception of Heidegger. I discuss the two main lines of criticism – which may be described as the Barthian and the neo-Thomist critique – before turning to the range of attempts to make Heidegger's work fruitful for theology. These are presented within the heuristic categories 'Existential Theology' (represented here by Rudolf Bultmann, Paul Tillich and John Macquarrie), 'Phenomenology and Thomism' (represented here by Karl Rahner and Edith Stein) and 'Post-Metaphysical Theology' (represented here in English by John Caputo and Merold Westphal, and in French by Jean-Luc Marion). I situate each vis-à-vis Heidegger's own development of thought, provide references to important work in the area, and then usually follow out a particular argument or strand of engagement, with the aim of showing some of the continuing potential of the relevant form of reception and whetting the reader's appetite for further work.

This book is written for (at least) two distinct types of readership. For students of theology who would like to know more about Heidegger, or students of Heidegger first encountering his engagement with theology, it aims to serve as a reliable introduction to this complex relationship in both its biographical and intellectual dimensions, in Heidegger's own life and work as well as its theological reception.

For specialists in the field, it aims to offer fresh information, interpretations and perspectives, often drawing on newly available source material, much of which remains untranslated into English. In this capacity, the book also aims to rectify a range of prevailing misconceptions and stale half-truths that have become entrenched in English-language scholarship on Heidegger and theology. The book avoids polemics that are, or hopefully soon will be, unnecessary, but the knowing and interested reader will find many implicit disagreements made explicit in the endnotes.

This dual implied readership means that although this book aims to cover the full range of Heidegger's engagement with theology, and theology's engagement with him, it pays relatively more attention to less-well-known texts and connections than to those about which a large volume of literature already exists: thus, for example, Heidegger's interactions with dialectical theology are treated in more detail than his reception by 'post-metaphysical' theologians, about which there is a large and ever-growing literature. Similarly, Heideggerian texts and testimonies that remain untranslated or hard to access – especially letters, manuscript notes and his earliest writings – are discussed more fully than the usual proof texts of theological discussions of Heidegger, for which particular aspects or lines of enquiry are highlighted, rather than basic summaries given. When this is the case, full bibliographies of extant secondary sources are provided in the endnotes.

A word about terminology and translation: Heidegger's language is notoriously difficult to translate. Sometimes this is for the usual reason that makes all academic German a headache for translators, namely its almost boundless tolerance for compound nouns or denominal adjectives. This means that even a notoriously long (but, to native speakers, otherwise entirely innocuous) compound such as *Donaudampfschifffahrtsgesellschaftskapitänskajüte* can function with all the grammatical versatility of a single noun, while the English equivalent, 'the cabin of a captain of the Danube Steamship Company' is an unwieldy string of prepositions or possessives. This is bad enough in the nominal form; but Heidegger, like most German scholars, has a predilection for using such compounds as denominal adjectives. Thus, he talks not only about *Seinsgeschichte* ('the history of being') but also, indeed more frequently, about *seinsgeschichtliche Entwicklungen* ('developments within the history of being'), *seinsgeschichtliche Einsichten* ('insights pertaining to the history of being'), etc. The English translator must either render these by means of intolerably clumsy adjectival phrases, or create direct calques that are grammatically manoeuvrable but semantically impenetrable: No doubt we would all dearly like to follow the commentator's advice, for example, to 'keep in mind the being-historical-enowning insight into the flight of gods and its implications' . . . if only we knew what he meant.[1]

However, what makes Heidegger not only predictably but also uniquely difficult to translate is that – partly owing to and partly fuelling his understanding of intellectual history – he sees it as one of his tasks as a philosopher to uncover again the intuitions and meanings already inherent in the German language or its source languages, and does so through a constant appeal to etymologies as well as the coinage of etymologizing neologisms. In his later work, Heidegger intensifies his idiosyncratic language use even further, because he comes to see language as, at its most authentic, evocative rather than denotative, and as aiming to lead us back to old-familiar truths rather than delineating new ones. All this means that Heidegger's philosophical insights are often instrumentally (and, sometimes at least, arguably also logically) dependent on the origins of particular German terms. Because the relevant English terms do not usually have the same etymology – English 'guilt' does not have the economic provenance of German *Schuld*, and English 'serenity' is not, like German *Gelassenheit*, a nominal version of the passive voice of 'to let be' – this kind of etymological use is impossible to render into English in a natural way. Retention of the etymologies contained in Heidegger's use is thus often purchased at the price of the word to which they were attached: monstrous calques like 'enowning' (for German *Ereignis*) and 'releasement' (for German *Gelassenheit*), designed to keep the German etymologies before the reader's eyes, have made 'Heideggerian' a byword for 'obscure' in non-Heideggerian philosophical circles.

Positively viewed, however, this makes translation a natural testing ground for the cogency of Heidegger's philosophy. It may be necessary to lose the insight (inherent, at its best, in Heidegger's philosophical etymologies) that a certain philosophical truth is already contained in an everyday German word. Nor is this a minor loss: part of Heidegger's argument, after all, is that we already have a pre-discursive (or rather, un-rationalized) understanding of being and its manifestations, and this is demonstrated in part by the words we already use every day, even if we are not always aware of the meanings embedded in them. Yet this claim, though by no means marginal, is to some extent subsidiary to the philosophical insights or claims themselves. And these insights ought, in principle, to be reconstructable even without the aid of etymology (even if etymology may first have set the philosopher on their trail).

It is in this sense that translation becomes a testing ground of the cogency of Heidegger's philosophy. Sometimes, removing the crutch of a language-specific double meaning makes the entire argument seem a bit shaky: Thus, the fact that the German word *Schuld* (debt/guilt) has its origin in the economic language of credit and debt is not in itself sufficient ground for arguing (as Heidegger does) that the Christian experience of guilt is merely a contingent or 'existentiell' outworking of the universal or 'existential' experience of debt which attends our being 'thrown into' a world not of our own making. At other times, however, arguments are less poetically satisfying but no less cogent when distilled from their etymological source: that serenity involves an ascetic letting-be of the world is perfectly comprehensible with or without philological prompting.

Although keenly aware of the central and irreplaceable role of Heidegger's original language, then, I think it is perhaps more important that readers (particularly students as yet relatively unfamiliar with Heidegger) see that Heidegger's philosophy retains much of its cogency in ordinary English language. Wherever possible in this book, therefore, I have translated key Heideggerian terms by ordinary English words. Where relevant, I note other common translations and briefly explain the additional meanings and connotations of the German originals, but I will generally not attempt to keep them continually before the reader's mind through idiosyncratic translations. This is not, of course, ultimately enough. Robert Frost's adage, 'poetry is what gets lost in translation', is as true here as ever, and if Heidegger believes, as he does, that man, at his truest, 'dwells poetically on earth', then some of the force particularly of his late thought can never ultimately be reproduced by translation, but only transposed – and thus at once validated and altered – by the utterance of a native English philosophical poetry. (A different sort of book than this one might, for example, make a case for T. S. Eliot's late poetry as an English, and religiously inflected, anticipation of Heidegger's German thought.) But just as Heidegger's philosophy aims to be an indication of 'paths, not works', this introductory volume will have done its work if it does no more or less than to set its readers on their own paths of engagement with Heidegger and theology.

Note

1 Parvis Emad, *On the Way to Heidegger's Contributions to Philosophy* (Madison, WI: University of Wisconsin Press, 2007), p. 178.

1

Heidegger's Catholicism
(1889–1915)

Heidegger's home: Ultramontanism and anti-modernism

Martin Heidegger was born in 1889 in the small town of Messkirch in Baden, a semi-autonomous Grand Duchy in Southern Germany. His father was sexton and cooper at the local Roman Catholic church, and the Heidegger family lived in a Church-owned house near the parish church. This was a difficult time for Roman Catholics. Historically a Catholic state, Baden still had a predominantly Catholic population: two thirds – rising to more than nine tenths in rural districts – were Roman Catholics.[1] However, the majority of Catholics were rural and other manual labourers who lived in villages and small towns away from the centres of power, and remained marginalized in the political and cultural life of the time. This marginalization also had to do with the resistance to current trends written into Roman Catholicism: the consolidation of the German *Reich* under Kaiser Wilhelm and Chancellor Bismarck did not sit well with traditional Catholic ultramontanism, that is, its general orientation towards the pope in Rome. Similarly, the liberalism of German Protestantism (which was also the driving force of national education and culture) went against the nineteenth-century Catholic resistance to modern trends. In the decades preceding Heidegger's birth, the Catholic Church had tried to gain more independence from the increasingly overbearing influence of Protestant Prussia and of Baden's own liberal Protestant cabinet, particularly by gaining or maintaining control of its denominational education and appointments. Although this *Baden Kulturkampf* was neither as drastic nor as hostile as Bismarck's own *Kulturkampf* in Prussia, it resulted in an increasing sense of marginalization and oppression on the part of Catholics, and so stoked a political and intellectual backlash in which the young Martin became directly caught up.

In Messkirch, and especially in the sexton's family, the ultramontanist and anti-modernist cause had a particularly high profile. In the decades before Martin's birth, a majority of the Messkirch population had, for a time, joined the Old Catholic movement, relinquishing strict adherence to Rome in favour of a more autonomous and local Catholic life. From the 1870s until the re-establishment of Roman Catholicism in 1895, Martin's father was among a small minority of ultramontanists, a commitment which incurred discrimination and even, for a while, the loss of the home (which belonged to the parish church).[2]

Martin could not fail to imbibe some of this entrenched religious commitment. The oldest son of the family, he was intended for the priesthood from an early age, and was sent to the (recently re-opened) episcopal schools in Constance and then in Freiburg from 1903 to 1909. The local community, once more rallied around Rome, also encouraged support for the ultramontanist cause by founding the Catholic daily *Heuberger Volksblatt* (1899). The ensuing (and locally famous) 'Messkirch newspaper war' between the *Volksblatt* and the liberal local daily *Oberbadischer Grenzbote* (founded 1872) continued until the demise of the Weimar Republic, and became the main local vehicle for carrying out the modernist controversy in Baden.[3] The *Volksblatt* was both Heidegger's first organ and one of our primary sources for his early public activities, which are often enthusiastically reported in its pages.

The dominant intellectual and cultural aspect of Heidegger's Catholic milieu was its so-called anti-modernism. The First Vatican Council of 1870, with its formal declaration of papal infallibility, had established the Catholic Church as a fiercely counter-cultural and, to some extent, counter-political body. In the intellectual sphere, this opposition was directed against a wide range of trends which were seen as threats to a traditional Catholic understanding of existence, knowledge, faith and morality. In 1907, Pope Pius XI published an encyclical entitled *Pascendi dominici gregis* ('Feeding the Lord's flock'), in which he summarized these trends and threats under the term 'modernism', slated as 'the synthesis of all heresies'.[4] The term 'modernism' remained notoriously multivalent throughout the ensuing *Modernismusstreit* (modernist crisis), but was generally agreed to include methodical agnosticism (the use of secular methods in theology), vital immanentism (an understanding of religion as primarily a matter of feeling and experience), symbolism (the view that doctrines are only symbols of inner beliefs) and evolutionism (the view that authority and dogma undergo historical development).[5]

At home and in school, Heidegger imbibed a distinctly anti-modernist attitude.[6] The pugnacious counter-cultural perfectionism of the anti-modernist movement suited his own temperament, and in his final school years, according to his headmaster's graduation report of September 1909, he decided to seek admittance to the Jesuits, the most vocally anti-modernist society within the Church.[7]

Martin's 'passion for apologetics'[8] soon came to public notice. On 6 September 1909, he presided over a 200th-anniversary celebration of Abraham a Sancta Clara (1644–1709), an Augustinian priest-orator from the nearby Kreenheinstetten. Abraham was revered as a patron by the literary circle surrounding the famous anti-modernist historian and writer Richard von Kralik,[9] whose project of a cultural renewal based on Catholic principles strongly attracted the 20-year-old Heidegger. At the anniversary celebration, he encouraged all young people present to subscribe to Kralik's journal *Gral* and 'become its disciples'.[10] The rival Catholic journal *Hochland*, Martin opined, should be shunned for 'sailing more and more in the fairway of Modernism'.[11] His speech was recorded enthusiastically in the *Heuburger Volksblatt*.

From 1909 to 1910, Heidegger also contributed directly to the 'newspaper war' by writing polemical pieces for the *Volksblatt* as well as several conservative Catholic journals, especially *Der Akademiker* and *Allgemeine Rundschau*.[12] The rhetoric of these essays is typical of the anti-modernist literature of the period, but also reflects emphases and concerns that are distinctly and recognizably Heidegger's. Modernist attitudes, in these short pieces, are to be despised because they emerge from and encourage weakness, delusion, and enslavement to the superficial, ephemeral and 'low'. Similar emphases, though with very different philosophical and political backgrounds, will persist in his critique of 'the crowd' (*das*

Man) in the late 1920s, and his short-lived support for National Socialism in the early 1930s.[13]

Heidegger's earliest known publication is a lyrical short story about the dramatic conversion of a young atheist on All Souls Day, published in November 1909. It opens with a damning description of the urban 'Moderns', whose wilful confusion of their 'passion [for] lust' for 'intelligence' and 'freedom' has so deluded and sapped their strength that they can no longer distinguish the 'dark, agonising night' from sunlight, and 'no longer hear the clangour' of the 'chains' in which they 'drag their tired, overwrought body through existence'.[14] In evading the divine judgement call that sounds in the bells of All Souls' morning, these 'Moderns' run away from 'seriousness', which 'only befits the strong': 'The feeble soul, the dull, creeping soul flees from the redemptive seriousness of life which is eager to overcome; it shirks the self-reflection which is glad to make sacrifices.'[15] In a book review in March 1910, Heidegger assimilates this contrast to Darwinist biology, which, during this period, he regards as a particularly fascinating corroboration of Christian belief.[16] Just as all 'higher life is predicated on the demise of the lower forms', he argues in the review, so the higher, 'spiritual life' requires the 'killing' of 'what is low' in oneself.

In a May 1910 review of a work by the moral philosopher Friedrich Wilhelm Foerster, Heidegger transposes these concerns to a philosophical register.[17] While the modernists demand free scientific enquiry and free thought, he argues after Foerster, true freedom of thought and joy of life require a habit of self-discipline: 'Truly *free* thinking', as Foerster puts it, 'presupposes an heroic act of moral self-liberation'.[18] Heidegger echoes this conviction almost *verbatim* elsewhere: 'Strict logical thinking that hermetically seals itself off from all affective influences of the emotions, all *truly* presupposition-less scholarly work, requires a certain fund of ethical power, the art of self-collection and self-emptying.'[19] Such self-liberation, however, according to Foerster, can only be achieved through obedience to the Catholic Tradition: 'Not *I* should judge the highest Tradition from my perspective, but I should learn to evaluate myself in a wholly new way from *its* perspective: That is true emancipation, that is the service which firm objective authority can render the personal life.'[20]

Intellectual honesty or objectivity is here coextensive with personal truthfulness or '*Wahrhaftigkeit*' (authenticity). Church doctrine is authoritative precisely because it contains not only factual truth but also the 'light of truth' that enables an authentic life. Heidegger echoes this idea in the conclusion of his Foerster review, borrowing the language of the Judeo-Christian Wisdom tradition. Here as ever after, Heidegger displays a remarkable sensitivity to the vision implicit in a particular language or semantic field; in this case, the fact that the biblical Wisdom genre inflects the classical ideal of knowledge with a specifically moral and spiritual emphasis culminating, for the Christian, in the Incarnation of the 'Wisdom of God' (1 Cor. 1.24):

> To him who has never set foot on straying paths [cf. Ps 1.1; Prov 1.15, 2.18, 4.14] and has not been blinded by the deceptive dazzle of the modern spirit; who can dare to walk through life in the radiance of truth, in true, deep, well-grounded offering-up of self [cf. Wis 9.11]; to him, this book bears tidings of great joy [cf. Lk 2.10], and conveys again with startling clarity the high joy of possessing the truth.[21]

Several themes with which readers of Heidegger will be familiar from his later work are reflected in this brief review of his earliest writings. The terms of his denunciation of 'the Moderns' are cognate with those he later develops in relation to 'the crowd' or *das Man*.[22] Similarly, his call to overcome this inauthentic mode of existence by opening oneself to the light of truth within which humans live and know anticipates his development, in the 1915 qualifying thesis and more radically in later writings, of the Scholastic doctrine of the convertibility of *ens* and *verum*, which implies (for Heidegger in 1915) that beings are 'true' (i.e. are capable of *manifestativa sui*) because they participate in Being (here associated with God), whose essence includes *communicabilitas sui*.[23] At the same time, these earliest texts present radically different requisites than Heidegger's later writings for the achievement of 'authenticity', or an existence true to one's 'essence' – differences signalled by the fact that 'authenticity' is not here characterized as '*Eigentlichkeit*' (mine-ness) but as '*Entselbstung*' (offering-up of self). These differences will concern us again in the next few chapters.

The 'Exciting Years' of 1910–1914

On 30 September 1909, Heidegger travelled to join the Jesuits, who at the time had their novitiate house in Western Austria, their German settlements still being banned by Bismarck. He completed a two-week candidacy for the novitiate, but was dismissed at the end of that period, probably because of an early manifestation of his chronic heart problems.[24] Martin nevertheless remained intent on becoming a priest, and in the winter semester of 1909/10 enrolled at the University of Freiburg as a student of Catholic theology – a course reserved, at the time, for candidates for the priesthood. However, in the middle of the third semester of the course, in February 1911, his career changed abruptly. Heidegger had to break off his studies due to a violent outbreak of his heart condition, and was forced to spend the summer semester in Messkirch to recuperate. When he returned to university in the winter semester of 1911/12, he did not continue his theology studies, but switched to the Philosophy Faculty and graduated in philosophy and mathematics in 1912. He completed a short doctoral dissertation in philosophy in 1913, and a *Habilitationsschrift* or 'qualifying thesis' – the customary post-doctoral thesis required to qualify as a university lecturer – on 'Duns Scotus' Doctrine of Categories and Signification' in 1915.[25]

The change of academic tracks marked a radical caesura in Heidegger's path, whose causes and reasons remain uncertain and controversial. Heidegger himself gave drastically differing accounts over the following ten years – accounts which may well map his shifting allegiances and aspirations over those years more accurately than they do the actual events of 1911. In a 1915 *curriculum vitae* submitted to the Catholic Philosophy Department in Freiburg, Heidegger presented the change as a forced decision, brought about by his heart condition, which, he was apparently informed at the time, rendered a clerical career 'extremely doubtful', and so practically barred him from continuing a vocational course in theology.[26] In a 1922 *curriculum vitae* sent to the Protestant philosopher Georg Misch, by contrast, Heidegger claimed that the decision was deliberate and decidedly theological:

> The direction in which my theological-philosophical studies led me during my first semesters was such that I left . . . in Spring 1911 and gave up my theological studies, because I could not

take upon myself the "Modernist oath" which had then been made mandatory.[27]

It should be noted right away that neither account can quite be taken at face value: both were written for specific purposes, one while Heidegger was still a Catholic and applying for funding from a Catholic foundation, the other when he had left the Catholic Church and was hoping for an academic post in a Protestant institution.[28] Still, the anti-Modernist oath mentioned in the 1922 CV clearly shook Heidegger, and it is worth probing a little further into this episode.

On 1 September 1910, Pope Pius X promulgated a *motu proprio* entitled *Sacrorum Antistitum*, which controversially demanded that 'all clergy, pastors, confessors, preachers, religious superiors, and professors in philosophical-theological seminaries' swear an 'Oath against Modernism'.[29] The oath committed its professors to reject the 'modernist' denials of the possibility of natural knowledge of God, of the unchanging truth of revelation and doctrine, and of the historical reality of miracles, prophecies and Christ himself. It also forbade Catholic scholars from acceding to the ill-conceived 'scholarly' demand that 'historico-theological subjects' should be investigated on purely historical-scientific principles, without regard for 'the supernatural origin of Catholic tradition or . . . the divine promise of help to preserve all revealed truth forever'. Against these 'errors', the oath affirmed the Church's divinely bestowed 'charism of truth', handed down 'absolute and immutable' from the apostles and therefore an incontestable criterion for all (Christian) scholarship.

In Freiburg as in many other universities, the promulgation of the anti-modernist oath incited a heated controversy between the Catholic-Theological Faculty and the Academic Senate over the question of scholarly objectivity, centring on the question whether or not theologians who took the oath thereby *mutatis mutandis* compromised their scholarly credibility. The controversy steadily intensified from November 1910 to March 1911, and was finally resolved in July 1911, when the local government in Karlsruhe enforced a compromise, allowing the continued appointment to academic posts of priests who had professed the oath. Even after this resolution, however, an ill-concealed animosity persisted between the Senate and the Catholic-Theological Faculty.[30]

Although Heidegger did not openly protest against the Oath (the 1922 *curriculum vitae* is the first indication of the possible magnitude of its impact on him at the time), the tone of his publications noticeably changes after its promulgation. His engagement with F. W. Foerster (as well as the Catholic scholars Carl Braig and Herman Schell) had given him the intellectual means for constructing an account of scholarly objectivity on which objectivity was not in conflict with, but rather facilitated by, Catholic commitment. Nevertheless, after 1911, Heidegger's attitude to this account was no longer the pre-critical triumphalism displayed vis-à-vis the 'Moderns' in the 1910 Foerster review. Rather than as an asset provided by the Church, the possibility of (objective) knowledge began to appear as a *question*. In a 1911 article in the *Heuberger Volksblatt*, Heidegger called upon Catholic scholars to confront this question: 'By freedom of research we understand freedom from all preconceived opinions and unproven assumptions in the examination of scholarly (specifically, philosophical-historical) questions. This is a problem that philosophical-theological epistemology has to solve.'[31]

Heidegger's formulation of the problem reveals his distance – less perhaps in substance than in methodology – from the papal position. By affirming the validity and urgency of 'philosophical-historical' questions, as well as the need for a 'philosophical-theological epistemology', Heidegger implicitly challenges Pius' dismissal of these subjects as deplorable outgrowths of 'Kantian philosophy', 'German Idealism', or 'Protestant theology' (terms Pius uses interchangeably in contrast to orthodox 'Scholasticism').

Indeed, it is critical to understand that in Pius' writings and the general discourse of the time, 'Scholasticism' came to refer as much to a methodology as to a philosophical system. And it was Scholasticism in this methodological sense which became, for the young Heidegger, unsustainable.[32] Thus, while he could quite truthfully assert in his 1915 CV that his 'fundamental philosophical convictions [have] remained those of Aristotelian-Scholastic philosophy', his best friend, Ernst Laslowski, also warned him in the same year to be '*careful* in judgments about Scholasticism' (here in a methodological sense) so as not to endanger his future career.[33] Heidegger made a similar distinction in a 1913 letter to Heinrich Rickert, his prospective post-doctoral supervisor. In response to Rickert's suggestion to take as his thesis topic an interpretation of Duns Scotus by means of modern (i.e. neo-Kantian) logic, Heidegger wrote: 'I must say that my own fundamental philosophical convictions are different at the same time, I certainly don't want to go along with the familiar, pathetic method of seeing in modern philosophy nothing but a string of "errors," a progeny of "godlessness" and so forth.'[34]

Pius X's *motu proprio 'Doctoris Angelici'* of 1914, declaring the teaching of Thomas Aquinas the sole authoritative philosophy of the Catholic Church, exacerbated this frustration with the perceived Catholic failure to engage with modern philosophy. In a letter to Engelbert Krebs in July of the same year, Heidegger acerbically commented: 'The *motu proprio* about philosophy was really the cherry on the cake. Perhaps you as an "academic" could apply for an even better procedure to gut the brain of anyone who dares to have an independent thought, and replace it with "Italian salad".'[35] His own ambition was a rejuvenation of Scholastic theology that would avoid the weaknesses of modernism (as diagnosed, not least, in his own earliest work) without being trapped in the stultifying overload of neo-Scholastic presuppositions. In this endeavour, he had a number of Catholic models, most importantly his teacher Carl Braig and the Würzburg apologist Herman Schell, whose efforts to integrate Scholastic metaphysics and the German Idealist tradition Heidegger followed with interest. But the young Heidegger also began to work out his own distinctive criteria for a Catholic philosophy that was both honest and robust – above all, its integration of the insights of modern discoveries in logic and history.

Models and sources

One of the results of Heidegger's philosophical studies was a mounting dissatisfaction with the inability or unwillingness of neo-Scholasticism as a philosophical method to 'encounter philosophical problems as problems'[36] – in other words, its tendency to gloss over, or presuppose simplistic answers to, basic questions such as the relation between objects and knowledge, or the human experience of time. These two seemingly disparate fields – knowledge (or logic) and history – played an increasingly important role in his thinking, and were intertwined in the theory of religious experience which

Heidegger began to develop in his post-doctoral thesis of 1915. It is worth looking at both of them in turn.

From 1912, Heidegger wrote a number of texts concerned with contemporary developments in logic, leading up to his doctoral dissertation *The Doctrine of Judgment in Psychologism* (1913) and his qualifying thesis *Duns Scotus' Doctrine of Categories and Signification* (1915, published with an added conclusion in 1916).[37] His leading philosophical question at the time was the relation between object and perception and between perception and thinking, as requisite for a theory of objects (*Gegenstandslehre*)[38] and of judgement.[39] At least until 1916, Heidegger was hopeful that his developing response could draw from and even strengthen Scholasticism as a philosophical system, whose fundamentally realist, anti-psychologistic perspective he regarded as indispensable, and as consonant with the 'critical realism' he was encountering in, among others, the work of Edmund Husserl.[40]

The importance of a realist attitude, for Heidegger, lay in its assertion that thinking is determined by the object, not *vice versa* – in other words, its rejection of psychologism and contrary assertion of the knowability of the world around us. One of the most consequential changes of mind Heidegger underwent as a student concerned the question whether or not Kant could be read as advancing a realist epistemology. In early 1912, Heidegger still regarded the Königsberg philosopher as irreducibly subjectivist.[41] In the ensuing year, however, his attitude to Kant shifted dramatically, bringing with it a host of other changes.

As already mentioned, after 1911 Heidegger became increasingly frustrated with the lack of an adequate epistemology within neo-Scholasticism, and with the resultant dogmatism both about the constitution of objects of perception and about the nature of judgements.[42] It was precisely these problems which he now found addressed in Kant's transcendental-logical discoveries, especially as interpreted by the Baden School of his own teacher Heinrich Rickert.[43] In late 1912, Heidegger explained to his Catholic readers that Kant's critique, interpreted correctly, did not (as he himself had previously believed) 'enquire after the psychological origin of knowledge, but after the logical value of its validity'.[44] In 1914, engaging with a recent Catholic work on Aristotle and Kant, he challenged the uncritical neo-Scholastic reliance on Aristotle, and called for a properly critical perspective among 'Aristotelian-Scholastic' philosophers.[45] Aristotle's (seemingly presupposition-free) acceptance of objects of perception as 'given' or 'complete', Heidegger now argued, in fact relied on his theory of movement and the first mover, and was thus 'heavily metaphysically loaded from the start'; consequently, his epistemology was 'much more encumbered by presuppositions' than Kant's, who succeeded in 'making the object of knowledge itself (not as really existing, but according to its significance), and with it the knowledge of the object, the problem'.[46] In his qualifying thesis, to which we will return in a moment, Heidegger developed his own provisional response to this problem in dialogue with both the Kantian trajectory – above all its renewal by Husserl – and medieval 'speculative grammar'.

Alongside his engagement with logic, Heidegger remembers an 'awakening interest' in Fichte, Schelling and Hegel in the years 1911–14.[47] This interest was mediated primarily through his dogmatics professor Carl Braig[48] and through Hermann Schell, a Würzburg apologist whose work Heidegger greatly valued as a student.[49] Both Braig and Schell were progenies of the mid-nineteenth-century Catholic Tübingen School, which Heidegger (who called Braig its last exponent) praised as giving 'rank and breadth to Catholic theology through engagement with Hegel and Schelling'.[50] Spearheaded by J. A. Möhler (1796–1838) and developed the following generation by J. E. Kuhn and others, the Catholic Tübingen School was a prominent school of speculative theology which sought an in-depth engagement of Catholic theology with contemporary philosophy, particularly German Idealism and Romanticism, in the service of a renewed appreciation of Catholic doctrine. Though it is now usually eclipsed by the more prominent contemporaneous Protestant movement of the same name, its importance for several generations of Catholic scholars was immense. Braig himself had studied with Kuhn in Tübingen, and continued his programme in his own dogmatics lectures, which Heidegger attended from winter 1910/11 to summer 1912,[51] remembering later how much their speculative approach and penetrating intelligence impressed him.[52] From Braig, Heidegger recalls in 1963, he 'heard for the first time about the significance of Schelling and Hegel for speculative theology as contrasted with the doctrinal system of Scholasticism'.[53] Concomitantly, Heidegger privately read the work of Hermann Schell (1850–1906), who had developed a speculative approach to apologetics which, in 1898, led to the temporary inclusion of several of his books in the Roman Index. In Schell, Heidegger confesses in his 1915 CV, he found a philosophical approach more satisfactory than those offered either in his prescribed philosophy lectures or in his private reading of 'Scholastic textbooks'.[54]

Both Braig and Schell emphasized the significance of temporality for an understanding of God. Braig, a strong opponent of psychologism, was particularly interested in the historically oriented idealism of Hegel.[55] Heidegger assimilated this interest sometime between 1912 and 1915, a process reflected in the stark contrast between his disparaging remarks about the Idealist philosopher in the 1912 essay 'The Problem of Reality in Modern Philosophy',[56] and the 1916 conclusion of his qualifying thesis, which culminates in the declaration that the great and immediate task of any 'philosophy of living spirit, active love, and reverential ardency for God' such as Heidegger envisions, is a 'fundamental critical engagement with that system of historical worldview which, exceeding all others in breadth and depth, wealth of experience and concept-formation, has sublated all previous fundamental philosophical problem-motifs into itself – that of Hegel'.[57]

Schell adhered to what he called a 'dynamic Thomism', which identified 'the true nature' of Thomism as 'trust in the power of reason, the absolute validity of the law of causality, [and] the strictly empirical foundation of all our scientific knowledge'[58] – in short, as rationalist realism. On this methodological understanding of *'philosophia perennis'*, the *perennitas* of Catholic truth manifests itself precisely in its ability to be applied to 'everything new and vigorous'.[59] The role of apologetics in relation to this truth is that of a 'philosophical critical-speculative *Begründungswissenschaft*' which can and must remain accountable to *'all the ideals and demands* of the scientifically and historically matured spirit'.[60] The theological correlate of this understanding, which at the same time served as its theological justification, was Schell's Hegelian re-conceptualization of the aseity of God in terms not of a static *ratio sui* but of a dynamic *causa sui*: for Schell, God is pure Being, positing itself and actuating itself in thought and act.[61] This dynamic conception of God (which was partly responsible for Schell's temporary inclusion in the Index) also facilitated a conception of Christian truth as inherently open to development.[62]

Alongside the discovery of Hegel and Schelling, Heidegger also mentions the publication of Dilthey's *Collected Works* as one of the events particularly noteworthy in the period 1910–14. This is not because they marked his first encounter with Wilhelm Dilthey (1833–1911), but rather because they made work he already prized significantly more accessible: Dilthey's hermeneutics were a significant influence on the young philosopher from 1909 onwards.[63] An important goal of historiography, for Dilthey, is to grasp the individual, who is 'an intrinsic value in the world of human spirit', rather than to reduce the individual to a part in some larger system.[64] This is the case because history is not brute facts, but both constituted and grasped in and by 'moods' (*Lebensstimmung*), 'colorations' (*Färbung*) or 'hermeneutics' (*Auslegung*) unique to each individual.[65] Consequently, we should first of all 'observe without prejudice the reality of our inner life and, proceeding from there . . . establish the meaning of nature and history for this inner life'.[66] Historical consciousness, according to Dilthey, finds its roots in early Christianity. Indeed, the irreducibility of 'personal experience' just *is*, for Dilthey, 'moral-religious truth'.[67] This personal element of faith (so well conceptualized by Schleiermacher)[68] is the distinguishing mark of primitive Christianity, medieval mysticism and Luther, and presents an enduring 'protest' against metaphysics.[69]

These concerns dovetailed, in Heidegger's developing view of history, with those of the Protestant 'history of religion' school, which Heidegger first encountered in 1910/11. According to the CV of 1922, the importance of this encounter cannot be overestimated: 'My engagement with primitive Christianity as approached by the history of religion school had rendered the [Roman Catholic position of faith] untenable.'[70] The 'history of religion' school was a late-nineteenth-century circle of Protestant theologians from Göttingen who conducted comparative studies of the history of religions, seeking to identify the common religious impulses underlying all religious texts, and the specific debts of early Christianity to Jewish and/or Hellenistic cultic and theological trends.[71]

Many scholars within this school, and some at its margins (most prominently Albert Schweitzer), were particularly interested in early Christian apocalyptic material, which they regarded as having defined the shape and direction of early Christian belief.[72] This also led to renewed attention to the notable differences between early

Christian eschatological fervour and the subsequent development of institutionalized liturgical forms, ethical teaching, and theology. Schweitzer, in particular, argued that these religious sensibilities were not merely different, but fundamentally incompatible: the second could only arise out of the failure of the first.

In this respect, Schweitzer agreed with Franz Overbeck, a New Testament and Patristics scholar of the previous generation (1837–1905), who had also done his post-doctoral work in Göttingen, though he taught for most of his working life in Switzerland. His most influential work, *How Christian is our Present-Day Theology?* (1873, 2nd edition 1903), particularly impressed Heidegger, who, as late as 1970, described it as 'establish[ing] the world-denying expectation of the end as the primary feature of the primordially Christian'.[73] In this work, Overbeck posits an absolute contrast between the ascetic apocalypticism of the earliest Christians, which represents a radical rejection of any hope of salvation within world and time, and the subsequent secularization (*Verweltlichung*) and historicization (*Vergeschichtlichung*) of Christianity, effected by the development of a Christian theology and (political) establishment. Any such development, in Overbeck's view, is fundamentally misguided, because it assumes the possibility of explaining or grounding faith intellectually, and of achieving within history what can only be attained by its End.[74]

For Heidegger, the significance of these insights was both material and methodological. Materially, the eschatological character of early Christian spirituality emerged as a kind of immediate, intuitive religious experience inherently resistant to ('metaphysical') systematization. While to Schweitzer or Johannes Weiss, this spirituality was nothing but a relic or even aberration to be left behind, to Overbeck and Heidegger, it became the paradigm of 'authentic' Christian experience, and as such formed the basis of a radical critique of 'metaphysicizing' neo-Scholasticism.[75] Methodologically, the 'history of religion' school both tacitly and explicitly described religion as an essentially human (rather than a [purely] supernatural) phenomenon, and highlighted the irreducible historical dimension of any manifestation of religious beliefs and practices. For Heidegger, these inquiries became a double call: first, for a religiosity marked both by such aboriginal experience and by truthfulness to the historical situation and development of its practitioners; secondly, for a theology capable of giving this experience expression from within, rather than imposing upon it a system from without which would, by its very nature, be untrue to the phenomenon it sought to describe.

The qualifying thesis of 1915

In his 1915 qualifying thesis, *Duns Scotus' Doctrine of Categories and Signification*, Heidegger follows and extends Schell and Braig's attempts to bring the neo-Scholastic practice of reading medieval texts with a direct view to contemporary concerns into alignment with the pneumatological and historiographical theories of Hegel, and the logical investigations of Kant and Husserl. His teacher Braig had already begun to integrate these two concerns by answering Kant's transcendental question after the condition of the possibility of knowledge with ultimate reference not to the laws of logic but to those of being: 'The laws of logic guarantee the substantial truth of their results, beyond the mere formal correctness of the procedure, only because the basic laws of thought coincide with the laws of Being of the thinking entity.'[76]

Simply put, it is the self-communication of Being – which Braig, like the Scholastics, identifies with God as the source of all beings – which enables man's passive and active intellect, that is, the self-manifestation of beings on the one hand and their perception/knowledge by man on the other. As Braig quotes Bonaventure:

> Just as the eye, when it turns towards the manifold differences of the colours, does not see the light. . . , so the eye of the mind, when it turns towards beings in particular and in general, does not notice being itself, . . . even though it is only through being that it encounters everything.[77]

Heidegger develops this strategy in his qualifying thesis. Taking up Husserl's challenge to create an 'indubitable foundation' for a 'general and, especially, an a priori grammar' through 'proof of a priori laws determining the possible forms of meaning',[78] he argues that such laws must transcend the sphere of logic: 'One cannot even begin to view logic and its problems in the right light if one does not recognize the context from within which they become visible as a trans-logical one.'[79] Ways of meaning correspond to ways of being. It is in this Bonaventurian sense that 'philosophy cannot, in the long run, do without its essential optics, i.e. metaphysics'.[80] Logic requires an ontological, indeed a spiritual, grounding:

> If one frames the concept of the object *transcendentally-ontologically*, . . . the problem of the "application" of the categories loses its meaning; the more firmly the more courageously one affirms the in-principle significance of the – not "individualistically" interpreted – *proposition of immanence*, whose ultimate grounding, which is in my opinion both necessary and ultimately achievable only metaphysically, can be managed through the already suggested concept of living spirit. If the partialness of a *solely* objective-logical treatment of the problem of categories is recognizable anywhere, then in the problem of the *application* of the categories.[81]

This living spirit, Heidegger continues, is 'by nature historical spirit in the widest sense of the word'.[82] Thus, a proper worldview is 'far removed from the merely punctual existence of a theory detached from life'. Rather, 'Spirit can only be grasped[83] if the whole abundance of his achievements, i.e. *his history*, is sublated into him; and this ever-growing abundance, philosophically grasped, offers an ever-increasing means of a living grasp of the absolute spirit of God.'[84]

God here is intrinsically a historical God, to be grasped in and through historical existence. In the years following his qualifying thesis, Heidegger will specify the disposition appropriate to such a temporal experience of God: affliction.

Notes

1   *Die Religionszugehörigkeit in Baden in den letzten 100 Jahren aufgrund amtlichen Materials* (Freiburg: Badisches Statistisches Landesamt, 1928).

2   See Rüdiger Safranski, *Ein Meister aus Deutschland: Heidegger und seine Zeit* (Frankfurt am Main: Fischer Verlag, 2001), pp. 19–20.

3   See Markus Vonberg, 'Der Meßkircher Zeitungskrieg: "Oberbadischer Grenzbote" und "Heuberger Volksblatt" im liberal-ultramontanen Streit', in Edwin Ernst Weber (ed.), *Renitenz und Genie: Meßkirch*

und der badische Seekreis zwischen 1848/49 und dem Kulturkampf (Konstanz: Gesellschaft Oberschwaben, 2003), pp. 153–87.

4 On the history of the ensuing modernist crisis in the Catholic Church, see Hubert Wolf (ed.), *Antimodernismus und Modernismus in der katholischen Kirche: Beiträge zum theologiegeschichtlichen Vorfeld des II. Vatikanums* (Paderborn: Schöningh, 1998); Otto Weiß, *Der Modernismus in Deutschland: Ein Beitrag zur Theologiegeschichte* (Regensburg: Pustet, 2001).

5 See Johannes Schaber, 'Martin Heideggers "Herkunft" im Spiegel der Theologie- und Kirchengeschichte des 19. und beginnenden 20. Jahrhunderts', in *HJB* 1, 159–84; pp. 162–3.

6 In Constance, for example, he received 'decisive spiritual influence' from the rector, Dr Conrad Gröber, an anti-modernist ultramontanist and later Archbishop of Freiburg (see Heidegger, 'Lebenslauf' (1915), GA 16, 37).

7 'Rektoratszeugnisse für die Abiturienten', 10 September 1909; quoted in Hugo Ott, *Martin Heidegger: Unterwegs zu seiner Biographie* (Frankfurt: Campus, 1988), p. 59.

8 Letter from Ernst Laslowski (Heidegger's closest childhood friend) to Heidegger, 20 April 1911; rpt. in *HJB* 1, 28–30; p. 29.

9 See Judith Beniston, *Welttheater: Hofmannsthal, Richard von Kralik, and the Revival of Catholic Drama in Austria, 1890–1934* (London: Maney & Son, 1998). Abraham a Sancta Clara was widely known in the German-speaking world for his rhetorical and literary work. Schiller praised him in a letter to Goethe as 'wonderful [in] originality' and 'not at all easy . . . to approach or surpass . . . in mad wit and cleverness'; Schiller to Goethe, 9 October 1798, in *Briefwechsel zwischen Schiller und Goethe in den Jahren 1794 bis 1805* (Stuttgart: Cotta, 1828–29), vol. 4, p. 335.

10 *Heuberger Volksblatt*, 10 September 1909; cited in Víctor Farías, *Heidegger and Nazism* (Philadelphia: Temple University Press, 1989 [1987]), p. 34.

11 *Hochland* was a Catholic monthly founded in 1903 and edited by Karl Muth for Kösel Verlag in Munich. Its contributors included Heinrich Finke and Herman Schell (about whom see below).

12 *Der Akademiker* acted as the official organ of the student association 'Catholic German Academics' (Katholischer Deutscher Akademikerverband). It strongly supported Pius X's interpretation of Vatican I and also attracted such contributors as Romano Guardini and Oswald von Nell-Breuning (see Ott, *Heidegger*, p. 63). The *Allgemeine Rundschau* was a 'weekly for politics and culture'

edited by the controversial Catholic intellectual Dr Armin Kausen.
It continued from 1904 to the eve of the accession of the Nazi Party,
and was directed particularly against what the editor perceived
as modernist 'immorality in life and art'. See Klemens Löffler,
'Periodical Literature (Germany)', trans. Douglas J. Potter, in *Catholic
Encyclopedia*, vol. 11 (1911), pp. 677–80; p. 679.

13 Victor Farías has made forceful efforts to popularize the claim that
Heidegger's early Catholicism, particularly his championing of
Abraham a Santa Clara, was already proto-Nazi in character (see his
Heidegger and Nazism, ch. 3). Although there are some dispositional
tendencies which surface in both Heidegger's Catholicism and his
later support for Nazism, Farías' point is untenable; see Chapter 5 for
a more detailed analysis.

14 Heidegger, 'Allerseelenstimmungen', *Heuberger Volksblatt*,
5 November 1909; rpt. In *HJB* 1, 18–21; p. 18. In a parenthetical
jibe at Nietzsche, Heidegger mocks these 'Moderns' for turning 'into
"blonde Beasts" when you dare to doubt the logic of their passions'
(18–19). Heidegger also gave a highly critical lecture on Nietzsche at
the *Katholische Gesellen- und Jünglingsverein* (Catholic Men's and
Boys' Club) of Messkirch in October 1912; see Alfred Denker and
Elsbeth Büchin, *Martin Heidegger und seine Heimat* (Stuttgart: Klett-
Cotta, 2005), pp. 127–8.

15 Heidegger, 'Allerseelenstimmungen' (1909), *HJB* 1, 18.

16 Heidegger, 'Per mortem ad vitam: Gedanken über Jörgensens
"Lebenslüge und Lebenswahrheit"', *Der Akademiker* 2, 5 (March
1910), pp. 72–3; rpt. in GA 16, 3–6; p. 3. Cf. Heidegger's statement
in a CV of 1915: 'Things said in RE classes . . . suggested to me a
more extensive study of the biological theory of evolution'; GA 16,
37. Heidegger also gave a talk entitled 'Die tierische Abstammung
des Menschen und das Urteil der Wissenschaft' ['The animal origins
of man and the verdict of science'] at the *Katholische Gesellen- und
Jünglingsverein* in Messkirch on 21 April 1912; see Denker and
Büchin, *Heidegger und seine Heimat*, pp. 126–7.

17 Heidegger, 'Förster, Fr. W. Autorität und Freiheit' (review), *Der
Akademiker* 2, 7 (May 1910), pp. 109–10; rpt. GA 16, 7–8.

18 Foerster, *Autorität und Freiheit: Betrachtungen zum Kulturproblem
der Kirche* (Kempten-Munich: Kösel, 1910), p. 28; quoted in Alfred
Denker, 'Heideggers Lebens- und Denkweg 1909–1919', *HJB* 1,
97–122; p. 104.

19 Heidegger, 'Zur philosophischen Orientierung für Akademiker',
Der Akademiker 3, 5 (March 1911), pp. 66–7; rpt. in GA 16,
11–14; p. 11.

20 Foerster, *Autorität und Freiheit*, 58; quoted in Denker, 'Denkweg', *HJB* 1, 104.

21 Heidegger, 'Zur philosophischen Orientierung für Akademiker' (1911), GA 16, 8.

22 For further examples, see also his August 1910 article 'Abraham a Sankta Clara: Zur Enthüllung seines Denkmals in Kreenheinstetten am 15. August 1910', *Allgemeine Rundschau*, August 1910; rpt. GA 13, 1–3; see esp. p. 3.

23 See Heidegger, *Die Kategorien- und Bedeutungslehre des Duns Scotus* (Tübingen: J.C.B. Mohr, 1916); rpt. in GA 1, 189–411; esp. p. 222. Cf. Richard Schaeffler, *Frömmigkeit des Denkens?: Martin Heidegger und die katholische Theologie* (Darmstadt: Wissenschaftliche Buchgesellschaft, 1978), pp. 22–8; esp. pp. 27–8.

24 See Ott, *Heidegger*, 59, and Denker, 'Denkweg', *HJB* 1, 100–1.

25 The author of *De modis significandi*, the primary source for Heidegger's account of Scotus' doctrine of signification, has since been determined to be Thomas of Erfurt, like Scotus a 'speculative grammarian'; see Jack Zupko, 'Thomas of Erfurt', *The Stanford Encyclopedia of Philosophy*, ed. Edward N. Zalta (Autumn 2008 edition), accessible online via <http://plato.stanford.edu/archives/fall2008/entries/erfurt/>

26 Heidegger, 'Lebenslauf' (1915), rpt. GA 16, 37–9; p. 38.

27 Heidegger, 'Vita' (1922), rpt. in GA 16, 41–5; p. 41. Additional autobiographical reminiscences of these years can be found in Heidegger's inaugural speech ('Antrittsrede') upon election to the Heidelberg Akademie der Wissenschaften in 1957, published in GA 1, 55–7; and in his 'Mein Weg in die Phänomenologie', in *Hermann Niemeyer zum achtzigsten Geburtstag am 16. April 1963* (private printing), rpt. In GA 14, 81–90.

28 A detailed evaluation of the 1915 and 1922 CVs and the plausibility of their claims can be found in Judith Wolfe, *Heidegger's Eschatology: Theological Horizons in Martin Heidegger's Early Thought* (Oxford: Oxford University Press, 2013), pp. 19–24.

29 *Sacrorum antistitum*; rpt. in *Acta Apostolicae Sedis* 2 (1910), pp. 655–80.

30 See Schaber, 'Herkunft', *HJB* 1, 164.

31 Heidegger, 'Dem Grenzbot-Philosophen zur Antwort', *Heuberger Volksblatt*, 7 April 1911; quoted in Schaber, 'Herkunft', *HJB* 1, 167.

32 A failure to distinguish between 'Scholasticism' as a method (marked by opposition to 'modernism') on the one hand, and as a set of

ideas derived from the Scholastic period on the other, has led some scholars to misinterpret many of Heidegger's texts and statements of that period. This is especially true of Hugo Ott's seminal biography of Heidegger and the many scholars who are indebted to it. For a good exposition of the (often conflicting) tendencies of early twentieth-century 'Scholasticism', explicitly aiming to correct Ott, see Robert Vigliotti, 'The Young Heidegger's Ambitions for the Chair of Catholic Philosophy and Hugo Ott's Charge of Opportunism', *Studia Phænomenologica* 1, 3–4 (2001), pp. 323–50.

33 Laslowski to Heidegger, 6 December 1915; rpt. in *HJB* 1, 52–3; p. 53.

34 Heidegger to Rickert, 12 October 1913, in *Heidegger/Rickert,* p. 12. Hugo Ott, in his biography of Heidegger, reads Heidegger's behaviour at this time as entirely opportunistic, designed to garner maximum financial and career support from Catholic sources.

35 Heidegger to Engelbert Krebs, 19 July 1914; rpt. *HJB* 1, 61–2; p. 62.

36 See Heidegger, 'Lebenslauf' (1915), GA 16, 38.

37 Heidegger, 'Die Lehre vom Urteil im Psychologismus' (1913), rpt. in GA 1, 59–188; *Die Kategorien- und Bedeutungslehre des Duns Scotus* (1916), rpt. in GA 1, 189–411. Preliminary reviews and articles include 'Das Realitätsproblem in der modernen Philosophie' (1912), 'Neuere Forschungen über die Logik' (1912), and 'Charles Sentroul, *Kant und Aristoteles*' (review, 1914).

38 Heidegger adopts this Meinongian term in his 1922 description of the aim of his qualifying thesis. See GA 1, 42; cf. Alexius Meinong, *Untersuchungen zur Gegenstandstheorie und Psychologie* (Leipzig: Barth, 1904).

39 See Heidegger, 'Das Realitätsproblem in der modernen Philosophie', *Philosophisches Jahrbuch der Görresgesellschaft* 25 (1912), pp. 353–63; rpt. GA 1, 1–15.

40 See Heidegger, 'Realitätsproblem' (1912), GA 1, 15. Heidegger mentions his early reading of Husserl in both the CV of 1915 (see GA 16, 37) and that of 1922 (see GA 16, 41).

41 'According to [Kant], the transcendental conditions of sensual and intellectual knowledge have a genetically a priori, subjective character'; Heidegger, 'Realitätsproblem' (1912), GA 1, 9.

42 See Heidegger, 'Lebenslauf' (1915), GA 16, 38.

43 Ibid. For a list of Rickert's seminars attended by Heidegger, see *HJB* 1, 15–17. On Heidegger's debt to Rickert's student Emil Lask, see Theodore Kisiel's oft-reprinted essay, 'Why Students of Heidegger Will Have to Read Emil Lask', e.g. in Theodore Kisiel,

Heidegger's Way of Thought: Critical and Interpretative Signposts, eds. Alfred Denker and Marion Heinz (London: Continuum, 2nd edn, 2002), pp. 101-36. On Heidegger's work on logic in the years 1912-16 more generally, see esp. Steven Galt Crowell, 'Making Logic Philosophical Again (1912-1916)', in Theodore Kisiel and John van Buren (eds.), *Reading Heidegger from the Start: Essays in His Earliest Thought* (Albany: State University of New York Press, 1994), pp. 55-72.

44 Heidegger, 'Neuere Forschungen über die Logik', *Literarische Rundschau für das katholische Deutschland* 38, 10 (1912), cols 465-72; no. 11 (1912), cols 517-24; no. 12 (1912), cols 565-70; rpt. in GA 1, 17-43; p. 19.

45 See Heidegger, 'Kant und Aristoteles von Charles Sentroul' (review), *Literarische Rundschau für das katholische Deutschland* 40, 7 (1914), cols 330-2; rpt. GA 1, 49-53; p. 53. This is a review of Charles Sentroul, *Kant und Aristoteles* (trans. L. Heinrichs; Munich: Kösel, 1911). Heidegger here explicitly criticizes Sentroul's psychologistic interpretation of Kant, following that of Schopenhauer; see GA 1, 51.

46 Heidegger, 'Kant und Aristoteles' (1914), GA 1, 50 (emphasis dropped).

47 See Heidegger, 'Lebenslauf' (1915), GA 16, 39; 'Vita' (1922), GA 16, 42; 'Antrittsrede' (1957), GA 1, 56.

48 In his 1957 inaugural speech ('Antrittsrede') upon election to the Heidelberg Akademie der Wissenschaften, which he included as a foreword to his early writings (GA 1), Heidegger declares that the 'decisive and therefore not definable determination for [his] own academic teaching activity' had come from Braig; see GA 1, 56-7.

49 See Heidegger, 'Lebenslauf' (1915), GA 16, 37.

50 Heidegger, 'Antrittsrede' (1957), GA 1, 57.

51 From 'Vorlesungsverzeichnis der Katholisch-Theologischen Fakultät', reproduced in Johannes Schaber, 'Der Theologiestudent Martin Heidegger und sein Dogmatikprofessor Carl Braig', *Freiburger Diözesanarchiv* 125 (2005), pp. 332-47; p. 337. See also Heidegger, 'Mein Weg in die Phänomenologie' (1963), GA 14, 82.

52 Heidegger, 'Mein Weg in die Phänomenologie' (1963), GA 14, 82.

53 Ibid.

54 Heidegger, 'Lebenslauf' (1915), GA 16, 37.

55 See e.g. Braig, *Vom Sein: Abriß der Ontologie* (Freiburg: Herder, 1896), esp. §§19-21.

56 Heidegger, 'Realitätsproblem' (1912), GA 1, 3.

57   Heidegger, *Kategorien- und Bedeutungslehre*, GA 1, 411. For
     an emphasis on Hegel's theological context, see also Heidegger,
     'Phenomenological Interpretations of Aristotle' (1921/22), GA 61, 7.

58   Schell, *Apologie des Christentums*, vol 1: *Religion und Offenbarung*
     (Paderborn: Schöningh, 1902), xiii; quoted in Schaber, 'Herkunft',
     HJB 1, 168.

59   Schell, *Religion und Offenbarung*, xxiv; quoted in Hans-Joachim
     Sander, 'Herman Schells Apologetik der pluralen Wahrheit des
     Glaubens', in Otmar Meuffels and Rainer Dvorak (eds.), *Wahrheit
     Gottes – Freiheit des Denkens: Herman Schell als Impulsgeber für
     Theologie und Kirche* (Würzburg: Schöningh, 2001), pp. 95–108;
     p. 102.

60   Schell, *Religion und Offenbarung*, xi; quoted in Meuffels and
     Dvorak, *Wahrheit Gottes*, p. 101.

61   See Raimund Lachner, 'Schell, Herman', *Biographisch-Bibliographisches
     Kirchenlexikon*, vol. 9, cols 88–99; Thomas Sheehan, 'Heidegger's Lehr-
     jahre', in John Sallis et al. (eds.), *The Collegium Phaenomenologicum*
     (Dordrecht: Kluwer, 1988), pp. 77–137; p. 92.

62   Schell, *Religion und Offenbarung*, xiii–xiv; cited in Schaber,
     'Herkunft', *HJB* 1, 168.

63   Responding to a request by Karl Löwith for the temporary loan of
     some volumes, Heidegger wrote on 3 September 1920, 'I don't have
     Dilthey's works, only detailed excerpts, in part hand-copied by me
     as a theologian in 1909–10, which are useful only if you know the
     context' (quoted in Theodore Kisiel, *The Genesis of Heidegger's
     Being and Time* [Berkeley: University of California Press, 1995],
     524n. 43).

64   Dilthey, *Der Aufbau der geschichtlichen Welt in den Geisteswissen-
     schaften* (1910), Gesammelte Schriften 7, ed. Bernhard Groethuysen
     (Stuttgart: B. G. Teubner, 8th edn, 1992), p. 212. The (so far) most
     detailed analysis, in English, of Heidegger's appropriation of Dilthey
     is Benjamin Crowe's *Heidegger's Religious Origins*, chapter 5, to
     which this paragraph is indebted. See also Rudolf A. Makkreel,
     'Dilthey, Heidegger und der Vollzugssinn der Geschichte', in *HJB* 1,
     307–21.

65   Dilthey, *Weltanschauungslehre: Abhandlungen zur Philosophie
     der Philosophie* (1931), Gesammelte Schriften 8, ed. Bernhard
     Groethuysen (Stuttgart: B. G. Teubner, 6th edn, 1991), p. 81.

66   Dilthey, *Einleitung in die Geisteswissenschaften* (1883), Gesammelte
     Schriften 1, ed. Bernhard Groethuysen (Stuttgart: B. G. Teubner, 10th
     edn, 2008), p. 408.

67 Dilthey, *Einleitung in die Geisteswissenschaften*, pp. 384–5.

68 See Dilthey, *Leben Schleiermachers* (1870), 2 vols, Gesammelte Schriften 13–14, ed. Martin Redeker (Stuttgart: B. G. Teubner, 1966 and 1985).

69 Dilthey, *Einleitung in die Geisteswissenschaften*, p. 385.

70 Heidegger, 'Vita' (1922), GA 16, 43.

71 See W. G. Kümmel, *The New Testament: The History of the Investigation of Its Problems* (trans. S. M. Gilmour and H. C. Kee; London: SCM, 1973 [1958]), chapter 5; see also Schaber, 'Herkunft', *HJB* 1, 180–1.

72 See esp. Hermann Gunkel, *Schöpfung und Chaos in Urzeit und Endzeit: Eine religionsgeschichtliche Untersuchung über Gen 1 und Apk Joh 21* (Göttingen: Vandenhoeck & Ruprecht, 1895); Wilhelm Bousset, *Der Antichrist in der Überlieferung des Judentums, des Neuen Testaments und der alten Kirche* (Göttingen: Vandenhoeck & Ruprecht, 1895), *Die jüdische Apokalyptik: ihre religionsgeschichtliche Herkunft und ihre Bedeutung für das neue Testament* (Berlin: Reuther & Reichard, 1903), and *Die Offenbarung Johannis: Kritisch-exegetischer Kommentar über das Neue Testament* (Göttingen: Vandenhoeck & Ruprecht, 3rd edn, 1906); Albert Schweitzer, *The Quest of the Historical Jesus* (trans. William Montgomery; London: A. & C. Black, 1910 [1906]).

73 1970 'Preface' to the 1927 lecture 'Phenomenology and Theology'; GA 9, 45–6 (followed by the lecture, 47–78). In the lecture itself, Heidegger distinguishes 'Christlichkeit' (Christianness) from 'Christentum' (Christendom) as the proper subject of theology.

74 Overbeck's summary term for these errors is 'Jesuitism', a term Heidegger uses repeatedly, e.g. in a 1932 letter to Elisabeth Blochmann, where he writes that communism is 'abhorrent', but Jesuitism 'diabolical'; Heidegger to Blochmann, 22 June 1932, in *Heidegger/Blochmann*, p. 52.

75 Cf. Kisiel, *Genesis*, p. 218.

76 Carl Braig, *Vom Denken: Abriß der Logik* (Freiburg: Herder, 1896), p. 9; quoted in Schaeffler, *Frömmigkeit des Denkens?*, p. 8.

77 Carl Braig, *Vom Sein*, pp. v–vi (original reference not provided).

78 Edmund Husserl, *Logische Untersuchungen* II/1 (Halle: Max Niemeyer, 1907), p. 287; quoted in Heidegger, *Kategorien- und Bedeutungslehre*, GA 1, 270.

79 Heidegger, *Kategorien- und Bedeutungslehre*, GA 1, 405.

80 Ibid., 406.

81 Heidegger, *Kategorien- und Bedeutungslehre*, GA 1, 407.

82 Ibid.

83 The German 'begriffen'/'begreifen', used twice more in the sentence, plays with the tension between the philosophical use of the term ('to conceptualize') and its visceral roots ('to grasp', 'to finger').

84 Heidegger, *Kategorien- und Bedeutungslehre*, GA 1, 407–8.

2

Heidegger's Protestantism
(1916–1921)

In the years 1916–19, Heidegger's dissatisfaction with the current state of neo-Scholasticism hardened into a full-scale estrangement from the Catholic Church. Many factors – personal, professional and intellectual – contributed to this change: the breakdown of his engagement to a Catholic, and his subsequent marriage to a Protestant who (despite early indications of such an intention) did not convert to Catholicism; the failure of his ambition to accede to the Freiburg Chair in Christian Philosophy, towards which he had been steering his career thus far; and above all his developing intellectual commitments and personal spirituality.

Despite the dramatic upheavals represented by these years, it is only at the point of Heidegger's more or less completed turn to Protestantism – coinciding professionally with having moved from being a 'protégé' of the Catholic historian Finke to being assistant to the Jewish-Lutheran phenomenologist Edmund Husserl – that engagement with his theological roots, at least in English-language scholarship, usually begins. One of the most damaging results of this foreshortening of Heidegger's religious-intellectual path is the common assumption that his interest in religion was secondary from the beginning: that Heidegger never regarded religion as more than one among many fields of phenomenological enquiry. Recently presented sources, however, suggest that, quite to the contrary, Heidegger discovered the phenomenological method, together with Protestantism, in large part as a means to adequately describing religious experience.

The religious origins of Heidegger's characteristic form of the phenomenological method, his 'hermeneutics of facticity', are attested both by Heidegger himself and by others. In a letter to Heidegger on 10 September 1918, Husserl affectionately calls him 'my phenomenologist of religion'.[1] And as late as 1921, Heidegger himself corrects his student Karl Löwith by insisting that he is not a philosopher but a 'Christian theologian'.[2] When he first presents his 'hermeneutics of facticity' publicly in 1923, Heidegger (sardonically) prefaces it with a partial genealogy: 'The companion of my search was the young Luther and its model Aristotle, whom the former hated. Kierkegaard provided impulses, and Husserl gave me my eyes.'[3] On other occasions, he mentions a number of other important Christian influences: St Paul, St Augustine, the medieval mystics (particularly Bernard of Clairvaux, Meister Eckhart and Johannes Tauler), Friedrich Schleiermacher, Fyodor Dostoevsky and Franz Overbeck.[4]

Recently published letters, notes and lecture transcripts from the period between 1915 and 1924 make it possible, for the first time, to determine and evaluate the substance of these Christian influences. The narrative that emerges is that of a dynamic reimagining of the basis of religious (and, with it, of all) experience – a re-imagining that lies at the root of Heidegger's great works of the 1920s, above all *Being and Time*.

Heidegger's main theological contribution of the years 1916–21 lies in adapting and revising Schleiermacher's basic religious experience of absolute dependency in line with Luther's and St Paul's emphases on crucicentrism and eschatological anxiety, presenting the basic religious experience (which is determinative of the phenomenological examination of religion) as *affliction* rather than dependency. This assimilation of Paul and Luther is, in turn, inflected by Heidegger's intense engagement, during the same years, with Romantic and post-Romantic poetry and, particularly, Friedrich Hölderlin. Through Hölderlin and his tradition, Heidegger arrives at an interpretation of (Christian) affliction neither as a result of sin nor as a participation in the suffering of Christ, but as the constitutive experience of irreducible human finitude – an experience which highlights the radical otherness of the human vis-à-vis the divine, but which alone also enables authentic existence.

This experience of human finitude, for the Heidegger of the late 1910s and early 1920s, has its horizon and paradigmatic expression in eschatological expectation. He works out this idea in his lecture series for the winter semester of 1920/21, Introduction to the Phenomenology of Religion, and refines it in his lecture series the following semester, Augustine and Neoplatonism.

This chapter traces the dramatic developments of the years 1916–21 in three parts: biographical, intellectual and textual. The first part charts Heidegger's dissociation from Roman Catholicism and turn towards an undogmatic Protestantism. The second part analyses two equally important trajectories in tandem: one, the thematic development of the question of what constitutes the basic religious feeling (indebted to both theology and Romantic literature), and two, the concomitant confirmation of his commitment to phenomenology as the philosophical method adequate to this kind of religiosity. The third part is a critical reading of Heidegger's two famous lecture series of 1920 and 1921, on the eschatology of Paul and Augustine, respectively.

A biographical sketch

In the years 1916–19, Heidegger's estrangement from the Catholic Church became definite and public. Heidegger navigated this move carefully, maintaining ties to Catholic scholarship while preparing the way for a professional existence within the Protestant academy, before openly declaring his break with Catholicism in 1919.

The professional difficulty attendant on Heidegger's changing religious views lay in his Catholic training. Even more consistently than today, German universities then conducted their theological research and teaching exclusively in confessional faculties, either Catholic (*katholisch*) or Protestant (*evangelisch*). Academic staff were expected to display their denominational allegiance in both their educational background and their personal commitment. Until the mid-1910s, Heidegger largely suppressed his growing scepticism of Roman Catholic scholarship in his academic work, because he was hoping for the vacant chair in Christian Philosophy at his native Freiburg. When this hope failed in 1916, Heidegger decided to attempt the jump to a Protestant department. Heinrich Rickert, the (nominal) supervisor of his qualifying thesis, had just moved to the Protestant Heidelberg, and Heidegger wrote to him in early 1917, expressing a wish to join him there. Rickert replied that Heidelberg was 'out of the question' for Heidegger, who, being 'a committed Catholic also in his capacity as a philosopher' could only serve at a Catholic theological faculty.[5] Heidegger replied defensively: 'I never have, and never would, maintain the *narrow* Catholic standpoint that the understanding and solution of problems should take their bearings from extra-scientific considerations, traditional or whatever. Rather, according to my free personal convictions, I will seek and teach the truth.'[6]

But the move did not happen. Instead, Heidegger tried to forge a closer association with Rickert's Freiburg successor Edmund Husserl, a Jewish convert to Protestantism. Husserl initially remained very lukewarm about Heidegger's work and person.[7] In October 1917, the (Protestant) Marburg philosopher Paul Natorp asked Husserl's opinion about Heidegger: Marburg was considering him for an associate professorship in philosophy, but was unsure about Heidegger's teaching experience and, in particular, the potential danger of 'confessional narrowness'.[8] Husserl replied evasively and with oblique dismissiveness. Heidegger's 'beginner's effort [*Erstlingswerk*]' on Duns Scotus was certainly 'a promising start for a historian of medieval philosophy', but Heidegger seemed too young and immature for a post, and had only mixed teaching success. In particular, however, he was clearly 'confessionally bound', being a protégé of 'our Catholic historian' Finke, who had recommended Heidegger as a 'confessionally suitable' candidate for the 1916 vacancy in Catholic Philosophy. The only counter-consideration, Husserl noted, was Heidegger's recent marriage to a Protestant woman, who had 'not yet' converted to the Catholic faith.[9]

Heidegger had indeed, after a failed engagement to a Catholic woman called Margarete Weninger,[10] chosen to marry the Protestant Elfride Petri – a move regarded with concern by his Catholic family and friends, and accepted only because of her alleged intention to convert to Roman Catholicism (which was never actualized).[11] It was Elfride who first voiced the couple's estrangement from the Roman Church to their Catholic friends. In a conversation with Engelbert Krebs on 23 December 1918, recorded in reported speech in Krebs' diary, she explained to the theologian priest why she and her husband could not in good conscience have their first child baptized within the Catholic Church:

> My husband no longer has his church faith, and I have not found it. Already when we got married, his faith was undercut with doubts. But I myself urged a Catholic wedding and hoped, with his help, to find faith. We have read, talked, thought and prayed a lot together, and the result is that we now both think in a Protestant way, that is, believe in a personal God and pray to him in the spirit of Christ, but without fixed dogmatic commitment, or Protestant or Catholic orthodoxy.[12]

Martin confirmed this representation to Krebs in a now famous letter less than a month later: 'Epistemological insights, extending to the theory of historical cognition, have made the system of Catholicism problematic and unacceptable to me – but not Christianity and metaphysics, these however in a new sense. . . .'[13]

This development soon became known more widely within the faculty. A few months after his dismissive letter to Natorp, Husserl learnt from a friend of Martin, Heinrich Ochsner, that Heidegger had in fact loosened his commitment to Catholic dogma already. Accordingly, in 1920, when Marburg was once more advertising its associate professorship in philosophy, Husserl sent Natorp a new report, proudly and pointedly declaring that already in late 1917, 'Heidegger had . . . detached himself from dogmatic Catholicism. Soon afterwards he accepted all the consequences and cut himself off from a safe and speedy career as a "philosopher of the Catholic worldview" – unequivocally, energetically, and yet tactfully.'[14] In a letter to Rudolf Otto around the same time, Husserl associated this conversion with Heidegger's increasing closeness to Husserl himself: 'Not without strong inner resistance did [Heidegger and Ochsner] gradually open up to my suggestions and also draw closer to me personally. At the same time, both underwent radical changes in their fundamental religious convictions.' He hurries to avow that

> [i]n arch-Catholic Freiburg I do not want to seem a tempter of young people, a proselytizer, an enemy of the Catholic Church. That I am not. I have not exercised the least influence on Heidegger's and Oxner's [sic] migration to the ground of Protestantism, although it can only be very pleasing to me as a

free Christian (if someone who uses that word in the sense of an ideal goal of religious desire and an infinite task, may call himself that) and an "undogmatic Protestant".[15]

The same year, Heidegger became Husserl's assistant, a post he held until his belated appointment to an associate professorship in Philosophy at Marburg in 1922. By that move, Heidegger was, as Rudolf Bultmann, the local New Testament professor, reported in a 1923 letter to Hans von Soden, 'thoroughly Protestant'.[16]

Intellectual developments

As already discussed, Heidegger remained, until about 1915, broadly committed to 'Aristotelian-Scholastic philosophy', but increasingly reinterpreted this thought system in the light of contemporary philosophy, particularly Husserlian phenomenology, which he had encountered via his training in neo-Kantianism.[17] In the conclusion of his qualifying thesis, *Duns Scotus' Doctrine of Categories and Signification*, he calls for an integration of medieval scholasticism and medieval mysticism, the latter of which he associates with a proper appreciation of the significance of the irreducibly temporal, individual experience of the believer for any understanding of God. This temporal experience is indispensable because it is the natural human counterpart of God's Spirit, which as 'living Spirit is . . . essentially historical Spirit'.[18] Consequently, theological philosophy 'as rationalistic construct detached from life is powerless'.[19] What is required is a 'philosophy of living Spirit, of active love, of reverential ardency for God'.[20]

Drawing on phenomenological ideas and methods, Heidegger devotes much of the years 1915–21 to the attempt to formulate a more authentic Christian theology, moving as an *exitus/reditus* from and to 'factic life experience'.[21] In this effort, he turns, among others, to the Protestant sensibilities of Schleiermacher, Kierkegaard and the early Luther. At the same time, his experience of World War I and his abiding interest in Romantic literature sensitize him to a decisive dimension of factic life experience: suffering or, more precisely, affliction. This experience of affliction, for the Heidegger of the late 1910s and early 1920s, finds its horizon and paradigmatic expression in eschatological expectation. The remainder of this chapter will follow Heidegger's development in both its theological-philosophical and its literary forms from his first interest in Schleiermacher to his 1920 and 1921 lecture series on Pauline and Augustinian eschatology.

The search for a basic religious feeling

On 1 August 1917, shortly after being passed over for the vacant Chair in Catholic Philosophy at Freiburg, Heidegger gave a private lecture on Schleiermacher's Second Speech on Religion, entitled 'The Problem of the Religious in Schleiermacher'.[22] This was a radical gesture for a Catholic scholar, and the first public indication of the break with Catholicism that followed two years later. No lecture notes or summaries are preserved, but Heidegger's approach to Schleiermacher's Second Speech can be gleaned from a set of notes that he took during the same year towards an ultimately cancelled lecture series on the philosophical foundations of medieval mysticism.[23] (Heidegger had announced the course for the winter semester of 1919/20, but asked the Faculty Board in late August 1919 to allow him to cancel it, explaining that he had not had enough time for an adequately rigorous review of the material.[24])

In Schleiermacher, Heidegger found a proto-phenomenological conception of religion as a 'disposition' or 'form of experience', which overcame the traditional conflation of religion with 'metaphysics'.[25] In his 1917 notes, he defined religion (after Schleiermacher's Second Speech, 'On the Essence of Religion') as 'the specific religiously intentional, emotional [gefühlsartige] relation of every experiential content to an infinite whole as [its] originary sense [Grundsinn]'.[26] This 'infinite whole', for Schleiermacher as read by Heidegger, is not the God of traditional theism, who is prior to and independent of the world, but the world itself in its infinite variety (for which 'God' is one appropriate 'auxiliary means of representation').[27] 'Religion', in the Second Speech, is the recognition of every finite being as a 'part', a 'cut-out', an 'imprint', or a 'representation' of that whole, and the consequent liberation of the 'believer' to 'love the World Spirit and joyfully observe its work'.[28] It is in this sense that, as Heidegger excerpts the Second Speech, 'history, in its most proper sense, is the highest object of religion; with [history] it begins and ends'.[29]

For Heidegger, one of the most important implications of this conception of religion is the dependence of the object of religious experience on the act of intuition. In the Second Speech, Schleiermacher notes: 'Intuition without feeling is nothing and can have neither the proper origin nor the proper force; feeling without intuition is also nothing: both are therefore something only when and because they are originally one and unseparated.'[30] Heidegger formalizes this thought as a phenomenological description of the way in which the content of religious experience is constituted: '*Mysterious* moment of unstructured unity between intuition [*Anschauung*] and feeling', he notes. '[T]he former is nothing without the latter. The noetic moment is itself constitutive of the noematic content [*Gesamtgehalt*] of the experience.'[31] This experienced co-originality of *noesis* and *noema* sharply distinguishes authentic religious feeling and its object (which are not transferable or delegable) from conventional religiosity, which, by merely appropriating the experiences, thoughts and precepts of others, inherently falls short of what is 'living' and 'holy'.[32]

The crucial task that any such approach to faith has to confront is the identification of the specific feeling that is (claimed to be) constitutive of religious experience. In order to form an adequate epistemological basis for religious faith, this feeling must be self-evident (or, in Cartesian terms, properly basic). For Schleiermacher, this basic feeling is (as an unargued matter of course) one of 'absolute dependence'.[33] But Heidegger will develop a different account of the basic feeling of religious experience, in conversation with his World War I contemporaries, (post-)Romantic poetry, and voices of the late Middle Ages and the Reformation.[34] This basic feeling is affliction, or, as he later terms it, 'care'.

Ascent and temporality

Husserl had adopted the motto 'To the things themselves!'. In other words, he called for a bottom-up approach to the description of objects, bracketing any pre-conceived notions or classifications in favour of concentrated attention to the way these objects are 'constituted' for the observer. Heidegger felt this method to be internally akin to religious experience as described by Schleiermacher and others, and so to be uniquely capable of illuminating that experience from within. Not only that: In 1919/20, he argued that it was in fact 'one of the inmost tendencies of phenomenology' to strive away from the metaphysization of Christianity that had occurred through its forced assimilation to Greek philosophy – a metaphysization only overcome partially and periodically by the medieval mystics, the young Luther, Schleiermacher and Kierkegaard.[35]

In the years 1915–19 and beyond, not only Heidegger but several of Husserl's students attempted to formulate phenomenological accounts of religious experience, often – as in the prominent cases of Adolf Reinach and Edith Stein – in response to personal conversion experiences. These young philosophers regarded as the primary task of such an account a description of the experiential constitution of 'God' as an object for the believer. Adolf Reinach, one of Husserl's most brilliant students, converted to Christianity in the trenches shortly before his death in 1916. (Edith Stein reports discussing his fragmentary work with 'little Heidegger' in 1919[36]). Reinach postulated that the constitutive experience of faith was that of a supernatural *Geborgensein*. The acknowledgement of the experience of 'being sheltered', and of one's own existential implication in that experience, became for him the epistemological condition for the recognition of God's existence: 'We have to distinguish two things: first the recognition of being sheltered, and secondly the recognition of the presence of God.'[37]

In a long note on Reinach's fragment, dated June 1918, Heidegger emphasizes the temporal (or 'historical') dimension of this statement, and sketches its implications:

> Our experiential conduct vis-à-vis God – which is primary, because it wells up inside us by grace – determines the direction of the specifically *religious* constitution of "God" as a "phenomenological object".... Therefore, determinations of the meaning of this, i.e. of the "Absolute", are only to be discovered in the specific structures of the constitutive experience.... The "Absolute" ... receives its full concretization within each sphere only by manifesting itself in a form of *historicity*; and accordingly, the analysis must manifest the "*historical*" as an element of living consciousness as such, bestowing basic sense and structure.[38]

In a contemporaneous note on Bernard of Clairvaux's third Sermon on the Song of Songs, Heidegger expounds the significance of such 'historicity' in the relevant (religious) context. He glosses Bernard's opening sentence, '*Hodie legimus in libro experientiae*', in a distinctly phenomenological way: 'Today we want to move with understanding (description) in the field of personal experience' – noting that a 'basic tendency' of human experience is the ability or wish to 'live more'.[39] This experience is central to the 'process of the constitution of God's presence', which is itself 'originary'.[40] In other words, God cannot be understood in the manner of a 'rationalist metaphysics' as an 'absolute', a 'highest measure' or 'measure *per se*'[41]; rather, the sense of the term 'God' is determined by the inherently temporal experience of perpetual ascent, which is nothing other than a recognition of one's interminable tendency to '*Mehr-Leben*' ('living more' or 'more life') in a specifically religious mood.

From 1918 onwards, Heidegger develops this sense of ascent or progress, in other words, of a specifically religious experience of one's own temporality, as defining the Christian life and life in general. In a 1918 letter to his friend and colleague Elisabeth Blochmann, he insists that an authentic life can only be lived in awareness of one's essential, dynamic God-directedness:

> Where belief in the proper value of one's own destiny is truly alive, everything unworthy in one's chance circumstances is overcome from within and forever. Every accomplishment achieves the character of finality in accordance with its authenticity, i.e. its inner belonging to the central "I" and its God-directed determination.[42]

However, Heidegger's sense of this 'God-directed determination' diverges from those of St Bernard and Adolf Reinach in the increasing displacement of the object or goal of this teleological process by the process itself. For both St Bernard and Reinach, the believer's ascent is directed both by and towards God, who is present and active beyond and independently of human comprehension. Thus, in his fourth sermon on Song of Songs, which immediately follows the sermon discussed by Heidegger, St Bernard emphasizes that the gradual human approach to God which he has just described is inferior to that of the 'dwellers in the heavens', who can 'read in the Book of Life without contradiction, and understand it without difficulty'.[43] Similarly, further on in the fragment discussed by

Heidegger, Reinach argues that the believer's experiential relation to God is determined by his or her actual position vis-à-vis Him.[44] For Heidegger, by contrast, there is no meaningful viewpoint outside the human: 'What does "position vis-à-vis God" mean? Meaningfully and constitutedly this can be formulated only as a disposition of consciousness, rather than, ontically, as being next to or "under" an (absolute) Being.'[45]

The fact that the Christian is always in movement towards God means that he or she can make no authentic assertions about God that do not arise from *within* this movement. It is these 'epistemological insights, extending to the theory of historical cognition', which – as Heidegger avows in the 1919 letter to Engelbert Krebs quoted earlier in this chapter – 'have made the system of Catholicism problematic and unacceptable' to him.[46] Indeed, in a letter to his wife Elfride in May 1918, Heidegger projects the development of a 'wholly original religious life' as the wellspring of his entire future work: 'The creation of a wholly original [alt.: originary] religious life of our own will succeed, and all our work will grow from it.'[47]

Temporality and affliction

One of Heidegger's declared companions in the endeavour of uncovering an 'originary' approach to religious life was the young Luther,[48] whom he had encountered as early as 1908 in Johannes Ficker's then new Weimar edition of the 'Lectures on Romans'.[49] In his interpretation of the Reformer's work, Heidegger strictly segregated the early, radical *theologia crucis* from Luther's later thought: 'In his first works, Luther opened up a new understanding of primitive Christianity. Later, he himself fell prey to the burden of tradition; this was the beginning of Protestant Scholasticism.'[50]

Luther formulated his theology of the cross in radical opposition to the Scholastic 'theologians of glory'. Its rejection of any continuity between natural human desires, ambitions and knowledge on the one hand, and a true knowledge of God on the other, is captured most succinctly in the proof of Theological Thesis XX of the 1518 Heidelberg Disputation:

> The nature of God which is turned towards us and visible to us – i.e. his humanity, weakness, foolishness – is opposed to the invisible nature of God, as 1 Corinthians 1.25 states of

divine weakness and foolishness. You see, because men abused the knowledge of God from his works, God wished now to be known through suffering. He wished to condemn such "wisdom of the invisible" through a "wisdom of the visible", so that those who did not revere God as He is revealed in His works would revere Him as the One Who is hidden in suffering [*absconditum in passionibus*].

In response to this and other sources, Heidegger came, increasingly, to regard the mood characterizing the human experience of ascent to the divine as one of *affliction* or *suffering*. Referring to Luther's interpretation of Romans 1, he wrote to his wife in September 1919:

Since I have read Luther's Commentary on Romans, much that was previously painful and dark to me has become luminous and liberating – I understand the Middle Ages and the development of Christian religiosity in an entirely new way, and wholly new perspectives on the problems posed by the philosophy of religion have opened up to me.[51]

But as much as it depended on Luther, Heidegger's interpretation of his *theologia crucis* also diverged significantly from its source. He was interested less in the specifically theological claims of Luther's thesis than in the experiential claim that God was 'to be known through suffering', which he interpreted largely anthropocentrically. In other words, Heidegger inflected Luther by relocating the centre of the revelatory significance of suffering from the passion of Christ to the passion of *man* in and from his own finitude – a finitude revealed particularly in the ascent character of religious experience.

The primary inspiration for this reinterpretation was Romantic literature, and in particular, Hölderlin.[52] Heidegger had read Hölderlin since first encountering him in a cheap Reclam edition in 1908[53]; but it was not until the war years that he discovered the poet's significance for a philosophical engagement with suffering. Years later, Heidegger remarked: 'During the campaign [of the Great War], Hölderlin's hymns were stuffed into one's backpack right along with the cleaning gear.'[54] In August 1918, he wrote to his wife Elfride from the front: 'Hölderlin is becoming a new experience for me at the moment – almost as if I am approaching him wholly originally (and) for the first time.'[55]

Arguably the main philosophical attraction of Hölderlin at this time was his justification of human suffering as the necessary supplement to divine perfection. Perfection, in Hölderlin's view, implies a complete being-at-rest in oneself, and consequently, beatitude. At the same time, however, complete self-sufficiency excludes self-awareness, because self-awareness can only arise in the space of an enduring self-difference, that is, within (or for) an incomplete self.[56] Although in one sense self-sufficient in themselves, the gods thus require humans to *witness* their perfection, and thus to supplement their lacking awareness of that perfection:

> The gods, however, are sufficient
> In their own immortality, and if
> The dwellers of heaven require one thing,
> It is heroes and humans
> And other mortals. For because
> The blessed do not of themselves feel,
> Someone else, if it is permitted
> To say so, must sympathetically feel on their behalf—
> That one they need. . . .[57]

More often than not, this vicarious (or 'participating') 'feeling' of humans for gods takes the form of suffering, which functions as a negative witness to divine perfection, and awakens the gods to their own contrasting blessedness. Hölderlin sees his own poetry as both evoking and continuing this witness, for example in 'Hyperion's Song of Fate', sung by the protagonist towards the end of the epistolary novel *Hyperion*[58]:

> You walk in the light above,
>   On soft ground, blissful spirits!
>   Bright divine airs
>   Touch you lightly
>   As the fingers of the harpist
>   her holy strings.
>
> Fatelessly as the sleeping
>   Infant, the heavenly ones breathe;

> Chastely preserved
> In a modest bud,
> Spirit blooms for them
> Eternally,
> And the blessed eyes
> Gaze in still
> Eternal clarity.

> But our fate is
> To find no resting place,
> Suffering humanity
> Faints, falls
> Blindly from one hour
> To the next,
> Like water flung
> From cliff to cliff,
> Year after year into the unknown.[59]

The temporal and restless existence of humans, in its difference and distance from divine peacefulness and stasis, is the main source of our suffering. However, in its role as witness, suffering, for Hölderlin, also becomes a source of joy for humans, because it constitutes their own proper participation in, indeed their excess over the divine, recalling the gods from the 'Nothing' of oblivion.[60]

Heidegger channelled this idea in his own religious programme, centred on bearing the burden of a perpetual 'titchdom'.[61] Soon after the May 1918 letter to Elfride announcing 'the creation of a wholly original religious life' as the wellspring of all his future work, Heidegger declared in a letter to Elisabeth Blochmann:

> Where a personal life, with inner truthfulness, is on the *way* to perfection – and we are, after all, always *essentially on the way* – it is necessarily beset by the asperity of tornness, of relapses and new attempts, and by an unstaunchable suffering from the problematic and questionable; these are essential components of the ethos of the truly scholarly and spiritual man.[62]

In 1919, Heidegger announced his break with institutional Catholicism. The language of his famous letter to Krebs echoes that of his recent correspondence: 'It is *hard* [*schwer*] to live as a philosopher: the inner truthfulness in relation to oneself and those one is called to teach requires sacrifices and renunciations and struggles which remain forever foreign to the mere scholarly craftsman.'[63] And in a 1921 letter to his student Karl Löwith, Heidegger recommends acceptance of this yoke as an active principle of the work of a theologian: 'We must *sacrifice* ourselves and find our way back into *existential* limitation and facticity, instead of deflecting these by programmes and universal problems.'[64] In the years following this breakthrough of 1918/19, Heidegger crystallizes this understanding of suffering in his interpretation of Christian eschatology.

The eschatological constitution of religious existence: Heidegger's readings of Paul and Augustine

Heidegger's dual concern with a religiosity marked by aboriginal experience and a theology capable of giving this experience expression from within culminated in the now famous lecture series of 1920 and 1921, Introduction to the Phenomenology of Religion and Augustine and Neoplatonism. There is a large and growing body of scholarship on both these lecture series. In this section, therefore, I am not concerned with full summaries of Heidegger's interpretations of these great Christian thinkers, but only with the main theological pressure points of these readings: what Heidegger regards as their main insights and errors, and in what ways his interpretations differ from their self-understanding or their more traditional Christian interpretation.[65]

Paul

Already in his winter semester 1919/20 lectures, Basic Problems in Phenomenology, Heidegger states that the consolidation of a *Selbstwelt* ('world of self') – a focus on the self as the locus of the expression and perception of 'being', which alone makes possible 'history' in a Hegelian sense – was a consequence of the emergence of Christianity. The basic disposition of this primitive Christianity, according to Heidegger, is *crede ut intelligas*, which he glosses: 'Live your self animatedly – and only on this ground of experience, your last and fullest experience of self, knowledge will grow.'[66] After the era of the early church, this basic disposition has been exemplified most strikingly by Augustine, the medieval mystics (Bernard of Clairvaux, Bonaventure, Eckhard and Tauler) and Luther. The phenomenological method is ally and handmaid of this Christian thought world, which alone has the inner power to deconstruct Aristotelian metaphysics. The emergence of Christianity, Heidegger writes, was

> [a] great revolution against classical science, particularly Aristotle, who, however, in the coming millennium, would once again triumph, indeed become the philosopher of official Christianity – such that the inner experiences and the new attitude to life [characteristic of Christianity] would be yoked to the forms of expression of classical science. [This is] a process, still showing deep and confusing repercussions, radical liberation from which is one of the innermost tendencies of phenomenology.[67]

In his lecture series Introduction to the Phenomenology of Religion (1920/21), Heidegger gives a fuller account of this convergence of Christian experience and phenomenology. Specifically, he seeks to show how the disposition towards temporality fostered by early Christian eschatology overlaps with – or motivates – the disposition necessary to be a true philosopher: a disposition of uncertainty, questioning and *Anfängertum* ('beginner-dom'). Philosophy, unlike the sciences, is not primarily there to 'sol[ve] . . . concrete problems', but to raise fundamental (and often seemingly preliminary) questions. This is a precarious task; but 'I, for my part, want to keep awake and acuminate this affliction of philosophy . . . to such an extent that it turns into a virtue'.[68] How semantically close this is to Heidegger's subsequent description of eschatological expectation will be apparent in a moment.

The standard of the 'sciences', Heidegger continues, is as inappropriate to religion as it is to philosophy.[69] He criticizes Ernst Troeltsch for treating the philosophy of religion as a *science* of religion, shaped by a scientific conception of philosophy as the perception or understanding of objects. In this false conception, religion becomes an 'object' for philosophy, and so is defined by 'contexts [lit.: object relations] which already existed *before* religion'.[70] By contrast, 'what characterizes a religion-phenomenological understanding is to lay the ground for an original/originary way of approach' to the Christian religion.[71]

This can only grow out of factic life experience, and therefore requires, first of all, an aboriginal approach to that experience: 'The meaning of temporality is defined by a basic relation to God – such, however, that eternity can only be understood through the practice of temporality.'[72] This, he believes, is the characteristic disposition of early Christian eschatological expectation.

Heidegger expounds on this by way of an exposition of Paul's exhortation regarding the Coming of Christ in Chapter 5 of the First Epistle to the Thessalonians. The relevant passage in Paul's Epistle is as follows:

> Now concerning the times and the seasons [of Christ's return], brothers and sisters, you do not need to have anything written to you. For you yourselves know very well that the day of the Lord will come like a thief in the night. When they say, "There is peace and security", then sudden destruction will come upon them, as labour pains come upon a pregnant woman, and there will be no escape! But you, beloved, are not in darkness, for that day to surprise you like a thief; for you are all children of light and children of the day; we are not of the night or of darkness. So then, let us not fall asleep as others do, but let us keep awake and sober.

For Heidegger, the phenomenological significance of this passage lies in the fact that Paul's expectation of the *parousia* is not controlled by speculation about the exact time of Christ's return but, on the contrary, effects a complete transformation of his experience of time or temporality as such. It calls forth a subjective experience of time 'without order and fixed spots, which cannot be grasped by any objective notion of time', and thus gives rise to eschatological 'affliction' (*Bedrängnis*), characterized by an existential insecurity or uncertainty which arouses an intense and undelegable 'watchfulness'.[73] It is this existential relation to time which characterizes primitive (and authentic) Christianity, and makes it a suitable model for phenomenology. It should be emphasized that this attitude contrasts sharply not only with a 'scientific' approach but also with later Christian attitudes. In his own day, Heidegger thinks, Christianity presents itself most commonly as a closed system of 'answers' precluding rather than opening existential uncertainty or questioning: It is thus as much in need of reform as most other (inauthentic) ways of living.

Heidegger is interested primarily in a *Befindlichkeit* or 'mood' – an intuitive, situated 'attunement' within and to the world.[74] Heidegger labels this disposition 'eschatological' affliction; however, his etymological understanding of *Befindlichkeit* (influenced by Schleiermacher)[75] as a function precisely of human situatedness *in* a world resists the inclusion of the traditional Christian object of this disposition, namely the anticipated irruption into the world from without of Christ's *parousia*, as a term of the analysis. Consequently, the object of eschatological 'care' or 'affliction' is no longer (as for Paul) the dark and death-filled world *inflected by* its imminent 'solicitation' by Christ, but only that world in its transience.

It is important to note that although Heidegger presents this as a phenomenologically precise representation of Paul's eschatology, which he has stripped only of its heuristic appeal to a specific object of anticipation (the *parousia*), his 'phenomenological reduction' in fact causes him to misidentify Paul's basic eschatological mood, which is not affliction but hope. Paul offers his discourse on the *parousia* to increase the hope of the faithful (1 Thess. 5.13), and closes it with an appeal, 'therefore', to persevere in faith, love and hope (5.8-11).[76] Nor is this misreading accidental. On the contrary, 'hope' (alone among the three theological virtues) is entirely absent from Heidegger's writings on the phenomenology of religion. The reason may be that Christian hope, as Henry Wansborough puts it, 'is to be confident of receiving the eschatological gifts'[77] – in other words, is inherently directed towards that which exceeds the 'naturally' human, and is gratuitously bestowed on *Dasein* by Another. What is more, Paul identifies precisely this hope as the 'ownmost' calling (*Beruf*) of the faithful, thus suggesting, paradoxically, that what is most proper to a person is also beyond his or her natural capacity – which is bounded by death – and must be received from Christ through his Resurrection and Return.[78] Heidegger's early phenomenology is fundamentally at odds with such a vision.

Augustine

A similar dynamic is at work in Heidegger's lecture series on Augustine's *Confessions* the following year. Augustine is a major interlocutor in the period of Heidegger's first formation as a phenomenologist. He appears in notes and lectures from as early as 1919, and a whole lecture series – Augustine and Neoplatonism – is devoted to him in 1921. In his winter semester 1919/20 lecture series Basic Problems of Phenomenology, Heidegger praises Augustine as 'elementally encompassing' the insight of primitive Christianity, which, as he emphasizes (correcting Dilthey), can never be merely epistemological, but must be 'lived': 'Augustine saw in the *"inquietum cor nostrum"* the great unceasing restlessness of life. He achieved a wholly original [alt.: originary] view which was not merely theoretical, but lived and brought to expression.'[79]

In his great reading of *Confessiones* X in the 1921 lecture series Augustine and Neoplatonism, Heidegger frames Augustine's marvelling discovery that the memory exceeds the grasp of the conscious spirit as a proto-phenomenological insight: '"*Penetrale amplum et infinitum.*" All this belongs to myself, and yet I do not grasp [or contain] it myself. The spirit is too narrow to possess itself.'[80] For Heidegger, it is precisely the self's non-coincidence with itself (contrasting with divine self-possession) which is at the root of Augustine's central insight into human facticity, '*inquietum est cor nostrum*' ('our heart is restless').[81] This non-coincidence enables and perpetuates the existential mood which Heidegger describes as eschatological affliction in the Introduction to the Phenomenology of Religion (1920/21), as *curare* or *Bekümmertsein* in the Augustine lectures, and as *Sorge* (care) in *Being and Time*.

However, for Heidegger this 'eschatological' affliction is radically compromised by Augustine's actual eschatological vision, centring on the eternal beatific vision of the *summum bonum*. In Augustine's work, this great eschatological theme frames the baring of his 'restless heart' in the exordium, and is developed in Book X: 'You have made us for yourself, O Lord, and our hearts are restless until they rest in you.'[82] But for Heidegger, the professed desire for the joyful contemplation of God is not an integral or authentic part of Augustine's insight into the human, but a Neoplatonic vitiation of his phenomenological analysis. In his reading, Augustine's 'beatific vision' is merely a version of the Neoplatonic notion of *theoria* or *contemplatio*, a static contemplation of God as a metaphysical object.[83] This passive vision of an objectified God, however, is inherently incompatible with the living experience of the holy which Heidegger has defined as authentic religion. Specifically, unlike the inherently 'unfulfilled' character of human willing (which is always directed to something it 'does not yet have' or 'not yet is'), contemplation of God as 'the greatest being' (*das Seiende selbst*) 'no longer points beyond itself, [but] is fulfilled in itself'.[84] Thus, it seems to betray the existential experience of eschatological 'affliction' or 'care' to which both Paul and Augustine himself have, in Heidegger's reading, testified.

Heidegger and Augustine's disagreement about the question of what constitutes human 'facticity' (and, consequently, what falls within the purview of phenomenological analysis) is closely related to their differing understandings of the relation (if any) between time and eternity. Both Augustine and Heidegger regard the ordinary concept of time as derivative of the existential experience of 'temporality' as a 'distension' of the soul.[85] However, they disagree about the source of this experience. Augustine (like Kierkegaard, as we will see in the next chapter) thinks that it is caused by the fact that, while within time, we strain towards eternity. Echoing Paul's commitment to 'stretch forward' towards the 'prize of the upward call of God in Christ Jesus' (Phil. 3.13-14), Augustine laments:

> You are my eternal Father, but I am scattered in times whose order I do not understand. The storms of incoherent events tear to pieces my thoughts, the inmost entrails of my soul, until that day when, purified and molten by the fire of your love, I flow together . . . into you.[86]

Heidegger radically disagrees with this. Just as Schleiermacher's religious feeling reveals Dasein as part of the world as an 'infinite whole', and thus cannot extend to 'the being of God before the world and outside the world', Heidegger's 'thrown projection' necessarily moves within the horizons of this world and this time.[87] In other words, *diastasis* is always an expression of what he calls 'diathesis' or *Befindlichkeit*: it is always a way of finding oneself *within* a world, and cannot be a relation to anything outside it.[88] As in his interpretation of Paul, therefore, Heidegger concludes vis-à-vis Augustine that not eternal life but death should function as the proper horizon of an authentic eschatology.

As is already the case in Heidegger's 1920/21 lectures, a dominant influence on this interpretation is Franz Overbeck.[89] In Overbeck's vision, the heart of Christianity lies in its 'eschatology', which he interprets as nothing other than a self-reflexive *memento mori* – in other words, an acknowledgement of the mortality of all things, which must necessarily include even the transience of Christianity itself. 'The highest wisdom' of Christianity, Overbeck writes, is found 'in [its] eschatology, that is, its *doctrine of the future* or of *death*. For Christianity is nothing other than the wisdom of death. It teaches us exactly what death teaches us, not more nor less'.[90] Heidegger intuitively agrees.

This shift of horizon, however, has far-reaching implications for Heidegger's theological-philosophical position more generally. Augustine's entire vision of man – both in the *Confessions* as a whole and in the philosophical account of Book X – is predicated on the belief that man was made for eternity. This claim has two main facets: First, that God dwells at the centre of each human heart and continually recalls it to him- (and thus it-)self.[91] Secondly, that death is not the natural end point of human existence, but an unnaturally imposed end consequent upon the Fall, which can and will be overcome in the eschaton. Given that Heidegger's phenomenological work at this time is still motivated by Christian commitment, his reinterpretation of eschatology as a 'doctrine of death' rather than an orientation towards eternal life therefore has to be fortified by a theologically responsible way to repudiate both these assumptions. Exactly this is what we see in the following three years: first, a defence of speaking under theological epoché, that is, within a procedural bracketing of the question of the God-directedness of man; secondly, a reinterpretation of death as the natural (rather than belatedly imposed) boundary of human existence. The next chapter follows out these developments.

Notes

1   Quoted in Kisiel, *Genesis*, p. 75. As late as 1931, Husserl told Dorion Cairns that he had long realized how far Heidegger was from him, and laid this to Heidegger never having freed himself completely

from his theological prejudices (as well as to the weight of the war on him); conversation on 13 August 1931, in Dorion Cairns, *Conversations with Husserl and Fink* (The Hague: Martinus Nijhoff, 1976), p. 9.

2 Heidegger to Löwith, 19 August 1921, in 'Heidegger/Löwith', pp. 28–9.

3 Heidegger, *Ontologie: Hermeneutik der Faktizität* (lecture series SS 1923), published as GA 63; here p. 5.

4 On Paul, Augustine, and the medieval mystics, see GA 60 (*passim*); on Schleiermacher, see 'Schriftenverzeichnis', *HJB* 1, 469 (discussed below); on Dostoevsky and Kierkegaard, see 'Antrittsrede' (1957), GA 1, 57; on Overbeck, see 'Vita' (1922), GA 16, 42 (and cf. the discussion of this reference in Wolfe, *Heidegger's Eschatology*, pp. 23–4).

5 Rickert to Heidegger, 3 February 1917, in *Heidegger/Rickert*, p. 40.

6 Heidegger to Rickert, 27 February 1917, in *Heidegger/Rickert*, p. 42.

7 See e.g. Husserl's letter to Heidegger concerning Heidegger's qualifying thesis, dated 21 July 1916, in Edmund Husserl, *Briefwechsel*, 10 vols, ed. Karl Schuhmann (The Hague: Kluwer Academic Publishers, 1994), vol. 4, p. 127. On Heidegger's early relationship to Husserl, see particularly Thomas Sheehan, 'Husserl and Heidegger: The Making and Unmaking of a Relationship', in *Edmund Husserl: Psychological and Transcendental Phenomenology and the Confrontation with Heidegger (1927–1931)* (ed. and trans. Thomas Sheehan and R. E. Palmer; The Hague: Kluwer Academic Publishers, 1997), pp. 1–40; esp. pp. 1–22.

8 Natorp to Husserl, 7 October 1917, in Husserl, *Briefwechsel*, vol. 5, p. 130.

9 Husserl to Natorp, 8 October 1917, in Husserl, *Briefwechsel*, vol. 5, p. 131.

10 Little is known about this engagement or its termination. A letter from Heidegger's friend Ernst Laslowski (responding to an unpreserved communication from Heidegger) suggests that Martin broke off the relationship for the sake of his philosophical vocation; Lawlowski to Heidegger, 21 November 1915, in *HJB* 1, 50–2; p. 51. (Note the arguable parallels to Kierkegaard's dissolution, after a year, of his 1840 engagement to Regine Olsen.)

11 A concerned letter from Laslowski dated 28 January 1917, as well as a series of diary entries by Heidegger's Catholic priest friend Engelbert Krebs concerning the difficulties of the marriage, are recorded in Ott, *Heidegger*, pp. 99–101 and 109.

12 Quoted in Ott, *Heidegger*, p. 108. Gerda Walther, a fellow student
    of Husserl, mentions Elfride's influence on her husband's turn from
    Catholicism in *Zum anderen Ufer: Vom Marxismus und Atheismus
    zum Christentum* (Remagen: Der Leuchter/Otto Reichl Verlag, 1960),
    p. 207; noted in Sheehan, 'Husserl and Heidegger', 12n. 33.

13 Heidegger to Krebs, 9 January 1919, in *HJB* 1, 67–8; p. 67.

14 Husserl to Natorp, 11 February 1920, in Husserl, *Briefwechsel*,
    vol. 5, p. 139.

15 Husserl to Rudolf Otto, 5 March 1919, in Husserl, *Briefwechsel*,
    vol. 7, pp. 205–8; pp. 205 and 207. See also Sheehan, 'Husserl and
    Heidegger', 12. Ochsner did not, in the end, convert to Protestantism,
    but came to form part of the progressive Catholic 'Freiburg Circle'
    which also included the Heidegger-influenced theologians Max
    Müller and Bernhard Welte (see Chapter 7).

16 Bultmann to Hans Freiherr von Soden, 23 December 1923; published
    in Antje Bultmann Lemke, 'Der unveröffentlichte Nachlaß von Rudolf
    Bultmann – Ausschnitte aus dem biographischen Quellenmaterial',
    in Bernd Jaspert (ed.), *Rudolf Bultmanns Werk und Wirkung*
    (Darmstadt: Wissenschaftliche Buchgesellschaft, 1984), pp. 194–210;
    p. 202.

17 Heidegger, 'Lebenslauf' (1915), GA 16, 38–9.

18 Heidegger, *Kategorien- und Bedeutungslehre* (1916), GA 1, 407.

19 Ibid., 409.

20 Ibid., 410.

21 See esp. Heidegger, *Einleitung in die Phänomenologie der Religion*
    (lecture series WS 1920/21), in GA 60, 3–125; pp. 9–14; and compare
    his 19 August 1921 letter to Karl Löwith, in which he affirms his
    commitment to his own 'facticity', which involves being 'a Christian
    theo*logian*' ('Heidegger/Löwith', p. 29).

22 'Das Problem des Religiösen bei Schleiermacher' (1 August 1917);
    attested in two letters by Heinrich Ochsner dated 2 and 5 August
    1917; see Curd Ochwadt and Erwin Tecklenborg (eds.), *Das Maß
    des Verborgenen: Heinrich Ochsner zum Gedächtnis* (Hannover:
    Charis-Verlag, 1981), p. 92 and 266; cited in 'Schriftenverzeichnis
    (1909–2004)', *HJB* 1, 469.

23 Heidegger, 'Zu Schleiermachers zweiter Rede "Über das Wesen
    der Religion"' (1917), in 'Die philosophischen Grundlagen der
    mittelalterlichen Mystik' (1916–19), GA 60, 301–37; pp. 319–22.

24 Heidegger to the Faculty of Philosophy, 30 August 1919; cited in
    GA 60, 348.

25 Heidegger, 'Zu Schleiermachers zweiter Rede' (1917), GA 60, 321.

26 Ibid., 322. (The term *Dasein*, so significant ten years later, is already used in this note for '[human] existence'.)

27 Friedrich Schleiermacher, *Über die Religion: an die Gebildeten unter ihren Verächtern*, ed. Günter Meckenstock (Berlin: Walter de Gruyter, 2001[1799]), pp. 82–3.

28 Schleiermacher, *Über die Religion*, pp. 80–2, 92.

29 Heidegger, 'Zu Schleiermachers zweiter Rede' (1917), GA 60, 322; citing Schleiermacher, *Über die Religion*, p. 100 (emphasis added by Heidegger).

30 Schleiermacher, *Über die Religion*, p. 89.

31 Ibid.; referring to Schleiermacher, *Über die Religion*, pp. 89–90 (emphasis added by Heidegger).

32 Heidegger, 'Mystik im Mittelalter' (1919), GA 60, 306–7; p. 307; and 'Zu den Sermones Bernardi in canticum canticorum' (1918), GA 60, 334–7; p. 336; cf. Schleiermacher, *Über die Religion*, p. 90.

33 Schleiermacher, *Der christliche Glaube nach den Grundsätzen der evangelischen Kirche im Zusammenhang dargestellt*, ed. Rolf Schäfer (Berlin: Walter de Gruyter, 2008[1830/31]), §4.

34 For an alternative account of Heidegger's 'basic experience', see Benjamin Crowe, *Heidegger's Religious Origins* (Indianapolis: Indiana University Press, 2006), pp. 29–37.

35 Heidegger, *Grundprobleme der Phänomenologie* (1919/20), GA 58, 61.

36 Edith Stein to Roman Ingarden, 8 June 1918, in ESGA 4, 85–6; p. 85.

37 Adolf Reinach, 'Das Absolute', in Karl Schuhmann and Barry Smith (eds.), *Sämtliche Werke* (2 vols; Munich: Philosophia Verlag, 1989), vol. 1, p. 610; quoted in 'Das Absolute' (1918), GA 60, 324–7; p. 327.

38 Heidegger, 'Das Absolute' (1918), GA 60, 324–5.

39 Heidegger, 'Zu den Sermones Bernardi' (1918), GA 60, 334 and 336.

40 Ibid., 336.

41 Heidegger, 'Das Absolute' (1918), GA 60, 325.

42 Heidegger to Blochmann, 15 June 1918, in *Heidegger/Blochmann*, p. 7.

43 Bernard of Clairvaux, Sermon IV, *Sermones super Cantica Canticorum*.

44 Reinach, 'Das Absolute', 10, quoted in 'Das Absolute' (1918), GA 60, 324.

45 Heidegger, 'Das Absolute' (1918), GA 60, 324.

46 Heidegger to Krebs, 9 January 1919, in *HJB* 1, 67.

47 Heidegger to Elfride Heidegger, 12 May 1918, in *Heidegger/Elfride Heidegger*, p. 66.

48 See Heidegger, *Ontologie: Hermeneutik der Faktizität* (1923), GA 63, 5.

49 See Otto Pöggeler, 'Heideggers Luther-Lektüre im Freiburger Theologenkonvikt', *HJB* 1, 185–96; p. 194.

50 Heidegger, *Augustinus und der Neuplatonismus* (lecture series SS 1921), published in GA 60, 160–299; pp. 281–2.

51 Heidegger to Elfride Heidegger, 9 September 1919, in *Heidegger/ Elfride Heidegger*, p. 100.

52 Although F. W. J. Schelling's *Freiheitsschrift* (*Philosophical Enquiries into the Essence of Human Freedom* [1809]) would seem a natural source for the ideas about to be sketched, Heidegger did not in fact read that text until 1926. In spring 1926, he wrote to his friend and colleague Karl Jaspers to thank him 'for the Schelling volume', noting: 'the treatise on freedom, I've only skimmed. It is too precious to first encounter in a raw reading' ('Sie ist mir zu wertvoll, als daß ich sie in einem rohen Lesen erstmals kennenlernen möchte'); Heidegger to Jaspers, 24 April 1926, in *Heidegger/Jaspers,* p. 62. Heidegger first held a seminar on Schelling's *Freiheitsschrift* the following year, 1927/28 (see *HJB* 1, 483), and later returned to it at least twice, in 1936 and 1941 (see GA 42 and GA 49).

53 See Heidegger, 'Antrittsrede' (1957), GA 1, 56, as well as Heidegger to Imma von Bodmershof, 12 July 1975, in Bruno Pieger (ed.), *Martin Heidegger/Imma von Bodmershof: Briefwechsel 1959–1976* (Frankfurt: Klett-Cotta, 2000).

54 Heidegger, 'Der Ursprung des Kunstwerkes' (1935/36), in GA 5, 1–74; p. 3.

55 Heidegger to Elfride Heidegger, 30 August 1918, in *Heidegger/Elfride Heidegger*, p. 77. Hölderlin again becomes vital to Heidegger's philosophy in the 1930s and beyond: see Chapters 5–6 below.

56 See Gerhard Kurz's marginal notes to 'Der Rhein' (1801), in Gerhard Kurz (ed.), Friedrich Hölderlin, *Gedichte* (Stuttgart: Reclam, 2003), pp. 162–6; p. 164. The following discussion and selection of quotes is indebted to Damian Love, 'Samuel Beckett and the Art of Madness' [unpublished DPhil dissertation, Oxford 2004], pp. 159–69.

57 'Der Rhein', ll. 105–14; in Hölderlin, *Sämtliche Werke und Briefe*, vol. 1, ed. Jochen Schmidt (Frankfurt: Deutscher Klassiker Verlag, 1992), pp. 328–34; p. 331.

58 Heidegger wrote to Hannah Arendt on 23 August 1925 that 'among
    the few books on [his] "desk" was Hölderlin's *Hyperion*'; in *Arendt/
    Heidegger*, p. 46.

59 Hölderlin, *Sämtliche Werke und Briefe*, vol. 2, pp. 157–8.

60 See esp. Hölderlin, *Sämtliche Werke und Briefe*, vol. 2, p. 164.

61 Heidegger to Matthäus Lang (who was, from 1905, the rector of
    Heidegger's grammar school in Constance), 30 May 1928, in Ott,
    Heidegger, pp. 55–6. By this 1928 letter, Heidegger associates this
    attitude firmly with philosophy (rather than, as in 1919, religious
    faith): 'Perhaps philosophy shows most strikingly and lastingly
    how much man is a beginner [*wie anfängerhaft der Mensch ist*]. To
    philosophize is ultimately nothing other than being a beginner. But if
    we remain true to ourselves in our titchdom [*Knirpstum*] and try to
    act from out of it, then even a little must be to the good.'

62 Heidegger to Blochmann, 15 June 1918, in *Heidegger/Blochmann*, p. 7.

63 Heidegger to Krebs, 9 January 1919, in *HJB* 1, 67.

64 Heidegger to Löwith, 19 August 1921, in 'Heidegger/Löwith', p. 31.

65 A good English-language introduction to the Introduction to the
    Phenomenology of Religion is S. J. McGrath and Andrzej Wiercinski
    (eds.), *A Companion to Heidegger's Phenomenology of Religious Life*
    (Amsterdam: Rodopi, 2010). Good English-language introductions
    to Augustine and Neoplatonism are Frederick van Fleteren, *Martin
    Heidegger's Interpretations of Saint Augustine* (Lewiston: Edwin
    Mellen Press, 2005); and Craig J. N. de Paulo (ed.), *The Influence
    of Augustine on Heidegger: The Emergence of an Augustinian
    Phenomenology* (Lewiston: Edwin Mellen Press, 2006).

66 Heidegger, *Grundprobleme der Phänomenologie* (1919/20), GA 58,
    61–2.

67 Ibid., 61.

68 Heidegger, *Einleitung in die Phänomenologie der Religion* (1920/21),
    GA 60, 4–5. Compare the quote from Kierkegaard, *Either–Or* I
    (Heidegger's German edition: *Entweder–Oder* I [Jena: Diederichs,
    1911], p. 35), which Heidegger chooses as a motto for his WS
    1921/22 lecture series Phenomenological Interpretations of Aristotle;
    see GA 61, 81.

69 For Heidegger's debt to Dilthey in the developing opposition between
    the explanatory and the understanding sciences, as well as in his
    account of intellectual history, see Kisiel, *Genesis*, pp. 101–8.

70 Heidegger, *Einleitung in die Phänomenologie der Religion* (1920/21),
    GA 60, 67.

71 Ibid.

72 Heidegger, *Einleitung in die Phänomenologie der Religion* (1920/21), GA 60, 117 (on 1 Thess. 3.3 and 5.9).

73 Ibid., 98 and 104; see also p. 105.

74 See *Sein und Zeit* (1927), now GA 2, §29. 'Attunement' is Stephen Mulhall's (Cavellian) translation of '*Befindlichkeit*' (see his *Heidegger and Being and Time* [London: Routledge, 2nd edn, 2005], p. 116). The German *Befinden* (from the verb *sich befinden*), from which *Befindlichkeit* is coined, means both 'residing' or 'being situated', and 'condition' or 'disposition'.

75 Kisiel cites Schleiermacher's 'felt intuition' as a precursor and model of Heidegger's *Befindlichkeit*, which enters his vocabulary in the 1919/20 lecture series Basic Problems in Phenomenology, a series which grew partly out of his engagement with Schleiermacher and medieval mysticism (compare his 1917–19 notes in GA 60, 301–37). In his 1924 lecture series Basic Concepts of Aristotelian Philosophy (published as GA 18), Heidegger identifies the term as an equivalent of Aristotle's '*diathesis*'. Cf. Kisiel, *Genesis*, p. 492.

76 Parallels can be found in all Pauline Epistles. See, among many other examples, Rom. 5.2, 8.18–23; 1 Cor. 15.19f; Gal. 5.5; Eph. 1.17f; Col. 1.5, 1.27; Tt 1.2, 2.13.

77 In his note to Rom. 5.2 in the *New Jerusalem Bible* (London: Darton, Longman & Todd, 1994), p. 1873.

78 See the verses listed above, especially 1 Cor. 15.19f. For the most influential formulation of this Christian position, see Thomas Aquinas, *Summa Theologiae* 1-2.114.2 ad 1. (*Beruf* is a favourite Heideggerian term, though he does not, of course, apply it to this context.)

79 Heidegger, *Grundprobleme der Phänomenologie* (1919/20), GA 58, 61–2. See also Heidegger, *Prolegomena zur Geschichte des Zeitbegriffs* (lecture series SS 1925), published as GA 20; here p. 418. For Heidegger's similar endorsement of Luther, see S. J. McGrath, 'The Facticity of Being God-Forsaken: The Young Heidegger and Luther's Theology of the Cross', *American Catholic Philosophical Quarterly* 79, 2 (2005), pp. 273–90; p. 285 (re-worked as chapter 6 of S. J. McGrath, *The Early Heidegger & Medieval Philosophy: Phenomenology for the Godforsaken* [Washington: Catholic University of America Press, 2006]).

80 Heidegger, *Augustinus und der Neuplatonismus* (1921), GA 60, 182, commenting on Augustine, *Confessiones* X. xvii [26]. Cf. Philippe Capelle, '"Katholizismus", "Protestantismus", "Christentum"

und "Religion" im Denken Martin Heideggers: Tragweite und Abgrenzungen', *HJB* 346–71; p. 362.

81 Augustine, *Confessiones* I. i (1).

82 Ibid. See also X. xxii (32) to xxiii (33).

83 See Heidegger, *Augustinus und der Neuplatonismus* (1921), GA 60, 199–203.

84 Heidegger, *Logik: Die Frage nach der Wahrheit* (lecture series WS 1925/26), published as GA 21; here p. 122.

85 See *Sein und Zeit* (1927), GA 2, §§65–71; Augustine, *Confessiones* XI. xxvi (33). Cf. Plotinus, *Enneads* 3.7.11 (cited in Augustine, *Confessions* [trans. and ed. Henry Chadwick; Oxford: Oxford University Press, 1992], 240n. 27).

86 Augustine, *Confessiones* XI. xxix (39); Chadwick's translation. There is no doubt about the Neoplatonic influence on this passage; nevertheless, it is not reducible to Neoplatonism. Cf. also Gregory of Nyssa's mystical appropriation of *epektasis*, curiously absent from Heidegger's catena of mystical sources.

87 Cf. Schleiermacher, *Über die Religion*, p. 82. Heidegger does not use the terminology of '*Geworfenheit*' and '*Entwurf*' until *Being and Time*; however, he expresses a similar concept from 1919 onwards. In the 1924 lecture series Basic Concepts of Aristotelian Philosophy, he thematizes this issue in relation to *Befindlichkeit* (see Kisiel, *Genesis*, p. 498).

88 *Grundbegriffe der aristotelischen Philosophie* (lecture series SS 1924), published as GA 18; here p. 122.

89 A discussion of the competing appropriations of Overbeck by Heidegger and Barth around 1920 can be found in Wolfe, *Heidegger's Eschatology*, pp. 90–2, 95, 97–102.

90 From the unpublished 'Kirchenlexikon' (a collection of several thousand index cards), on a series of cards entitled 'Christentum Eschatologie Allg.', 2–3; quoted in Rudolf Wehrli, *Alter und Tod des Christentums bei Franz Overbeck* (Zürich: Theologischer Verlag, 1977), p. 229. Cf. Franz Overbeck, *Christentum und Kultur*, ed. C. A. Bernoulli (Darmstadt: Wissenschaftliche Buchgesellschaft, 1963), pp. 297–8.

91 See esp. Augustine, *Confessiones* X. xx (29).

3

The emancipation of philosophy (1921–1929)

During the 1920s, Heidegger turned from the development of a phenomenology of religion to that of a principled 'a-theistic' method – a philosophical methodology, that is, which brackets God from its analyses, without necessarily implying an atheistic worldview.[1] Until the mid-1920s, Heidegger regarded this a-theistic philosophy as a *preparatio evangeliae*, a phenomenological groundwork for understanding the existential situation of man into which God irrupts. However, already by 1927, this view gives way to a prioritization of philosophy as a competitor or successor to the role of mediatrix of an authentic life.[2]

Heidegger's development of this position comprises three main stages: The first stage, already discussed in the last two chapters, was to prioritize the earliest, eschatologically oriented Christian experience as capable of disclosing the deepest structures of existence, namely eschatological affliction or anxiety. This prioritization consistently comes with a critique of Christianity as quickly abandoning its earliest eschatological experience for secure philosophical and political *systems* (represented in Heidegger's own time by neo-Scholasticism). The second stage is a more systematic 'deconstruction'[3] of these systems through the postulate of a constitutive and absolute *rift* between God and man – a rift that perpetuates affliction or anxiety as the proper mood both of human existence and of theological enquiry. In this emphasis, Heidegger draws on the anti-metaphysical tradition in Christianity, especially St Paul, Augustine, Martin Luther, Søren Kierkegaard, Franz Overbeck and Fyodor Dostoevsky: theologians who think that the arrogation of a God's-eye view of human existence is a basic betrayal of the true Christian condition, a hubristic 'theology of glory'. Ironically, however, the radical externality of God, for Heidegger, comes to imply that God's agency must remain irretrievably beyond the purview of the phenomenological method: what originally attracted Heidegger as a method adequate to describing Christian faith now emerges as a demarcation of the philosopher's territory against that of the theologian. The third stage, then, is the emancipation of philosophy from theology as an independent mediatrix of authentic existence. This step has a thematic and a methodological component: Thematically, Heidegger goes through an intensive engagement with the question of sin, which ends in rejecting revelation and grace as the appropriate horizon within which to interpret sin. Methodologically, Heidegger formulates a more fully worked-out distinction between 'ontic' and 'ontological' sciences, coming to see theology as only one among many 'ontic' sciences that must be 'ontologically' grounded in the questions raised by philosophy.

This chapter tracks this development through its successive stages, using Heidegger's lectures, seminars, letters and other sources to document his reception of Luther and Kierkegaard, as well as the way his thematic concerns develop in tandem with his methodological commitments. The next chapter presents a reading of key theological terms in *Being and Time*, Heidegger's *magnum opus*, written at the nadir of this development and encapsulating his reinterpretation of sin and death, and of the relationship between philosophy and theology.

It might be useful for readers (particularly those coming from Heidegger to theology rather than vice versa) to have to hand a short summary of traditional Christian understandings of sin and death before reading further into the particularities of Heidegger's and his interlocutors' treatment of them. Such a summary is provided here.

Any Christian account of death must include reference to sin. The causal connection between sin and death (at least 'as it meets us'[4]) in the source texts is inescapable: '[S]in came into the world through one man, and death came through sin, and so death spread to all because all have sinned' (Rom. 5.12); 'For the wages of sin is death' (Rom. 6.23). This New Testament correlation – consistently accepted by the Christian tradition – is a complex interpretation of Genesis 2.16-7 and 3.1-24 in the light of the Christ event. God had declared upon placing the newly created man in Paradise, 'You may freely eat of every tree of the garden; but of the tree of the knowledge of good and evil you shall not eat, for in the day that you eat of it you shall die' (Gen. 2.16-7). Man, having trespassed the command, incurred the curse of mortality: 'By the sweat of your face you shall eat bread until you return to the ground, for out of it you were taken; you are dust, and to dust you shall return' (Gen. 3.19).

Whether death here is an intrinsic or punitive consequence of sin remains a matter of theological debate, closely connected, of course, to the concurrent debate on how to interpret the Atonement.[5] But the general claim, only rarely contested until recently, is that mortality is not a natural feature of human life, but a violation of that life in its original (that is, prelapsarian) integrity – and that the primary significance of Christ's Incarnation, Death and Resurrection is precisely the overcoming of death: '[W]here sin increased, grace abounded all the more, so that, just as sin exercised dominion in death, so grace might also exercise dominion through justification leading to eternal life through Jesus Christ our Lord' (Rom. 5.20-1).[6] This victory over death is conceived both in individual and in cosmic terms: as an eternal life with God after death, consequent upon the forgiveness of one's sin through faith in Christ (Jn 3.16, 11.25; etc.), and as the general resurrection of all the dead unto divine judgement and eternal life with or punished by God (1 Cor. 15.12-28, 50-7; Rev. 20.11-15; etc.).

The *temporality* of human existence is not directly linked with sinfulness in the Old or New Testaments; nevertheless, its inescapable association with mortality[7] means that it, too, is envisioned as being overcome by the eschatological defeat of death: 'time shall be no more' (Rev. 10.6).[8] The question whether this anticipated timelessness is a return to prelapsarian existence or a radically new mode of human existence – in other words, whether Biblical anthropology is in this respect fundamentally nostalgic or dynamic ('evolutionary') – is never raised in the source text, but becomes an important underlying concern in the Reformation Era.

It is on this background that Paul and Augustine await with hope the 'coming of the Lord' and eternal 'rest in [him]'. For both thinkers, a description of what it is to be human must involve an account of the *disruption* of human existence by sin and consequently death, and of the hoped-for restoration of authentic human existence through an outstripping of that disruption. Heidegger's developing vision is very different.

Philosophy under theological epoché

As we saw in Chapter 2, Heidegger developed during World War I a theological sense of human existence as ascent – of being essentially 'on the way'. This also determined the basic religious feeling: a dynamic affliction with one's own finitude. Until about 1920, this description of human existence seemed to Heidegger to necessarily include reference to God. Thus, in mid-1918, he wrote to Elisabeth Blochmann that '[e]very accomplishment achieves the character of finality in accordance with its authenticity, i.e. its inner belonging to the central "I" and its God-directed determination'.[9] A year later, he assured Blochmann of the 'mystery and grace-character of all life',[10] calling her to 'trust . . . in [her] inner calling'[11] and 'quiet humility before the Spirit':[12] 'I have firm faith in the Spirit and his power – whoever lives in him and for him will never fight a losing battle.'[13]

But already in his winter semester 1919/20 lecture series Basic Problems in Phenomenology, this view changes. Heidegger now begins to emancipate phenomenology, which he describes as the 'original' or 'originary science of life',[14] from the experience and elaboration of religious faith, which becomes one field among others in which the 'ultimate questions' analysed by phenomenology can arise. Such faith is authentic when it is the case that 'in religion . . . the ultimate questions are alive and in some way answered'.[15] However, theology (and religion in general) must remain in some sense secondary to phenomenology because its impetus is always to *answer* those 'ultimate questions', not, like phenomenology, to sustain them *as questions*. It is precisely because of this that Heidegger writes in preparation for his summer semester 1922 lecture series Phenomenological Interpretations of Aristotle:

Questionability is not religious, but is rather what leads to a situation of religious decision in the first place. I do not act religiously in philosophizing, even if I, as a philosopher, can be a religious person. But the art lies in philosophizing and in this being truly religious, which means factically taking philosophizing as one's worldly, historical task, in . . . a concrete world of action, not in religious ideology and fantasy.[16]

One model for Heidegger's re-conception of philosophy, here, as a perpetual 'titchdom' is Kierkegaard.[17] Among Heidegger's mottos for his 1921/22 lecture course Phenomenological Interpretations of Aristotle are two passages from Kierkegaard that emphasize the methodological implications of our constitutive 'paltriness' or 'puniness'. 'But what philosophy and the philosopher find difficult', writes Kierkegaard, 'is to stop'.[18] Rather than retaining a proper dread in the face of inescapable doubt, modern philosophy tends to 'float, as abstract, in the indeterminacy of the metaphysical'. 'But instead of admitting this of itself, and so to point men (the single man) to the ethical, the religious, the existential, philosophy has created the illusion that men. can, prosaically put, speculate themselves out of their skin into mere appearance.'[19]

However, what Heidegger regards as the great temptation of theology – to 'curry favour with our needs'[20] and claim a knowledge it cannot really attain – Kierkegaard regards as the typical failing of philosophy, to be overcome only by a sincere religiosity. True faith, for Kierkegaard, is marked by a recognition of one's own finitude as limitedness and burden, a recognition that overcomes the natural human arrogation of metaphysical insight into the transcendent. However, for Kierkegaard this experience arises from a conviction of our own depravity, and should lead the believer to a humble and trusting turn towards God in expectation of His help – a help which comes as a radical antithesis to the natural order of the world.

For Heidegger, by contrast, Kierkegaard's position seems, increasingly, to imply the need for a route different from that taken by the theologian himself. Kierkegaard's interpretation of the natural human state as sinful, Heidegger begins to argue in 1920/21, is itself a secondary and partly imposed description from the perspective of already achieved salvation. This salvation, however, because it is granted as a gift by an external source, is not itself part of the primordial human condition which is the task of phenomenology to investigate. While Heidegger continues to regard talk of 'sin' and 'salvation' as justified in the sphere of theology, he comes to regard it as the more basic philosophical task to describe the 'sinful' state in which humans naturally find themselves *from within*. If this implies a moral imperative, it is to acknowledge and work with the *Schwere* (heaviness/difficulty) of human existence rather than to wish to neutralize it. To work philosophically, he writes in 1922, is to sustain the fact that 'factic life has the ontological character of being heavily burdened with itself'.

This approach, Heidegger comes to think, has the paradoxical result that it is at the same time a more human way of being true to the acknowledgement of God than theology itself (because it does not seek to exceed the limits of the human, and so implicitly acknowledges the absolute transcendence of God), and a rebellion against God (because it resists His intervention). To sustain this paradox is the 'specific factic "ascesis" of the scientific life'.[21] Philosophy, Heidegger concludes, 'must, in its radical, self-reliant questionability, be in principle *a-theistic*. It must, precisely in light of its basic tendency, not falsely claim to have God or to determine God', 'keeping itself free from the temptations [of] only talking glibly about religiosity'. The more authentic it is, 'the more determinedly it is an "away" from [God], and precisely in the radical execution of the "away" a difficult "with" him'.[22] Later the same year, Heidegger adds provocatively, 'Could it be that the very idea of a philosophy of religion, and especially if it does not take into account the facticity of human being, is pure nonsense?'[23]

Our readings of Heidegger's engagements with St Paul, Augustine and Kierkegaard make it clear that both Heidegger's methodological commitment to 'existential limitation' and his thematic commitment to an eschatology oriented not towards eternal life but towards death are in implicit conflict with the doctrinal positions of his theological models, particularly their close identification of both ignorance and death with sin. This implicit conflict becomes a dominant concern of the philosopher's work in the years 1921–25. Especially following his move to Marburg and the establishment of a close working relationship with his theological colleague Rudolf Bultmann, Heidegger begins to work systematically through the problem of sin and its philosophical implications.

Luther and the problem of sin

Heidegger developed his understanding of the relation between sin, death and philosophy in direct engagement with Martin Luther. After an initial immersion in the work of Luther in his early student days, Heidegger returned to the Reformation theologian around 1919.[24] Karl Jaspers recalled that, during his visit in Freiburg in April 1920, he 'sat alone with [Heidegger] in his den, watched him at his Luther studies, and saw the intensity of his work'.[25] To his wife Elfride, Heidegger wrote in late 1920 that his 'edition of Luther' had become 'indispensable' to him.[26] After his move to Marburg in 1923, Heidegger attempted a more systematic engagement with the Reformation thinker, in dialogue with his theological colleague Rudolf Bultmann. Bultmann wrote at the time that Heidegger 'not only [had] excellent knowledge of Scholasticism, but also of Luther' – so much so that he 'rather put' the resident church historian Heinrich Hermelink 'on the spot'.[27] His student Karl Löwith recalled attending a joint seminar by Heidegger and Bultmann on the young Luther,[28] and Heidegger lectured on Luther at least twice in Bultmann's New Testament seminar: on 'The Problem of Sin in Luther' in 1924, and on Luther's commentary on Paul's Letter to the Galatians in 1927.[29]

In the last lecture series before his move to Marburg, Ontology: Hermeneutics of Facticity (1923), Heidegger first explicitly engages with the Christian understanding of sin as the state in which postlapsarian humanity finds itself, that is, the *status corruptionis*. In seeking to isolate 'the idea of facticity and the concept of man', Heidegger vigorously criticizes Max Scheler's 'phenomenological' claim that man's difference from the rest of the animal kingdom rests not in his rationality but in his perception of spiritual values and of God for its insufficient differentiation between theological and philosophical claims.[30] Especially Scheler's definition of man as an '"intention and gesture of 'transcendence' itself," a "God-seeker"'[31] is ridiculed for importing theological categories without observing the fundamental theological distinction between human existence in its prelapsarian integrity, its postlapsarian corruption, its Christian state of grace and its eschatological glory: '[W]hat gets overlooked again is that . . . in theology, man's various states, modes of being, must in principle be distinguished (*status integritatis, status corruptionis, status gratiae, status gloriae*) and that one cannot arbitrarily exchange one for the other.'[32]

Heidegger then draws special attention to Luther's understanding of the *status corruptionis*:

See Luther: *Porro caro significat totum hominem, cum ratione et omnibus naturalibus donis*.[33] This flesh is in a *status corruptionis* which is from the start fully defined: to it belong *ignorantia Dei, securitas, incredulitas, odium erga Deum*, a definitely negative relation to God in which man stands against God. *This* is as such *constitutive!*'[34]

In his supplementary notes to the lecture series, Heidegger isolates the essential difference between a Scholastic and a Lutheran understanding of the *status corruptionis* – a dispute in which he firmly sides with Luther.[35] For Scholastic theology, the Fall into sin impaired but did not obliterate human nature as it was constituted before the Fall. There was for Scholasticism, consequently, a large degree of continuity between man's prelapsarian and postlapsarian states, which expressed itself primarily in his continued ability to discern God by natural reason (as affirmed in Rom. 1.18-20).[36] For Luther, by contrast, the term 'flesh' (as opposed to 'Spirit') now encompasses 'the whole man with his reason and all his natural endowments': The *status corruptionis* 'is as such *constitutive*'; human nature as originally created 'in the image of God' (Gen. 1.27) is obliterated. In his supplementary notes, Heidegger explains the Christological rationale for this radical position: 'the more originally [or: originarily] and absolutely [salvation] is understood, the weightier sin must be. But it can have such weight only if the Fall is absolute, . . . its result [being] pure sinfulness'.

In his February 1924 seminar presentation on the problem of sin in Luther, Heidegger elaborates on the radical rift between pre- and post-lapsarian existence. In seeking to give a theological elucidation of Luther's understanding of sin, he reiterates the Christological reasoning cited in the earlier lecture notes:

The more the radicalness of sin is underestimated, the more salvation is undervalued and God's Incarnation stripped of its necessity. Thus, one finds in Luther the basic tendency: The *corruptio* of the being of man can't be understood radically enough; this in contrast to Scholasticism, which had always spoken of an attenuated *corruptio*.[37]

This position – that the 'nature of man is corrupt' – is then translated into characteristically Heideggerian language: 'The being of man as such is sin. . . . In other words, it does not attach itself to the moral make-up of man, but is his actual [or: authentic] core.

Sin, in Luther, is an existential term.'[38] Defining this state of sin as 'nothing other than the opposite of faith',[39] Heidegger comes to the startling conclusion that 'one can only understand faith if one understands sin, and one can only understand sin if one has a correct understanding of the being of man itself'.[40]

This conclusion confirms Heidegger in his commitment to an a-theistic phenomenology. If sinfulness is the mode of being in which humanity today always already finds itself, then it is precisely this sinful existence which it is phenomenology's primary task to interpret. Furthermore, this sinful existence is also the only soil on which any understanding of 'faith' can grow: faith must always be understood by contrast to sin. The constitutive significance of this interpretation of Luther for *Being and Time*'s discussion of *Verfall* (which, though in a Heideggerian context usually clumsily translated into English as 'falling', is merely a German rendering of the Latin *corruptio*) is one of the concerns of the next chapter.

The emancipation of philosophy

The pressing question now becomes: Is this phenomenological analysis of the *status corruptionis* (as the state in which humanity always already finds itself) a *preparatio evangeliae* – a Christian's analysis, in his capacity as philosopher, of the state from which (faith in) God alone can save? Or is it much rather an alternative to salvation? While Heidegger still tends towards the first view in his 1924 texts, he begins to shift towards the second view in the years following. An important step within this development is his formulation of a systematic distinction between 'ontic' and 'ontological' sciences, which builds on his earlier distinction between philosophy's role as raising and sustaining questions, and the role of theology and other discourses as attempting answers. In his 1927 lecture 'Phenomenology and Theology' (published in 1970 with a dedication to Rudolf Bultmann), Heidegger defines 'science' as the 'disclosure of a particular, circumscribed field of being or of what-is, for the sake of that disclosure itself'.[41] However, this means that every science relies on the prior demarcation of a particular area of being as its field of enquiry: science is 'positive' or 'ontic' in the sense of dealing with a *positum* or given subject. The only science that differs from this model (and is thus not in the same sense a science) is philosophy. Philosophy in its purest form is ontology, the study not of any predefined area of what-is, but of being itself. In seeking to clarify the ontological ground and constitution of all that is, philosophy is foundational for all other sciences. Theology, on this model, is the scientific investigation of the particular field of existence we call faith. Although faith itself is independent from philosophy, its systematic investigation, if it wishes to lay claim to being scientific, must appeal to the ontological groundwork laid down by philosophy.[42] This distinction between ontic and ontological also allows Heidegger to pinpoint what it is that makes St Paul, Augustine, Luther, Kierkegaard *et al.* ultimately inadequate to his own level of enquiry: they remain on an ontic level of analysis.

Although 'Phenomenology and Theology' casts philosophy as a potential help for theological enquiry, this presentation is in fact in conflict with the substance of Heidegger's argument. He himself recognized this. Heidegger wrote his lecture at the invitation of the Lutheran Theological Faculty in Tübingen, who also prescribed its subject matter. After delivering it, he wrote to Elisabeth Blochmann that its very remit, namely to make philosophy fruitful for theology, placed him 'as a philosopher in a terribly skewed light . . . and [made] the whole thing into an apology for Christian theology rather than', as it should be, 'a confrontation'.[43] Later in the letter, Heidegger felt compelled to return to the subject: The lecture, a 'document of my *Marburg* time', was merely meant to show '*how, given* that someone stands in the Christian Protestant faith and busies himself with theology, he ought to take philosophy, assuming that he wants it to be a help and not', as it really is, 'a fundamental agitation'.[44]

Heidegger's rejection of God as the horizon of an interpretation of human existence, then, is more than a declaration of allegiance to one field rather than another: It implies a revaluation of theology as at best an ontic science, one that already takes for granted the being of its object. But in tending to *claim* the place of the ontological science, it can be pernicious – indeed, can be the very embodiment of evil, claiming a grasp of that which must be acknowledged as ungraspable.[45] Consequently, in a 1928 letter to Julius Stenzel, one of the reviewers of *Being and Time*, Heidegger writes that 'in the *philosophical* problem of existence there is necessarily . . . an absolute opposition to all Christianity'.[46] The continuation of this trajectory will be followed out in Chapter 6.

Heidegger and Kierkegaard

Of particular importance for Heidegger's parallel concern with sin and eschatology is Kierkegaard's *Concept of Anxiety* (1844). In *Being and Time*, he commends the book in no fewer than three of his notoriously sparse footnotes: 'The one who has penetrated the phenomenon of anxiety [*Angst*] furthest is S. Kierkegaard', though his 'existential interpretation' of the phenomenon remains deficient.[47] The book, and Heidegger's reading of it, is a useful locus for focusing many of the issues we have been concerned with in this and the last chapter.

In *Concept of Anxiety*, Kierkegaard's pseudonym Vigilius Haufniensis – conscious that he is speaking psychologically of a matter that cannot adequately be discussed other than dogmatically[48] – posits anxiety (Heidegger's *Angst*) in the face of future possibility as the psychological condition (or environment) of sin.

Essential to Vigilius' claim is his understanding of temporality. Sin happens in a 'moment' (*øieblik*) of decision; it is a 'leap' not conditioned by anything but itself.[49] But the term *øieblik* so innocuously deployed here is by no means simple; on the contrary, it is the lynchpin of Vigilius' whole concept of temporality. As for Heidegger, Augustine and (Heidegger's) Paul, temporality, for Vigilius, is the specifically *human* existence in time, which is characterized by awareness of its own transience, or of itself as temporal; and as for Augustine and Paul (but by contrast to Heidegger[50]), this awareness – and with it the whole human phenomenon of temporality – can only arise in the background of the eternal, in which man also participates:

> The moment is that ambiguity in which time and eternity touch each other, and with this the concept of *temporality* is posited, whereby time constantly intersects eternity and eternity constantly pervades time. As a result, the above-mentioned division acquires its significance: the present time, the past time, the future time.[51]

Vigilius finds the Biblical source for this idea in Paul's eschatological vision of the resurrection, which is to happen 'in a flash, *in the twinkling of an eye* [Danish: *i et øjeblik*], at the last trumpet' (1 Cor. 15.52): 'With this', he claims, Paul 'also expresses the fact that the moment [øieblik] is commensurate with eternity, since the moment of destruction at that same moment expresses eternity'.[52]

Psychologically, the øieblik as a moment of decision requires a particular relation to the future. The reason is that to the human subject, eternity appears, for the time being, primarily as the not-yet: 'The eternal means first of all the futural'; or, expressed differently, 'the futural [is] the incognito . . . under which the eternal, being incommensurable with time, nevertheless keeps company with time'.[53] Vigilius is ambiguous here: for on the one hand, he talks ('objectively') of that 'fullness of time' which, for human beings, still lies in the future,[54] and on the other hand, he talks ('subjectively') of the future as *possibility*, which is infinite in two senses: the uncountable number of possible events and choices, and the 'limitlessness' (i.e. lack of delimitation) of 'possibility' as a term whose criteria include lack of realization (and so, to a certain extent, concretization).

It is the second, subjective sense – in which 'infinity' is quietly substituted for 'eternity' – which gains precedence in the following discussion. For the øieblik turns out to be simultaneous with the awakening of the human spirit (in Adam and in each person) as the synthesis of body and soul, or of time and eternity.[55] The human spirit awakens in its realization of the infinity of its own potential (*mulighedens selviske uendelighed*).[56] But this self-revelation is always already, psychologically speaking, anxiety: Anxiety 'is freedom's actuality as the possibility of possibility';[57] it 'is defined as freedom's disclosure to itself in possibility'.[58] To enter a conscious relation to one's own future is here inherently self-reflexive,[59] and to come to oneself in this way is full of anxiety because it is to confront Nothing in a double sense: as the 'nothing' of events and choices that are not yet and may never be, and vis-à-vis which the human spirit experiences its own immense (creative) infinity;[60] and as the 'nothing' of possibility which the human spirit itself *is*. 'The actuality of the spirit constantly shows itself as a form that tempts its possibility but disappears as soon as it seeks to grasp it, and it is a nothing that can only bring anxiety.'[61]

It is in the 'vertigo' induced by finding oneself thus between infinity and Nothing that one makes the leap of sin,[62] which is the attempt to stave off these enormities by positing as absolute something that, in reality, is merely finite. But this sin produces more anxiety, epitomized in the anxiety of death as punishment.[63] 'The moment sin is posited', Vigilius puts it radically, 'temporality is sinfulness.'[64] For Luther, the *status corruptionis* was 'as such constitutive'; for Vigilius, that sinfulness is inextricable from temporal existence itself. 'Authentic selfhood', as Heidegger will say, 'is an existentiell modification of the "they" as an essential existentiale'.[65]

But although anxiety is the psychological condition of sin, it is also potentially redemptive precisely because it 'consumes all finities, uncovers all their deceptions',[66] and reveals the human subject to himself not only in his actual but also in his possible existence. 'Whoever is educated by [anxiety] is educated by possibility, and only [he] who is educated by possibility is educated according to [his] infinitude.'[67]

The potential benefit is twofold. First, anxiety teaches the true power of faith:

> However, in order that an individual may thus be educated absolutely and infinitely by the possibility, he must be honest toward possibility and have faith. By faith I understand here what Hegel somewhere in his way correctly calls the inner certainty that anticipates infinity. When the discoveries of possibility are honestly administered, possibility will discover all the finitudes, but it will idealize them in the form of infinity and in anxiety overwhelm the individual until he again overcomes them in the anticipation of faith.[68]

Secondly, anxiety allows the human person to gather up his entire self and surrender himself to God in faith *in his entirety*: 'In that very moment, he is absolutely identified with the unfortunate man; he knows no finite evasion by which he may escape. Now the anxiety of possibility holds him as its prey until, saved, it must hand him over to faith.'[69]

In Heidegger's development of an eschatology without eschaton, Kierkegaard's analysis of anxiety was formative but not definitive: it lacked, Heidegger claimed, an ontological perspective, and remained on an ontic level insufficient to Heidegger's own existential analytic.[70] This, according to Heidegger, was particularly true of Kierkegaard's understanding of eternity: 'Kierkegaard probably penetrated the *existentiell* phenomenon of the moment most deeply – which doesn't mean that his existential interpretation was equally successful. He remains stuck in the vulgar concept of time, and defines the moment by way of the now and eternity.'[71] For Heidegger, this definition of time vis-à-vis a postulated eternity was a structural correlate of Kierkegaard's definition of man vis-à-vis a postulated Absolute or God. Both are ontologically unnecessary: the *Christian* sense of anxiety as related to sin is merely one ontic manifestation of – indeed, one religious attempt to answer the question posed by – that anxiety which is an *ontological* moment of man. Heidegger, consequently, attempts a more radically ontological/phenomenological account of anxiety which does not appeal to extraneous postulates such as eternity or God, but reveals the structural 'self-sufficiency' of factic life.[72]

The central move of this reworking is the replacement of the Absolute (God) with Nothing. Heidegger shares Kierkegaard's correlation of authenticity and wholeness: as for Kierkegaard, it is, for Heidegger, a vital concern for the human subject to 'take the measure of himself', even if this leads only to the realization that he cannot complete that action. But, Heidegger argues, this does not require the final term of Kierkegaard's analysis. For Vigilius, anxiety (once sin is posited) is and remains part of the sinful state; salvation is through the faith that overcomes anxiety by consuming what anxiety has gathered up – the infinite possibility of human existence. For Heidegger, anxiety is enough.

It is important to pinpoint in which ways this is an astute and penetrating reinterpretation of Kierkegaard, and in which ways it is problematic. In Vigilius' analysis, although anxiety is penultimate, it comes first, that is, before faith. The human subject is alone with it until – once anxiety has searched out and burnt away all mere 'finities' of his being – he can hand over the whole he has thus gathered up to God in faith and hope of salvation. The criteria of 'salvation', here, are wholly external to the terms of the psychological analysis: they are imported from traditional Christian belief and 'take over' once the psychological analysis is complete. *Within* that analysis, there is an implicit, competing conception of 'salvation', namely 'wholeness', achieved by a grasping of one's own infinity. Vigilius' protestations that this is merely a penultimate term are unlikely to stick with the phenomenologist Heidegger.

But there is a deeper level of analysis, for Kierkegaard is perfectly aware of this importation. What justifies it, in his view, is that the very concept to which he attempts a psychological approach is a concept only given by Christian belief. He could not attempt an analysis of sin without the concept of 'sin' – as a moment of decision within the free will of the human subject, not fully conditioned by anything outside itself – having been revealed by Christian doctrine. The handing over of his subject to dogmatics after the completion of the psychological analysis thus merely completes the circle. There is an obvious parallel between this practice and the Lutheran account of consciousness of sin discussed above: for Luther, the significance of sin could only be revealed (in history and in each individual's consciousness) through faithful contemplation of Christ, the magnitude of whose deed revealed, by implication, the corresponding magnitude of man's corruption. Both thinkers' appeal to 'phenomenology' (or 'psychology') in recognizing that sin is firmly rooted within the phenomenon of faith.

Although Heidegger wishes to draw a firm line between the 'ontic' level of faith – which postulates entities such as God to resolve the questions posed by factic life – and the 'ontological' level of his own analysis, the distinction between corruption (*Verfall*) and authenticity which is so central to that analysis is dependent, at least genealogically, on Christian belief, and hovers uncomfortably between it and his professed a-theism.

Notes

1   Those chiefly responsible for advancing knowledge of Heidegger's religious origins in the English-language academy are John van Buren, Thomas Sheehan, and more recently Benjamin Crowe and S. J. McGrath; see van Buren's translations of early Heideggerian writings in *Supplements: From the Earliest Essays to Being and Time and Beyond* (Albany: SUNY Press, 2002), as well as his own *The Young Heidegger*; Sheehan, 'Heidegger's *Lehrjahre*'; Crowe, *Heidegger's Religious Origins* and *Heidegger's Phenomenology of Religion: Realism and Cultural Criticism* (Indianapolis: Indiana University Press, 2007); McGrath, *The Early Heidegger & Medieval Philosophy: Phenomenology for the Godforsaken* (Washington: Catholic University of America Press, 2006).

2   Owing to the paucity of source material available until recently, there has been much uncertainty among scholars whether Heidegger maintained a view of philosophy as *preparatio evangeliae* throughout this period or whether he regarded it as theology's rival or successor (as well as whether, when and how he shifted his view). Among those

who espouse the former are, e.g. Hans Meyer, *Martin Heidegger und Thomas von Aquin* (Munich: Schöningh, 1964), Maurice Corvez, *L'être et la conscience morale* (Louvain: Editions Nauwelaerts, 1968), and Schaeffler, *Frömmigkeit des Denkens*. Among the latter are van Buren, *Young Heidegger*; Kisiel, *Genesis*, and McGrath, *Heidegger: A (Very) Critical Introduction* (Grand Rapids: Eerdmans, 2008).

3   Heidegger first borrows this phrase from Luther in the 1923 lecture series *Ontologie: Hermeneutik der Faktizität*, published as GA 63.

4   Karl Barth, *Church Dogmatics* III/2: *The Doctrine of Creation*, eds. G. W. Bromiley and T. F. Torrance (trans. H. Knight, G. W. Bromiley, J. K. S. Reid, and R. H. Fuller; Edinburgh: T&T Clark, 1960), p. 596.

5   The key text for this debate in the twentieth century, though it has undergone severe and justified criticism, is still Gustaf Aulén, *Christus Victor An Historical Study of the Three Main Types of the Idea of Atonement* (trans. A. G. Herber; London: SPCK, 1931; New York: Macmillan, 1969).

6   Schleiermacher makes an early attempt at reframing death not as an imposition but as the natural and necessary limit of human life since its creation; see Schleiermacher, *The Christian Faith* (Edinburgh: T&T Clark, translated from the 2nd [1830] edn, 1928), pp. 243–4. Karl Barth's position on the subject is somewhat ambiguous, but the passages in the *Church Dogmatics* directly relating to the subject are clear in their conception of death 'as it actually meets us' as 'the sign of divine judgement', 'standing [under which] is not something intrinsic to our human nature'; Barth, *Church Dogmatics* III/2, pp. 596–7.

7   See, among many other examples, Ps. 90.10 and Ecclesiastes (*passim*).

8   'χρόνος οὐκ ἔσται ἔτι'. Some recent translations have rendered the verse, 'there shall be no more delay', but this is an ideologically motivated translation with no influence on the relevant Christian tradition.

9   Heidegger to Blochmann, 15 June 1918, in *Heidegger/Blochmann*, p. 7.

10   Heidegger to Blochmann, 1 May 1919, in *Heidegger/Blochmann*, p. 14.

11   Ibid.

12   Heidegger to Blochmann, 2 October 1918, in *Heidegger/Blochmann*, p. 9.

13   Heidegger to Blochmann, 6 November 1918, in *Heidegger/Blochmann*, p. 10. For earlier comments in this vein, see particularly the epilogue of Heidegger's qualifying thesis (GA 1) and his 1917

note 'Phänomenologie des religiösen Erlebnisses und der Religion',
GA 60, 322–4.

14 'Ursprungswissenschaft vom Leben', in Heidegger, Grundprobleme
(1919), GA 58, 42.

15 Heidegger, Grundprobleme (1919), GA 58, 42.

16 Heidegger, Phänomenologische Interpretationen zu Aristoteles
(1922), GA 61, 197 (loose leaf entitled 'Zur Einleitung').

17 Heidegger to Matthäus Lang, 30 May 1928, in Ott, Heidegger,
pp. 55–6. See also Heidegger, 'Anmerkungen zu Karl Jaspers'
Psychologie der Weltanschauungen' (1919/21), in GA 9, 1–44; 42.

18 Quoted in Heidegger, Phänomenologische Interpretationen zu
Aristoteles (1922), GA 61, 182 from Kierkegaard, Entweder-Oder I
(trans. H. Gottsched and C. Schrempf; Jena: Diederichs, 1911), p. 35.

19 Kierkegaard, Einübung im Christentum (Diederichs IX, 1912), 70;
quoted GA 61, 182.

20 Heidegger, 'Phänomenologische Interpretationen zu Aristoteles'
('Natorp Report') (1922), published in Dilthey-Jahrbuch 6 (1989),
pp. 236–74; rpt. In GA 62, 346–75; p. 349.

21 Heidegger, Phänomenologische Interpretationen zu Aristoteles
(1922), GA 61, 198.

22 Ibid., 197.

23 Heidegger, 'Phänomenologische Interpretationen zu Aristoteles'
('Natorp Report') (1922), GA 62, 363.

24 Heidegger's early reading of Luther is documented in Otto Pöggeler,
'Heideggers Luther-Lektüre im Freiburger Theologenkonvikt', HJB 1,
185–96.

25 Quoted in van Buren, Young Heidegger, 149; no reference is
provided. Julius Ebbinghaus similarly recounted that after the war, his
friend and colleague Heidegger 'had received the Erlangen edition of
Luther's work as a prize or gift – and so we read Luther's reformatory
writings for a while in the evenings we spent together', a practice
from which his own essay 'Luther and Kant', as well as a joint
colloquium on the influence of Luther on Kant and German Idealism
more generally emerged. See Ebbinghaus, 'Julius Ebbinghaus', in
Ludwig Pongratz (ed.), Philosophie in Selbstdarstellungen (vol. 3;
Hamburg: Felix Meiner, 1977), p. 33. Ebbinghaus' essay on Luther
and Kant is found in Ebbinghaus, Interpretation und Kritik, eds.
Hariolf Oberer and Georg Geismann (Bonn: Bouvier, 1981). The
joint colloquium was entitled 'Die theologischen Grundlagen von
Kant, Religion innerhalb der Grenzen der blossen Vernunft', and

held in SS 1923 (see 'Schriftenverzeichnis', *HJB* 1, 476). A proposed journal article by Heidegger on 'The Ontological Foundations of Late Medieval Anthropology and the Theology of the Young Luther' never appeared; see van Buren, *Young Heidegger*, p. 149.

26 Heidegger to Elfride Heidegger, 20 August 1920, in *Heidegger/Elfride Heidegger*, pp. 111–12; p. 112.

27 Bultmann to Hans Freiherr von Soden, 23 December 1923; published in Bultmann Lemke, 'Der unveröffentlichte Nachlaß von Rudolf Bultmann', in Jaspert (ed.), *Rudolf Bultmanns Werk und Wirkung*, p. 202. Bultmann gives a similar account in a letter to Friedrich Gogarten dated 22 December 1923; see *Bultmann/Gogarten*, p. 53.

28 In Löwith, *Mein Leben in Deutschland vor und nach 1933. Ein Bericht* (Stuttgart: J.B. Metzler, 1986), p. 29.

29 The first is reprinted as 'Das Problem der Sünde bei Martin Luther', in Bernd Jaspert (ed.), *Sachgemäße Exegese: Die Protokolle aus Rudolf Bultmanns Neutestamentlichen Seminaren 1921–1951* (Marburg: Elwert, 1996), pp. 28–33. The second is reported by Heinrich Schlier, 'Denken im Nachdenken', in Günther Neske (ed.), *Erinnerungen an Martin Heidegger* (Pfullingen: Neske, 1977), pp. 217–21; p. 219.

30 See Heidegger, *Ontologie* (1923), GA 63, 25–6.

31 Heidegger, *Ontologie* (1923), GA 63, 26; quoting Max Scheler, 'Zur Idee des Menschen', *Abhandlungen und Aufsätze* (Leipzig: Weisse Bücher, 1915), p. 346.

32 Heidegger, *Ontologie* (1923), GA 63, 27.

33 'Flesh means further the whole man with his reason and all his natural endowments'; Luther, *In Esaiam Prophetam Scholia praelectionibus collecta, multis in locis non parva accessione aucta* (1534), ch. 40; in *Exegetica opera latina*, vol. XXII, ed. H. Schmidt (Erlangen, 1860), p. 318.

34 Heidegger, *Ontologie* (1923), GA 63, 27. Cf. Luther's *Lectures on Genesis Chapters 1–5*, p. 166.

35 Ibid., p. 111 (appendix X).

36 There were significant internal disagreements whether the 'original justice' of Adam was natural (i.e. inherent to his existence) or supernatural (i.e. superadded from without), that is, whether the Fall reduced man *from* his natural state (Aquinas) or merely from the supernatural state of Adam *to* a natural state (Scotus). These disputes, however important, are not immediately relevant to the present discussion.

37 Heidegger, 'Das Problem der Sünde bei Luther' (1924), p. 29. Cf., for example, Luther's *Lectures on Genesis 1–5*, p. 142.

38 Heidegger, 'Das Problem der Sünde bei Luther' (1924), p. 31. Later, Heidegger will say, 'das eigentliche Selbstsein ist eine existenzielle Modifikation des Man als eines wesenhaften Existenzials'; *Sein und Zeit* (1927), GA 2, §27, p. 130 (see below).

39 Heidegger, 'Das Problem der Sünde bei Luther' (1924), p. 31.

40 Ibid., p. 33.

41 Heidegger, 'Phänomenologie und Theologie' (1927), published in GA 9, 47–78; p. 48.

42 Heidegger, 'Phänomenologie und Theologie' (1927), GA 9, 61–5.

43 Heidegger to Blochmann, 8 August 1928, in *Heidegger/Blochmann*, pp. 24–6; p. 24.

44 Ibid., p. 26.

45 For an analysis of this Heideggerian concept of evil (though without reference to theology as a possible instantiation of it), see Bernd Irlenborn, *Der Ingrimm des Aufruhrs: Heidegger und das Problem des Bösen* (Vienna: Passagen Verlag, 2000), ch. 1.

46 Heidegger to Stenzel, 14 April 1928, in Ott, *Heidegger*, p. 159.

47 Heidegger, *Sein und Zeit* (1927), GA 2, §40, n. 4; §45, n. 6; §68, n. 2.

48 Søren Kierkegaard, *Begrebet Angest: En simpel psychologisk-paapegende Overveielse i Retning af det dogmatiske*, attr. to Vigilius Haufniensis (Copenhagen, 1844), Introduction.

49 Kierkegaard, *Begrebet Angest*, ch. 1, §2. I take it that this is a definitional rather than an empirical statement: If the relevant act were thus conditioned, it could not be called 'sin', and its relevant discourse would no longer be dogmatics, but psychology, sociology or medicine. The impossibility of Vigilius' project rests precisely in the attempt to speak psychologically of *sin*, which by definition can only be discussed ethically or dogmatically.

50 Cf. Heidegger, *Sein und Zeit* (1927), GA 2, §68, n. 2.

51 Kierkegaard, *Begrebet Angest*, ch. 3. ET: *The Concept of Anxiety* (trans. and ed. Reidar Thomte; Princeton: Princeton University Press, 1980), p. 89.

52 Kierkegaard, *Begrebet Angest*, ch. 3, n. 30 (ET 88).

53 Ibid. (ET 89; my translation).

54 Ibid. (ET 89).

55 Ibid. (ET 88).

56 Kierkegaard, *Begrebet Angest*, ch. 2, §2 (ET 61).

57 Kierkegaard, *Begrebet Angest*, ch. 1, §5 (ET 42).

58 Kierkegaard, *Begrebet Angest*, ch. 4 (ET 111).

59 In Adam's innocence, by contrast, his spirit was 'dreaming'; Kierkegaard, *Begrebet Angest*, ch. 1, §5 (ET 41).

60 Kierkegaard, *Begrebet Angest*, ch. 2, §2 (ET 61).

61 Kierkegaard, *Begrebet Angest*, ch. 1, §5 (ET 42).

62 Kierkegaard, *Begrebet Angest*, ch. 2, §2 (ET 61).

63 Kierkegaard, *Begrebet Angest*, ch. 2 (ET 53); ch. 3, n. 32 (ET 92).

64 Kierkegaard, *Begrebet Angest*, ch. 3 (ET 92).

65 *Sein und Zeit* (1927), GA 2, §27, p. 130 (emphasis removed).

66 Kierkegaard, *Begrebet Angest*, ch. 5 (ET 155; my translation).

67 Ibid. (ET 156).

68 Ibid. (ET 157).

69 Ibid. (ET 158).

70 See Heidegger, *Ontologie* (1923), GA 63, 30. Cf. also *Sein und Zeit* (1927), GA 2, §40, n. 4; §45, n. 6; §68, n. 2.

71 Heidegger, *Sein und Zeit* (1927), GA 2, §68, n. 2.

72 Cf. Heidegger, *Grundprobleme* (1919/20), GA 58, 42. An insightful discussion of Heidegger's (very partial) emancipation from the Christian Kierkegaard is found in Stephen Mulhall, *Philosophical Myths of the Fall* (Princeton: Princeton University Press, 2005), pp. 46–66.

4

Theology in *Being and Time*

The question of being

In his most famous work, *Being and Time* (1927), Heidegger calls for a renewal of the question of being: Not only, he argues, do we not know what Being is, we don't even know how rightly to *ask* what it is. Why does Heidegger think the question of the meaning of 'Being' an important question, and why does he insist that we need to learn not only how to answer it, but how to ask it in the first place? We can begin to unpack this double question by looking at two very different traditions of thought that have gone into Heidegger's approach: medieval theology and Kantian philosophy.

For the Scholastics of the High Middle Ages, Being is nothing less than another name for God himself. There was perhaps no other biblical passage that fascinated the medieval philosopher-theologians as much as God's declaration to Moses: 'I am who I am.' Being Aristotelians as much as Rabbis, they understood this as saying that God is Being itself. Mixed into Aristotelian metaphysics, this declaration yielded, for the most famous of medieval philosophers, Thomas Aquinas, the formula that in God, existence and essence were identical – *deus, cuius essentia est ipsummet suum esse*.[1] All created beings, by contrast, are defined by essences that must be realized (or brought alive) by Being. (How to understand the relationship between the Being that is God and the Being that gives existence to things – whether they are one and the same Being, or whether there is such a thing as 'created Being' in contradistinction to God's own 'uncreated Being' – has been a bone of contention among Thomists ever since.) For Thomas, as for his

Franciscan contemporary Bonaventure, this ontological fact is also an epistemological one: Being is not only the ground of our existence, but also the ground of our knowledge.

However, if 'Being' is the ground of everything, it cannot be understood by the usual means of a definition. Definitions always mark out particular bits of the world over against others: 'This is a cow, not a cat'. But Being cannot be marked out against any particular things or ideas, because it is the 'instantiation' or realization – the condition of the actuality – of *every* thing. Being, Bonaventure therefore argues, can never be a direct object of knowledge or apprehension, but can only come into view indirectly as that which makes apprehension of everything else possible. As the Franciscan puts it, in a passage that Heidegger liked:

> Just as the eye, when it turns towards the manifold differences of the colours, does not see the light. . . , so the eye of the mind, when it turns towards beings in particular and in general, does not notice being itself, . . . even though it is only through being that it encounters everything.[2]

This description is methodologically, although not substantively, proleptic of the philosophical method of Kant, transcendental enquiry. 'Transcendental' here refers to the intellectual discipline of 'transcending' the things apprehended towards that which makes those apprehensions possible: the logical or ontological conditions of the possibility of their appearance. (Note that this has little to do with 'transcendence' in the traditional sense of 'the supernatural'.) However, Kant radically rejects the substantive implication of the Scholastic philosophy that 'Being' might be one of these conditions. Rather, Kant argues, the term 'being' (*sein*) is simply an indication that a concept is instantiated: that a copper penny with the king's image on it is not simply a means of payment – it is that by definition, whether or not I have one – but is in my pocket – right here, right now – to buy an apple. For Kant, whether or not something exists does not change anything about *what* it is, only *whether* it is. 'Being' is therefore not only not apprehensible directly: there is simply nothing to apprehend, whether directly or indirectly. 'Being' is a marker of instantiation, but there *are* only things; and the 'are' in this sentence has nothing to do with metaphysics, only with grammar or logic.

Heidegger follows Kant's transcendental method, but rejects his analysis of the ontological vacuity of Being in favour of a re-centralization of the question of Being: One might say that he inherits the Scholastics' project in a decidedly post-Kantian way. And this brings us back to his insistence that we need to learn not so much how to answer the question of Being, as how to ask it. If Being realizes and illuminates everything, but is itself no thing, then we cannot start with an analysis of what Being 'is' – because to ask 'what is Being?' is at worst nonsensical (because Being *isn't* anything), and at best already presupposes what it tries to find out (because to ask what Being 'is' already presupposes an intuitive understanding of the very term we're asking after, 'to be'). So we have to ask first how to ask about Being.

But if this seems like a hopeless being-stuck in preliminaries, it soon turns out that the emphasis on *asking* in fact already contains one of the central insights of *Being and Time*. The question of Being, Heidegger comes to realize, cannot ultimately be raised or answered conceptually at all, but only in and through a life. It is by living honestly, not trying to ward off the precariousness of existence by false securities (whether practical or conceptual), that we acknowledge the question of being as what it is: a question that engages us in our entirety, in which our own existence is at stake. This is what Heidegger means when he describes his analysis as a 'formal indication': his philosophy can do no more than to 'formally indicate' a task, a way of living the questions implied in his philosophical analyses.

However, Heidegger's position is even more radical than that – because a radical pursuit of this approach, he thinks, reveals that our own existence is a question that can never be answered. To answer the question who we are, we would have to see our life as a whole; but the moment our life is 'whole' – that is, the moment of death –, we are no longer there to live or see it. Thus, 'being-unto-death' – neither denying the question of our own existence nor pretending that we shall be able to answer it – is at the heart of authentic existence.

And this indicates Heidegger's central conflict with Christianity. Within the scheme just outlined, religion (and particularly Christianity) is in its basic tendency inimical both to philosophy and to an authentic life, because it insists on jumping to answers: it is (or seems to Heidegger) a way of trying to escape the very precariousness and uncertainty of our existence by positing secure conceptual or metaphysical as well as practical or moral frameworks in which there is no room for doubt or anxiety. 'To question', by contrast, 'is the piety of thinking'.[3] This contrast is concentrated in Christianity's promise of an eternal life after death. Christianity, Heidegger thinks, makes an authentic life impossible by masking the painful truth at the heart of our existence by illusory promises of a continuation of life after death.

And yet Heidegger's analysis also conceals significant parallels with Christianity which he does not dwell on. Some of these parallels are relevant to a critical enquiry, some to a constructive engagement. Among the former, the question of the origins of Heidegger's analysis and terminology is foremost. As has already become clear, Heidegger developed much of the philosophical method of *Being and Time* directly from Christian sources, and the question to what extent he succeeds in coherently severing these sources from their theological origins, or divesting them of their theological meaning, rightly remains a subject of debate.[4] We will look more closely at theology-derived terminology in *Being and Time* in the next section below.

But there are also constructive parallels which it is worth following out. Just as for Heidegger, the question of Being can only be raised in and through a (properly questioning) life, so for Christianity, the question of God can never be raised purely conceptually, but only in and through a life of faith. This is because to regard God as an object of rational comprehension is to distort from the outset what one is trying to understand: It is to pretend that there can be a 'neutral' place of rational contemplation from which God can be evaluated and defined – whereas in fact, a necessary implication of the idea of God is that there can be no such 'neutral' place, that God can never be thought of in the third person as an object of ratiocination, that he encompasses our entire existence and can only be addressed doxologically, by an 'I', as a 'Thou'. The only way to engage with his reality is a life of faith, whose course any discussion can only ever 'formally indicate'.

Origins and ends: Eschatology and original sin in *Being and Time*

The goal of *Being and Time* is a renewal of the question of the meaning of 'Being'; and this means first of all the attempt not to answer a long-standing question but to find the right way of asking it. The ability to ask the question of Being, so Heidegger, has been stunted since after Plato and Aristoteles by the uncritical assumption of a particular mode of being, namely 'presence' (Greek: παρουσία; German: *Gegenwart* or *Vorhandensein*), as Being *per se*. This assumption, determinative of ontology from classical and medieval times even to the most influential philosophical projects of modernity, those of Descartes and Kant, has made 'being' the most *general* term, neither requiring nor allowing any further definition. Heidegger, instead, proposes to return to Bonaventure's transcendental conception of being as illumination. For Bonaventure as for Heidegger, a transcendental viewpoint, which seeks the conditions of the possibility of all knowledge, does not discover a new entity, but asks after that which is no entity and yet makes possible all intentionality – and this is Being itself.

For Heidegger, consequently, Being cannot come into view directly at all, but only indirectly through an analysis of the existential constitution of that being 'for whom its being is about that being': the human being or *Dasein*.[5] This analysis reveals at least two structures that are revelatory of Being in a different way than expected by the champion of 'presence', Descartes: Human existence is always *possibility*, and it is always *being-in-a-world*. As we will see in a moment, both are intimately related to the two central theological loci of Heidegger's intellectual development, eschatology and original sin.

Possibility and death

At its simplest, Heidegger's account of human existence in *Being and Time* is 'eschatological' because it envisions the possibility of authentic existence as dependent on a certain (existential) relation to one's future. Because existence, in Heidegger's phenomenological analysis, constitutes essence, the 'essence' or identity of each person remains continually dependent on a future that she can neither fully know nor fully control.[6] 'If the being of Dasein is determined by existence, and its essence is constituted partly by its capability [literally: possibility] of being, then Dasein must, as long as it exists . . . *not yet be* something.'[7]

Part I's interpretation of Dasein's constitutive 'not yet' begins from a formalization of the fact that how Dasein is to be the next moment, and whether it is to be the next moment, are never simple givens for it: Dasein always faces its future first and foremost as a range of possibilities, only some of which are under its control. In his 'existential analytic',[8] Heidegger is less interested in the *particular* choices a Dasein will make, events it will experience, and changes it will undergo in the future, than in the *fact* of these possibilities as a permanent structural constituent of human existence. Dasein, he specifies, is not an independently existing thing which, in addition to existing, has possibilities – 'it *is* first and foremost possibility'.[9]

'Possibility', here, must be interpreted not as a deficient form of reality ('something not yet real and never inevitable'), but as a wholly different mode of being: Dasein's 'possibility of being is never still outstanding as something not yet present, but . . . rather *is* with the being of Dasein (*viz*, existence) *as* essentially never present'.[10] Or, put differently: 'The being for whom its being is about that being engages with its being as its ownmost possibility. Each Dasein *is* its possibility and does not merely "have" it, as if that possibility were an attribute of an [independently] existing thing.'[11] Possibility, then, is an 'existentiale' – in fact, 'the aboriginal and final positive ontological determination of Dasein'.[12]

In Part II, Heidegger concretizes his analysis of possibility by reference to death. In Part I, he had described possibility as that which, rather than 'not yet [being] real',[13] already '*is* with the being of Dasein *as* essentially never present'.[14] Now, he replaces the subject of this definition: '*Death* is not something not-yet-present, not something outstanding until the last, but rather an imminence [*Bevorstand*].'[15] Death, as he follows up more explicitly, is Dasein's last and 'un-overtakable possibility'.[16] Like all possibility, it must therefore be understood as an 'existentiale', an aspect of the existential constitution of Dasein:

> Just as Dasein always *is*, as long as it is, already its not-yet, so also it always *is* already its end. The ending meant by death is not the being-at-an-end of Dasein, but the *being-towards-the-end* of this being. Death is a way of being which Dasein assumes as soon as it is.[17]

But death, as the horizon of possibility as futurity, is also its negation. 'As long as Dasein *is* as a being', Heidegger summarizes starkly, 'it never attains its "fullness". And once it attains it, this attainment turns into the loss of being-in-the-world *per se*'.[18] Put in the constitutive terminology of possibility, Dasein's last and 'un-overtakable possibility' is that of 'no-longer-being-able-to-exist', the 'impossibility of existing'.[19]

This 'possible impossibility' demands a reformation of one's ordinary understanding of 'possibility' – a reformation which, for Heidegger, must become paradigmatic for *all* possibility. In ordinary experience, possibility tends to be understood 'teleologically', that is, by reference to its realizable content. Dasein, as Heidegger puts it, looks to the possible 'not in terms of its possibility *qua* possibility, but in such a way that it circumspectly looks *away* from the possible to the possibility-of-*what*'.[20] But death cannot be treated this way. 'Death as possibility gives Dasein nothing that it can "realize," nothing that it could, if it were real, itself *be*.'[21] Any attempt to 'realize' the possibility of death (e.g. by suicide) would merely 'dissolve the ground of Dasein's existent being-unto-death'.[22] Rather, death must be understood as 'pure' possibility: 'Being-unto-death . . ., if it wants to disclose the described possibility *as such*, must robustly under-stand, develop and *bear* this possibility *as possibility*.'[23] In other words, Dasein must engage with death in and through its being-in-the-world; Heidegger calls the appropriate attitude the 'anticipation of' or 'running-forward to' the possibility of death.[24]

Corruption and the fall

But such anticipation or mindfulness of death does not come easily to human beings, who are, naturally and for the most part, fully immersed in the world and dispersed in its cares and pleasures.[25] While such immersion or being-in-the-world is initially described as a neutral status quo, the imperative to be mindful of one's death makes it appear as an avoidance rather than a merely neutral stance.[26] 'The crowd', Heidegger writes in a typically ironic formulation, 'suppresses the courage to dread death'.[27] The term he coins for this kind of dispersion is *Verfall*, which is a Germanization of Luther's Latin word *corruptio*, semantically and pragmatically related to *Fall* ('fall' into sin) but also bearing the ordinary meaning of 'addiction'.

Heidegger's rejection of the dogmatic framing of Luther's understanding of corruption as constitutive of human existence, that is, as the state man always already finds himself in in this postlapsarian world, is repeated forcefully in his introduction of the concept *Verfall* in Part I of *Being and Time*. 'The name [*Verfall*], which does not express a negative valuation, means: . . . Dasein has always already fallen from itself as the possibility of authentically being itself, and fallen to the "world".'[28] This must be understood as a permanent structural constituent of human existence, not as 'a "fall" from a purer and higher "original state"'.[29] The postulation of such a Fall, he expounds, is philosophically empty, because Dasein, 'as existing, can never go behind its being-thrown[-into-the-world]'.[30] But philosophy is an 'analysis of existence which affixes the guiding line of philosophical questioning to the place whence it arises and whither it returns', namely that existence itself.[31] Consequently, it 'not only [does] not (ontically) have any experience of such a thing [as a primordial Fall]; [it] also do[es] not (ontologically) possess any possibilities or guidelines for interpreting it'.[32]

Heidegger therefore positions his analysis as ontologically prior to the Christian understanding of the Fall: 'This existential-ontological interpretation makes . . . no ontic statement about the "corruption of human nature," not because the necessary evidence is lacking, but because its set of problems occurs *before* any statement about depravity or undepravedness.' 'Ontically, we are not deciding whether man "wallows in sin" (i.e. in the *status corruptionis*), walks in the *status integritatis*, or finds himself in an intermediary state, the *status gratiae*.' Quite the reverse: 'faith and "worldview," in talking about Dasein as any of these and as being in the world, provided they wish to make any claims to *conceptual* understanding will have to take recourse to the existential structures we have uncovered'.[33]

Guilt and the call of conscience

This non-moral account of 'original sin' is both intensified and complicated by the fact that not only Heidegger's term 'falling' or 'corruption' (*Verfall*) *but also* the positive term 'being-unto-death' are modelled on theological descriptions of original sin: 'Being-unto-death' (*Sein zum Tode*) is coined in parallel to Kierkegaard's 'sickness-unto-death' (translated into German in 1911 as *Die Krankheit zum Tode*).[34] The alternative formulation 'anticipation of [lit.: running-forward towards] death' (*Vorlaufen zum Tode*) is an almost direct translation of Luthers *cursus ad mortem*.[35] But both theological terms describe the outworking of original sin. Can the provenance of the borrowing be accidental?

It soon turns out that it is not; for on the deeper level of Part II, being-unto-death itself is an affirmation of 'sinfulness'. After his existential analysis of being-unto-death, Heidegger raises the question of the *existentiell* attainment of authenticity – the question not of whether being-unto-death is theoretically possible but whether it is practically possible. For Heidegger as for Paul, this practical turn must be occasioned by the call of a voice already aware of the coming end, recalling the hearer from his or her entanglement in the world to anticipation and wakefulness. In 1 Thessalonians 5, Heidegger's source text in formulating his understanding of eschatological anticipation in 1921, Paul himself takes the role of that caller. For Heidegger, the matter is more complicated. Because it is 'lost in the crowd', Dasein 'must be "shown" to itself in its own potential authenticity'; it 'requires testimony to its capability [lit.: possibility] of being itself, which, in potentiality, it already is'.[36] But because authenticity is Dasein's ownmost and non-relational possibility,[37] this testimony cannot be given by an external, but only by an internal voice: 'The call [cannot] come from another who is in the world with me. The call comes *from* me and yet *over* me.'[38] Heidegger finds an existentiell pointer to the possibility of such an inner voice in Dasein's ordinary understanding of conscience.[39] He now reinterprets this voice of conscience existentially as the internal, eschatological call of Dasein *as* already 'in the depth of its uncanniness'[40] to itself *as* still lost in the crowd.[41]

Following the ordinary intuition that conscience speaks of guilt (*Schuld*),[42] Heidegger pursues his analysis of conscience through an ontological analysis of guilt, that is, one that reveals the existential ground of ordinary sensations and postulations of guilt: 'Being-guilty', is his guiding assumption, 'does not first result from having incurred guilt [or: an indebtedness]; on the contrary: this incurrence is only possible "on the basis of" an original/originary being-guilty'.[43] Such existential guilt cannot be understood as a 'lack' in the sense of 'the absence of a mandatory something'[44] any more than Dasein's perpetual 'unfinishedness' can be understood as a 'something yet outstanding'.[45] These senses of incompleteness accrue only to modes of being – being-to-hand or being-at-hand – that are not defined from out of themselves, but by reference to a pre-defined use or essence. Rather, Dasein's guilt, like its unfinishedness, is a distinguishing mark of Dasein's *existential* finitude.

As inescapably 'thrown into the world', Dasein is always 'in debt' for its existence: to parents and shaping influences too numerous and diffuse to count; to the world as a whole.

> Being [*viz*, existing], Dasein is thrown, not brought into existence [lit.: into its "there" (*Da*)] by itself. Being, it is defined as a capability-of-being that belongs to itself yet has *not* given itself as itself. Existing, it can never go behind its being-thrown, so that it might dismiss this "that it is and is called to be" from *its being*-itself into the There. . . . *As this entity*, committed to which it can only exist as the entity that it is, *it is, existing*, the ground of its capability of being.[46]

The primary import of this difficult quote is this: The existentiell possibility of being-unto-death is grounded precisely in the fact Heidegger had claimed earlier, namely that Dasein is shaped and comes to know itself from within a 'world'. The call of *conscience* is the summon to acknowledge this fact as a *task* rather than a puzzle that does or even could have an answer. Dasein's origin in the world is not a defined 'there' onto which, as the causal 'explanation' of its existence, Dasein can slough off responsibility for that existence. Rather, that ungraspable origin functions precisely as the bar to any belief that existence can be *known* rather than or before it is lived, any belief that existence is explicable by a 'ground': Dasein itself *in existing* is the 'null ground' of its own being.

But to shoulder that existence is not to redress that nullity. On the contrary, authentic existence consists, practically, in a perpetual series of choices, each of which rejects or makes impossible other choices: 'Not only is the projection always, as thrown, determined by the nullity of its being-[its-own-]ground; it is also, *as projection*, itself essentially null.'[47] The determination of life by death only acuminates this point: The final ground and purpose, the uttermost depth of Dasein (the German *Grund* carries all three meanings) is its thrownness into death: 'The nothingness before which dread brings us reveals the nullity that determines life in its *ground* [depth/ essence/purpose], namely thrownness into death.'[48]

The entire being of Dasein as a 'thrown projection' (*geworfener Entwurf*), then, is 'the null ground of a nullity'.[49] The call of conscience, although away from 'corruption' as dispersion in the world, is therefore not away from 'being guilty', but *towards* it: It is a call to accept the 'heaviness' or 'difficulty' (*Schwere*)[50] of being the 'null ground' of an existence pervaded by nullity. The voice of conscience is 'a summons to be guilty'.[51]

> Does not the being of Dasein [being-there] become more mysterious with the explication of the existential constitution of the being of its "there" as thrown projection? Indeed. We must first allow the full mysteriousness of this being to become apparent, if only to be able truly to fail in [or: be shipwrecked against] its "solution" and begin to ask the question of the being of the thrown-projecting being-in-the-world anew.[52]

Authenticity and wholeness

However, Heidegger's understanding of guilt and conscience, with its startling formulation of Dasein's being as 'the null ground of a nullity', is predicated on the unspoken assumption that the *wish* for a ground and a goal remains constitutive of Dasein. To become oneself, indeed, is to accept that one is *neither* grounded in a definite origin (or even able coherently to express what such a ground would be), *nor* able to escape the desire for a ground; neither moving towards fulfilment (or even able coherently to express what such fulfilment would be), nor able to escape that desire. To become oneself, in other words, is to accept as a *task* rather than a mere refutation of one's desire the fact that one cannot access such a beginning or end. The crowd is a temptation because it provides either a distraction from the question of wholeness, or an illusion that Dasein is already part of a whole that is unproblematically and already 'there'. Being-guilty and being-unto-death, by contrast, arise from the wish for wholeness coupled with an acknowledgement of the fact that beginning and end are ontologically inaccessible: that we *must* but cannot be whole.

This is Heidegger's eschatological reformulation, against the horizon of Nothingness, of Kierkegaard's definition of faith as

relating oneself absolutely to the absolute precisely by relating
relatively to all relative things.[53] As Heidegger writes,

> The anticipating becoming-free *for* its own death liberates
> [Dasein] from its lostness in possibilities arbitrarily crowding
> in by allowing it, for the first time, to authentically understand
> and choose the factic possibilities that precede the unovertakable
> [one]. Anticipation opens up to existence, as its uttermost
> possibility, [the possibility of] self-surrender, and so breaks every
> stiff focus on the existence already achieved. . . . [Dasein becomes]
> free for its ownmost possibilities, defined from their *end*, that is,
> understood as *finite*.[54]

In Heidegger's reanalysis of Kierkegaard, in other words, things
appear as finite not by contrast to the infinite, but as illuminated from the horizon of the end or *finis*. We can now
understand better Heidegger's position, two years later, in 'What
is Metaphysics?'(1929). Here, *Dasein* 'transcends' that-which-is.
But 'to transcend' (for Heidegger as for Scholastic thought) means
not only 'to surpass' but also 'to gather up': by acknowledging its
own 'ownmost and deepest finitude',[55] Dasein also leads all other
beings to themselves: 'Only in the Nothing of Dasein does that-
which-is come to itself according to its ownmost possibility, i.e. in
a finite way.'[56]

The meaning of Dasein, then, is care,[57] the meaning of care is
temporality,[58] and the meaning of temporality is finitude.[59] This
is not an intellectual but an existential 'meaning', one that cannot
be known, but only lived – in that sense also is it eschatological.
Heidegger summarizes starkly:

> Only a being that is essentially, in its being, *futural*, i.e. able,
> available for its death, to let itself be shattered against that
> death and thrown back on its factic "there" – only a being, in
> other words, which, as futural, is equally originally/originarily
> *past* [or: has been] – can assume its own thrownness by passing
> on to itself its inherited possibility, and so be [or: exist] for "its
> time" *in the moment*. Only authentic temporality, which is at the
> same time finite, makes destiny, that is, authentic historicality,
> possible.[60]

An eschatology without eschaton?

Speaking on a more general level, Heidegger's project in *Being and Time* can be viewed as an ethical inflection of the Kantian problem of metaphysics, centring on a morally charged description of 'the human' as most vitally defined by the tension between ineluctable finitude and the equally persistent desire to transcend it. The aim of both speculative and moral philosophy is here no longer to aspire to a transcendent ideal, but to sustain an 'authentic' human existence by refusing to collapse this constitutive tension into either a metaphysical meta-narrative or an (apathetic or 'sceptical') denial of its allure.

But while Heidegger's analysis is a virtuoso *plaidoyer* for the ineluctable finitude of human existence, its pathos depends on the assumption of a desire to transcend finitude which the analysis itself cannot and does not attempt to account for. The passionate acts of 'shattering oneself against death' or bearing its 'affliction' which characterize authentic human existence are predicated on a contrary longing which is as consistently assumed as it is obfuscated by Heidegger's analysis.

A pressure point is the analysis of the experienceability of death in §47. Heidegger claims that an existential experience of death can only be gained by anticipating one's own death, never by witnessing another's. But as both Edith Stein and more recently Simon Critchley have countered from different perspectives, it is not one's own death but the death of others – specifically, that of loved ones – which is most immediately disclosive of finitude.[61] In an inversion of Heidegger's assertion, Nothing can only show up against the horizon of Being. If Being can only appear 'as' threatened by Nothing, then at the same time, Nothing can appear only *as* a threat. But only what is valued can be threatened, and if the threat makes the value amply clear, it does not in itself create it. To love, as Heidegger himself realized in analysing his love for Hannah Arendt, is to say '*volo ut sis*'.[62] Only in one's love for another can death appear as the horrendous negation it is. But this implies that the apprehension of being which is always already constitutive of Dasein includes a *desire* that being should be infinite which is not easily dismissed as a mere misanalysis of our finitude.

The experience of Christian eschatology takes seriously that desire as well as that impossibility. The problem with theology, from

Heidegger's perspective, is one of two things: Either, like Roman Catholic 'theologies of glory', it assumes an uncomplicated continuity between earthly existence and heavenly – an assumption that must be deconstructed by reminders of the ultimacy of death (ontological critique). Or, like a Lutheran 'theology of the cross', it assumes a complete break between this life and the next – an assumption that must be deconstructed by an analysis of how constitutive *this* life is for anything we might mean by 'human' (grammatical critique). Those are formidable challenges; nevertheless, Heidegger's own configuration cannot escape the constitutive significance of desire, which he assumes from his eschatological sources, but never successfully re-situates.

If human existence teaches us that we can never attain fulfilment but also that we seek it, that we can never find our ground but also that we crave it, then the phenomenological conclusion cannot *simply* be a denial of the object. C. S. Lewis gives a perhaps more accurate phenomenological summary:

> [I]f a man diligently follow[s] . . . desire, pursuing the false objects until their falsity appear[s] and then resolutely abandoning them, he must come out at last into the clear knowledge that the human soul was made to enjoy some object that is never fully given – nay, cannot even be imagined as given – in our present mode of subjective and spatio-temporal experience.[63]

These conflicting accounts remain to be followed out.

Notes

1 Thomas Aquinas, *De ente et essentia*, caput 5.

2 See Chapter 1 above.

3 'Die Frage nach der Technik' (1953), in GA 7, 9–40; p. 40.

4 See Chapters 7 and 8 below.

5 Heidegger, *Sein und Zeit* (1927), GA 2, §9, 42–4. In *Being and Time* and other important texts, Heidegger uses the term *Dasein* (literally: 'being-there') both in its conventional meaning of '(human) existence' and in the idiosyncratic sense of 'human being'/'person'. The elision is not accidental, but implies that the human being is determined by his/her existence rather than a pre-defined 'essence'. English-language

Heidegger scholarship has, for the most part, adopted the term 'Dasein' (not italicized) rather than attempting a translation. I have followed that practice when discussing *Being and Time* and Heidegger's phenomenology in general.

6 See Heidegger, *Sein und Zeit* (1927), GA 2, §9, 42 and §45, 233.

7 Heidegger, *Sein und Zeit* (1927), GA 2, §45, 233.

8 Ibid., §4, 13.

9 Ibid., §31, 143.

10 Ibid., §31, 144.

11 Ibid., §9, 42.

12 Ibid., §31, 144.

13 Ibid., 143.

14 Ibid., 144.

15 Heidegger, *Sein und Zeit* (1927), GA 2, §50, 250 (emphasis added).

16 Ibid., 250.

17 Heidegger, *Sein und Zeit* (1927), GA 2, §48, 245.

18 Ibid., §46, 236.

19 Ibid., §50, 250.

20 Ibid., §53, 261.

21 Ibid., 262.

22 Ibid., 261.

23 Ibid., 261.

24 Ibid., 262.

25 Ibid., §§25–7.

26 See e.g. Heidegger, *Sein und Zeit* (1927), GA 2, §50, 252 and §53, 263.

27 Heidegger, *Sein und Zeit* (1927), GA 2, §51, 254 (emphasis omitted).

28 Ibid., §38, 175.

29 Ibid., §38, 176.

30 Ibid., §58, 284.

31 Ibid., §7, 38 (emphasis omitted).

32 Ibid., §38, 176.

33 Ibid., §38, 179–80.

34 Kierkegaard, *Die Krankheit zum Tode* (Jena: Diederichs, 1911), being Volume 8 of Kierkegaard, *Gesammelte Werke* (12 vols; trans. H. Gottsched and C. Schrempf; Jena: Eugen Diederichs, 1909–22).

35   'Vorlaufen zum Tode' appears in *Sein und Zeit* (1927), GA 2, §53, 263; §62, 305.

36   Heidegger, *Sein und Zeit* (1927), GA 2, §54, 268.

37   See e.g. Heidegger, *Sein und Zeit* (1927), GA 2, §50, 250–1.

38   Heidegger, *Sein und Zeit* (1927), GA 2, §57, 275.

39   See Heidegger, *Sein und Zeit* (1927), GA 2, §54, 268.

40   '. . . im Grunde seiner Unheimlichkeit sich befindend'; *Sein und Zeit* (1927), GA 2, §57, 276. The nuances of the German (which obliquely draws Heidegger's key concepts *Grund* and *Befinden* into the analysis) are, as so often, lost in any English translation concerned (as it must be) with readability.

41   It is notoriously unclear in what sense Heidegger regards this as a *practical* solution to the problem of the possibility of authenticity. Stephen Mulhall, in his introduction to *Being and Time*, consequently offers a Cavellian reading of the section, in which the 'friend' or 'mentor' replaces an internal conscience, as the only practically viable interpretation. (See Mulhall, *Heidegger and Being and Time* [London: Routledge, 2nd edn, 2005], pp. 143–5.) Simon Critchley, by contrast, criticizes Heidegger's 'autarkic' conception of conscience, and proposes its replacement by a (Freudian) conception of conscience as essentially relational. (See Critchley, 'Originary Inauthenticity— on Heidegger's *Sein und Zeit*', in Simon Critchley and Reiner Schürmann, *On Heidegger's Being and Time*, ed. Steven Levine [London: Routledge, 2008], pp. 132–51; pp. 145–7.)

42   The translation of Heidegger's *Schuld* is notoriously difficult. Like the cognate Old English *scyld*, German *Schuld* acquired its theological (and by Heidegger's time dominant) meaning 'guilt' from its primary, economical meaning 'debt', and retains a strong etymological association with that root. English 'guilt' has no similar etymology, although it is sometimes falsely traced to the Old Teutonic root *geld-, gald-, guld-*, 'to pay' or 'yield'. See Grimm, *Deutsches Wörterbuch*, vol. 15, col. 1870, and John Simpson and Edmund Weiner (eds.), *The Oxford English Dictionary* (Oxford: Oxford University Press, 2nd edn, 1989), 'guilt'.

43   Heidegger, *Sein und Zeit* (1927), GA 2, §58, 284. For conscience as speaking of guilt, see *Sein und Zeit*, GA 2, §57, 279.

44   Ibid., §58, 283.

45   Ibid., §48, 242.

46   Ibid., §58, 284.

47   Ibid., §58, 285.

48 Ibid., §62, 308.

49 Ibid., §58, 285.

50 Ibid., 284.

51 Ibid., 287.

52 Heidegger, *Sein und Zeit* (1927), GA 2, §32, 148.

53 Cf. Mulhall, *Heidegger and Being and Time*, p. 137.

54 *Sein und Zeit* (1927), GA 2, §53, 264.

55 Heidegger, 'Was ist Metaphysik?' (1929), GA 9, 118.

56 Ibid., 120.

57 See e.g. Heidegger, *Sein und Zeit* (1927), GA 2, §39, 182.

58 Ibid., §65, 326.

59 See e.g. Heidegger, *Sein und Zeit* (1927), GA 2, §65, 331.

60 Heidegger, *Sein und Zeit* (1927), GA 2, §74, 385. Compare Karl
    Barth's assertion that man 'shatters himself' on God (*The Epistle to
    the Romans* [trans. E. C. Hoskyns; Oxford: Oxford University Press,
    1965], p. 43).

61 See Critchley, 'Originary Inauthenticity', pp. 143–5; Stein, 'Martin
    Heideggers Existenzphilosophie', ESGA 11/12, 475–6. Despite some
    fine observations, Critchley's account of Heidegger's 'authenticity' is
    too distorting, and his own suggested 'inauthenticity' too polemical
    and ambiguous, to constitute a formidable overall critique of
    Heidegger.

62 Heidegger to Arendt, 13 May 1925 and 7 December 1927, in *Arendt/
    Heidegger*, p. 31 and 59.

63 C. S. Lewis, *The Pilgrim's Regress* (London: J. M. Dent, 3rd edn,
    1943), preface.

5

Heidegger between Hitler and Hölderlin (1930–1935)

No other question surrounding Heidegger was and has remained as hotly debated as that of his relation to National Socialism in the years 1933–34 and beyond. The publicly known facts – his controversial rectorship of the University of Freiburg (1933) and premature resignation from it (1934), various lectures and newspaper articles extolling Hitler during and after the rectorship, and his forced retirement (*Emeritierung*) during the denazification of the German academy – are indicting, but also open to a wide range of interpretations. These interpretations, in turn, can be weighted in very different ways within an assessment of his philosophy: as a more or less direct outgrowth of his 'fundamental ontology'; as a more or less radical departure from his earlier philosophical path which, however, determines his later path to a lesser or greater extent; or as a personal lapse of judgement which should be kept separate from his philosophy altogether. These questions have spawned a flood of books and articles over the years, many of which (often the most popular) are not much more than inflammatory polemic, and most of which are trading on research that has not been updated in decades.[1] Meanwhile, the excellent archival research undertaken by German scholars in the last few years, and the publications to which it has led, have not yet been appropriated by English-language scholarship at all.[2] A book like this one cannot, of course, undertake to (re-)evaluate Heidegger's relation to National Socialism in its entirety: my concern here is only with the theological dimension of his life and thought under Nazi rule. Nevertheless, a clear and well-informed account of this aspect will, I hope, also shed new light on the 'Nazi question' more generally.

Two points should be clarified right away. First, Heidegger's institutional involvement with Nazi rule – specifically, his agreement to become rector of Freiburg University in 1933 – was motivated less by ideological agreement than by practical contingency. The inadequacy of the modern university (which, in Heidegger's view, was becoming a polytechnic rather than a place of learning for its own sake), and the need to understand the task of philosophy anew and to organize university teaching and administration in accordance with it, had been a constant concern of Heidegger's since the beginning of his university career.[3] It had gained new urgency in 1931/32, when the Prussian Concordat with the Lutheran Church, and the Baden Concordat with the Catholic Church, consolidated church control over theological appointments: a development that incited him to renewed expressions of the dream of a wholesale university reform.[4] At the time of his rectorship, the Nazi Party had not yet developed a unified educational policy, and it is clear from his inaugural address and from the letters surrounding his acceptance of the post that Heidegger was hoping to seize this opportune moment to put into action the intellectual renewal he had been talking and writing about for a decade.[5] That he was soon disappointed in this hope becomes clear both in a series of disappointed letters to friends (complaining that a very differently-minded candidate had been appointed Minister of Education and that he, Heidegger, had not been invited to any educational policy meetings at the higher level), and in his premature resignation from the rectorship in early 1934. Heidegger consistently stayed away from party politics from that point onwards.

Secondly, it is important to emphasize at the outset that Heidegger's assessment of Christianity in general was entirely at odds with the dominant Nazi view of the early 1930s. Heidegger's sympathies within Christian thought, as has already become clear, lay firmly with Paul and with Luther's *theologia crucis*. By contrast, the dominant Nazi view of religion in its early years was of Paul as the 'corruptor of Christianity', and of Germany as called to a return to the pure 'Aryan' fighting ethics of Jesus.[6] The influential leader of the German Christians in Berlin, Dr Reinhold Krause, singled out the recent emergence of dialectical theology as a development in direct opposition to this properly German religion. In his infamous speech to 20,000 people at the *Sportpalast* stadium on the occasion of the 450th anniversary of Luther's birth in 1933, Krause called for a categorical rejection of a Pauline 'theology of scapegoats and inferiority complexes'.[7] 'The entire development of dialectical theology from Paul to Barth' had 'made our Father God into a brainteaser'.[8] But while this theology attempted to separate God and man, Jesus' own teaching knew of no such separation – and it was this teaching which must once again become the foundation of the German Church. 'If we take from the gospels the things that speak to our German hearts', Krause encouraged his audience, 'then the essence of Jesus' teaching shines forth clearly and radiantly: a teaching (and we may be thoroughly proud of this) that accords perfectly with the demands of National Socialism'.[9] When this happens, he announced, 'the affinity between the Nordic Spirit and the heroic spirit of Jesus will be revealed', and the 'final victory of the Nordic Spirit' will be 'the fulfilment of Martin Luther's Reformation'.[10] Heidegger's own residual religious sensibilities were very different.

If we speak about the theological dimension of Heidegger's brief convergence with Nazi thought, therefore, we must mean something else. The main claim I will stake in this chapter is that in the early 1930s, Heidegger's de-theologized eschatology began to intersect with an eschatological consciousness that had shaped German self-understanding since the Romantic era, and was also being appropriated by Nazi leaders and intellectuals. However, though Heidegger temporarily thought to be finding in Nazism a spiritual ally – a movement bold enough to realize the intellectual ambition he was projecting – he was soon disappointed by the crass, militant apocalypticism into which the eschatological tradition of Fichte, Hegel and Hölderlin was here being shaped, and dissociated himself from the party programme in favour of an apophatic eschatology centred on a very different reading of Hölderlin.

This is a large claim, and several steps will be required to substantiate it. The first step will be a brief survey of German nationalism as, from its beginnings in the Napoleonic Wars to World War I, a vision of the apotheosis of the German 'spirit'. This vision found philosophical expression in G. W. F. Hegel's account of growing German intellectual and political power as the advancement of the 'absolute rule' of the Spirit, in which 'all peoples [would] find their salvation'. It was popularized by J. G. Fichte, F. Hölderlin, E. M. Arndt and others, and had a wide-ranging influence on nineteenth-century German philosophy, theology, political thought and literature. Although originally conceived as primarily an educational (and only secondarily a political) programme, this nationalist vision was inflected militaristically during World War I. Thus, Pastor Karl König, representative of hundreds of speakers and writers, could declare, 'This army is an embodiment of our national spirit'.

After the failure of the German Empire, this apocalyptic interpretation of German history was not abandoned, but only refocused in the early writings, speeches and spectacles of Hitler, Goebbels and Arthur Moeller van den Bruck. The second step of my argument is to discuss this legacy of apocalyptic nationalism within Nazi thought, rhetoric and culture, especially programmatic National Socialist writings such as Arthur Moeller van den Bruck's *Third Reich* (1923), Hitler's *Mein Kampf* (1925–27), Alfred Rosenberg's *The Myth of the Twentieth Century* (1930) and the poetry of Herbert Boehme and Gerhard Schumann.

One crucial shift here is that whereas earlier nationalism, carried by the *Bildungsbürgertum* (educated middle class), defined the German people by its national spirit, the nationalism of the Nazi Party, carried primarily by the proletariat, defined it by its blood: in Hitler's words, 'the people as such is a substance of flesh and blood'.[11] As we will see, Heidegger's initial support for, but repeated discord and progressive disappointment with the Nazi Party, like that of other intellectuals, is explicable at least in part by the fact that he retains the conception of the *Volk* (people) championed by Hölderlin, Hegel and Fichte, as an entity of *Geist* (spirit) called to a rule of spirit. A test case for this claim are various Nazi-era treatments of Hölderlin, who had long been regarded as a singular prophet of the (eschatological) union of *Volk* and *Geist*.

The third step of my argument is to set Heidegger's Rectoral Address (1933) and other texts of the 1930s in the context both of this German nationalism and of his own developing sense of eschatology. As we have seen, Heidegger's early work is in part a reshaping of Christian eschatological thought into an 'eschatology without eschaton' of affliction and struggle. In *Being and Time* and related texts, the main focus of this eschatological perspective is the individual and his or her mortality. Towards the end of *Being and Time*, however, Heidegger shifts his attention away from individual existence towards collective or national life, aiming to repeat on that level the question of what a fundamentally temporal existence can mean.[12] Within the incomplete framework of *Being and Time*, this communal perspective is never fully worked out, but a vague appeal to 'destiny' begins to be formulated which he begins to work out, in proximity of the Nazi party, in the early 1930s.[13] In the years 1933–34, the impossibility of fulfilment that has been such a central characteristic of Heidegger's eschatology is briefly submerged by a (short-lived) hope for fulfilment of national and individual destiny in the National Socialist state. But already in 1934, Heidegger becomes disillusioned with the regime, and begins, primarily via his readings of Hölderlin, to reassert the uncertainty and (perhaps perpetual) futurity of his vision of individual and communal existence.

Apocalyptic nationalism in Germany

As Klaus Vondung and others have documented, an apocalyptic imagination suffused and shaped German nationalism from its beginnings in the Napoleonic Wars.[14] I take 'apocalypticism' here to mean the expectation of a salvation which is characterized by three main features: it encompasses both the individual and the community; it consists in an integration of the spiritual and the political; and it is the fruit of a radical upheaval or reversal that entails struggle and suffering.

Napoleon's reign was interpreted apocalyptically by a wide range of German writers, including J. G. Fichte and F. Schlegel.[15] At first glance, this response resembled the outbreaks of apocalyptic fervour that had accompanied so many political and social upheavals in medieval and Reformation Europe.[16] Seen as events so terrible and incomprehensible that they could only be contained in an apocalyptic vision, Napoleon's defeat of Austria and Prussia in 1805 and 1806 led to visionary proclamations of the coming turn of the age:

> Indeed, if just beings animate and judge the world, then there is now more hope than ever, seeing how thick a cloud of presumption and iniquity, of lies and injustice, the most ruinous of goddesses, the beguiling ancient one, has gathered over the head of the great slayer. This will, indeed it must, erupt in thunder and lightning, and devastate him and the world together.[17]

But alongside the relatively simplistic Biblicist millenarian interpretations already familiar from the Turkish invasions, the Peasant Wars, the Siege of Muenster, and so forth,[18] a new, 'Romantic' nationalist eschatological narrative emerged from the Napoleonic Wars. It was this which came to define German nationalism from the Rhine Confederation to the World Wars.

In his influential pamphlet collection *Spirit of the Age* (1809–14), the prominent political writer Ernst Moritz Arndt (1769–1860) developed an apocalyptic account of the Napoleonic age as the 'Last Holy War' against the 'Prince of Darkness and Enemy of the Sons of Light'.[19] Although clearly influenced by Biblicist millenarianism,[20] Arndt here formulates a substantially different vision by shifting the traditional Biblical vocabulary of a judging God to one of 'Spirit': the 'judging Spirit that moves through history'; 'the gigantic spirit that . . . rides through time'.[21] This quasi-divine Spirit, entrusted with world judgement, is at the same time the national spirit of the Germans. 'Believe', Arndt exhorts Germany, 'this time is your time, its God and its Spirit are your God and your Spirit, and you will lead the radiant round dance of the new century. . . . You are the Spirit and Soul of the new history.'[22] This 'new century', rising from the turmoil of the French Revolution, is to be a 'third epoch of Christianity', under the rule of God as a national, 'German' deity.[23]

Divine spirit and German spirit

The origin of this conflation of divine 'Spirit' and German national 'spirit' had been not so much political as intellectual and educational. The education-oriented nationalism of Herder and Fichte, among others, aimed at the formation of the entire nation in its 'national spirit', which was encapsulated in German language and culture, and was representative of Spirit as such. The aim of this nationalist movement was the institution, as Fichte put it, of an entirely 'new creation', based on the rule of Spirit and reason, after the devastation of the Napoleonic Wars.[24]

In his *Addresses to the German Nation* (1808), delivered in the aftermath of Napoleon's defeat of Prussia, J. G. Fichte (1762–1814) develops J. G. Herder and J. G. Hamann's claim that 'not man speaks, but human nature speaks in him, and proclaims itself to those like him'.[25] This 'human nature' is manifest not only or primarily on the level of individual speech, but also on that of a national language. Every language develops through the fortunes and encounters of a people, and is therefore 'necessarily' what it is: 'not the people expresses its knowledge [Erkenntnis], but its knowledge itself expresses itself in them'.[26] The German people is superior to other Germanic tribes because it alone, among them, has retained its primordial, 'necessary', organic language, whose acquisition educates or forms all Germans in the spirit of the German nation, which is a manifestation of Spirit per se.[27] As its language, so the German people itself is a pure and primordial one – 'a primordial people, the people as such'.[28] The Slavs and other 'tribes', by contrast, have adopted the language of another people.[29] The difference is absolute: 'the German speaks a language which is alive right down to its emergence from the power of nature'; the 'other Germanic tribes', by contrast, speak a language which 'stirs on the surface, but is dead at its root'.[30] In practice, this means that among Germans, all communal (that is, lingual) life is already 'intellectual formation [Geistesbildung]', and is, accordingly, saturated by a sense of purpose, seriousness and diligent labour. Among other Germanic tribes, by contrast, life and intellectual formation remain separate, and its members 'drift through life unawares'.[31] Fichte is, in effect, sketching a national version of Heidegger's description, on the individual level, of authenticity as contrasted with absorption in the 'crowd'.

This primordial relation to Spirit singles out the German people for a historical destiny: no less than 'to found the kingdom of Spirit and reason as such'.[32] This is the meaning of this desperate age: Not until the despair and disintegration following Prussia's defeat by Napoleon could this Spirit fully reveal itself to the people. The 'forefathers' who fought in the wars of the Reformation 'did not quite know what [they] were fighting for': in addition to their own conscience, a 'higher Spirit compelled [them], which never fully revealed itself to [them]'. It is for the self-realization, the growth to 'autonomous existence' of this Spirit that German 'blood has flown' throughout history. 'It is up to you', Fichte exhorts his compatriots, 'to justify this sacrifice and realise its meaning by instating this Spirit in the world dominion destined for it'.[33] This is the telos of the entire history of the German people.[34]

Again and again, Fichte describes this task in deliberately apocalyptic language, for example, as the resurrection of a 'glorious form' from the corpse of Germany, stepping into the 'dawn of the new world' which has already risen.[35] The conclusion to his *Addresses to the German Nation* is equally explicitly apocalyptic: 'You are adjured by providence itself, by the divine plan for the world set in place at the creation of mankind, which only exists to be thought by humans and to be realized by humans, to save its honour and its existence.' To the Germans it is given 'to pass Last Judgement [*letztes Endurteil*]' on the question whether man is called to 'rise up to higher worlds' or to 'continue to slumber in a mere animal or plant-life'.[36]

> Among all the newer people it is you in whom the seed of human perfection is most decisively planted, and to whom progress in this development is entrusted. If you perish in this your essence, then all hope of the entire human race for salvation from the depths of its evils perishes with you.[37]

A decade later, G. W. F. Hegel (1770–1831) develops a more systematic, detailed and wide-ranging version of the idea of national spirits. In the *Philosophy of Right* (1821), Hegel defines world history as the 'interpretation and actualization of the universal spirit'.[38] This happens through the dialectic interplay of the several 'national spirits'. In each age, one national spirit is the vehicle of that moment of the world spirit. During its epoch, 'that nation reigns in world history', exercising the 'absolute right' of the world spirit, while 'the spirits of the other nations are without rights, and . . . count no longer in world history'. The last and highest of these vehicles is the 'Germanic empire' [*das Germanische Reich*], which completes the realization of the world spirit, so fulfilling 'world history, which is the Last Judgement' or 'judgement of the world'.[39]

This vision is immediately absorbed into the prevailing eschatological nationalism of the German Romantics. In 1848, quoting Schiller via Hegel, Ernst Moritz Arndt writes, 'World history is the Last Judgement *of the peoples*.'[40] Knowing himself an exponent of the dominant power of this last age of the history of the world spirit, and therefore as holding the interpretative key of history, he continues: 'With the judge, world history, I declare at the outset [of this tract]: the Poles and the whole Slavonic tribe are inferior to the Germans.'[41] Like Fichte, Arndt holds it as central that the national spirit must be realized or fulfilled through political action; in an 1810 speech, he exhorts the German people, 'You must lend this Spirit a body.'[42]

Messianic suffering

Besides the fusion of 'world spirit' and political action, a second focus of Romantic nationalism is the rise of the people, or its eschatological manifestation, from and in suffering. In part, this emphasis is a natural concomitant of the circumstances of the birth of German nationalism in the turmoil of the Napoleonic Wars, interpreted through the lens of the Christian apocalyptic tradition. Two of its most influential manifestations are found in the philosophical system of Hegel and the poetic vision of Hölderlin.

Friedrich Hölderlin (1770–1843) emphasizes suffering as the initial condition of the coming (or return) of god. In 'Bread and Wine' (1800), to which he returns often from the 1940s to his death,[43] Hölderlin divides time into two past and one prophesied eras: the golden age of ancient Greece, when the gods were present on earth, and raised man to an almost divine height of artistic and cultural achievement; the night following the departure of the gods; and their anticipated return.

> But friend! we come too late. The gods do live,
> But above our heads, up in another world.
>
> . . .
>
> In the meantime, I often think it
> Better to sleep than to be thus without companions,
> To wait thus; and what to do and to say in the meantime
> I don't know, and wherefore poets in destitute times?
> But they are, you say, like the holy priests of the wine-god,
> Who travelled from land to land in holy night.

One of the striking features of this as of many Hölderlinian poems is its transposition of the Judeo-Christian idea of the suffering that the Messiah has (or had) to undergo into a destiny for Germany and the German poet. This suffering, which in the Biblical books of Isaiah and the New Testament was the result of the Messiah's rejection by his people, is here the fate of the few who are conscious enough to notice the absence of the gods. This painful consciousness, for Hölderlin, is itself a quasi-messianic task; for here and elsewhere in his poetry, the return of the god is predicated precisely on the human realization of his absence. This, indeed, is the role of the poet 'in time of scarcity': to expose himself to the darkness of the present night and proclaim that darkness to his fellow men, even at the risk of being overpowered by it (a popular aetiology of Hölderlin's madness by his followers, including Heidegger).[44]

G. W. F. Hegel, too, presents suffering as both the condition and the continuing character of Germany's realization of Spirit. After rehearsing three previous stages in world history – those of the 'Oriental', 'Greek' and 'Roman' empires – Hegel, in the last part of his *Philosophy of Right*, turns to the final phase of the self-realization of Spirit, the age of the 'Germanic empire'. The paragraph is worth quoting in full:

[With the disintegration of the Roman empire,] spirit and its world are . . . both alike lost and plunged into . . . infinite pain. . . . At this point, spirit is pressed back upon itself in the extreme of its absolute *negativity*. This is the absolute *turning point*; spirit rises out of this situation and grasps the *infinitepositivity* of this its inward character, i.e. it grasps the principle of the unity of the divine nature and the human, the reconciliation of objective truth and freedom as the truth and freedom appearing within self-consciousness and subjectivity, a reconciliation with the fulfilment of which the Nordic principle . . . of the Germanic peoples, has been entrusted.[45]

This fulfilment comes about only through a 'stern struggle [*Kampf*]' between spiritual and worldly forms of the realm, culminating in the establishment of the State.[46]

World War I

Receding during the time of the German Confederation and much of the German Empire, this apocalyptic vision – centred on the German national spirit as that which will, in its political self-fulfilment, bring salvation to the whole world – was revived during World War I. Hundreds of war poems, sermons and lectures invoked it, frequently with reference to Fichte, Hegel and Arndt.[47] However, an important shift had occurred: What was required to bring the German spirit to fulfilment, now, was not merely educational or even political action, but military action; the suffering exacted was death on the battlefield.

Friedrich Gogarten described the German national spirit as bearer of revelation and so agent of salvation: 'To our highest thoughts, the German people and the German spirit are the revelation of eternity.'[48] Sociologist Johann Plenge described the war as a 'crusade in the service of World Spirit', whose highest developmental stage was represented by Germany – for which reason the German crusade would 'redound to the salvation of the world'.[49] Pastor Karl König, having equated 'the history of the divine spirit [göttliche Geistesgeschichte]' with 'the history of the human spirit', states his conviction that the latter would find its fulfilment in the German spirit. Germany, consequently, had to win the apocalyptically interpreted war, 'simply because this is a necessity of the history of the human and divine spirit on this earth'.[50] Philosopher Rudolf Eucken, too, insisted that Germany must win the war, as a defeat would 'rob world history of its deepest meaning' and 'signify the downfall of human history'.[51] Philosopher Adolf Lasson concurred in this spiritual interpretation of Germany's military power: 'Our army and navy too are a spiritual power.'[52] And König again: 'This army is an embodiment of our national spirit.'[53] Indeed, the attitude was so common as to be satirized in Karl Kraus' Last Days of Mankind, in whose epilogue 'Dr.-Ing. Abendrot of Berlin' appears as a self-declared 'Knight of the Spirit', who concocts lethal gas 'to finally gain the final final victory, and therefore finally infinitely to triumph'.[54]

This is the quasi-religious nationalist imagination that National Socialist thinkers such as Arthur Moeller van den Bruck, Adolf Hitler, Alfred Rosenberg and Joseph Goebbels received and refashioned.

National Socialism as a messianic ideology

That Nazi ideology and rhetoric included an explicit apocalyptic dimension is now well established by historians and political theorists.[55] Inheriting the nationalist tradition reviewed above, the Nazi regime deliberately projected the political and military consolidation of a 'messianic kingdom' that was informed by a vision of the final state of history, born through struggle and suffering, and centred around a messianic *Führer* figure. However, the Nazi development of German apocalyptic nationalism was complicated by a persistent tension between opposing definitions of the German *Volk*. As we have seen, Germany's eschatologically inflected nationalism had been driven, in the era of Hegel, Fichte and Hölderlin, by an understanding of the *Volk* as primarily an entity of spirit called to a spiritual destiny. By contrast, leading Nazi thinkers such as Hitler, Goebbels and Alfred Rosenberg described the *Volk* not as a spiritual entity but as a body defined by 'blood and soil', a 'race'. Intellectuals and artists including Heidegger, Gerhard Schumann, Herbert Böhme and others persisted in the older tradition – a persistence which often led to increasing conflicts with the party programme.

A foundation stone of National Socialist ideology, at least in its early years, was the identification of the projected state or nation with the eschatological kingdom of Christ. Thus, the term 'Third Reich' as an epithet for the Germany of the future was chosen not only by analogy to the two preceding 'German' empires, but also, and more significantly, with explicit reference to the 'Third Kingdom' prophesied by the twelfth-century Christian apocalypticist Joachim of Fiore: the millennial kingdom of the Spirit.[56] In his programmatic book *The Third Reich* (1923), Arthur Moeller van den Bruck draws on the entire tradition of apocalyptic nationalism, in a synthesis that is worth quoting in full:

> Instead of government by party we offer the ideal of the Third Empire. It is an old German conception and a great one. It arose when our First Empire fell; it was early quickened by the thought of a millennium; but its underlying thought has always been a future which should be not the end of all things but the dawn of a German Age in which the German People would for the first time fulfil their destiny on earth. . . .

> [However,] the thought of the Third Empire – to which we must cling as our last and highest philosophy – can only bear fruit if it is translated into concrete reality. It must quit the world of dreams and step into the political world. It must be as realist as the problems of our constitutional and national life; it must be as sceptical and pessimistic as beseems the times.[57]

Until 1939, Hitler habitually adopted this terminology: in September 1933, for example, he officially announced that the state he was leading would be a 'Third Reich' that would last 'a thousand years'.[58]

The Antichrist of this national apocalypse was, unsurprisingly, the Jew, deploying Marxism as his tool of deception and domination. In his tellingly titled speech 'The Decisive World Struggle' ('Der entscheidende Weltkampf'), given at the Party Congress in Nuremberg in 1936, then-*Reichsleiter* Alfred Rosenberg characteristically refers to the Soviet Union as 'Soviet-Judea'[59]; and Goebbels writes about Russian Bolshevism: 'Thus may the devil rage when he rules the world. The Jew must be the Antichrist of world history.'[60] Hitler uses the same imagery in *Mein Kampf*:

> If the Jew, with the aid of his Marxist creed, should triumph over the peoples of this world, then his crown will be the dance of death of humanity, then this planet will once again, as millions of years ago, move through the ether devoid of human life.
>
> Eternal nature mercilessly avenges the violation of her laws.
>
> Thus I believe myself to be acting on behalf of the almighty Creator: By resisting the Jew, I fight [*kämpfe*] for the work of the Lord.[61]

Hitlerite apocalyptic nationalism also incorporated the idea of suffering in both its aspects: that of the 'infinite pain' out of which the German spirit wrests its identity, and that of the 'struggle' [*Kampf*] involved in this wresting – an agonizing struggle to weld together spirit and political reality. Arthur Moeller van den Bruck describes the condition from which this *Reich* will be born as one of pain and mourning:

> Over Germany, to-day only one flag is flying, the token of mourning and the symbol of our life: one only flag, which tolerates no colour near it, and robs the people who move below its sable folds of all their joy in merry pennons and in gaudy standards: only the black flag of need, humiliation and an utter bitterness – a bitterness which clothes itself in self-control lest it should pass into despair.[62]

Hitler and Goebbels concretized this idea of the birth of an eschatological kingdom from suffering (symbolized, for van den

Bruck, by the 'sable flag'), in the ritual celebration of the (failed) Beer Hall Putsch of November 1923, presented as the birth pangs or messianic woes of the coming kingdom. Only at these celebrations was the 'flag of blood' carried at the putsch displayed to the public,[63] and the quasi-liturgical texts accompanying them presented the death of 16 of Hitler's followers as a sacrifice necessary for the subsequent victory. In correspondence with the 'sacral event' of 1923, Vondung argues, 'Hitler's seizure of power was interpreted as a second sacral event which made true the revelation of 9 November. The content of this revelation was the *Reich* under National Socialist rule. . . . As an eternal *Reich* it was considered to be the final period of the National Socialist "history of salvation".'[64]

The vision of the nation as both the subject and the object of an eschatological faith, born from, and in, suffering and struggle, pervades Gerhard Schumann's poetry, often focused emblematically in Hitler as the suffering messiah.[65] The seventh sonnet of Schumann's cycle *Songs of the Reich* (1935) places Hitler in the Garden of Gethsemane:

Then night came. The one stood, wrestling in mortal agony.
Blood flowed from the eyes which, seeing,
Died in the face of the terror
That rose from the valleys to the peak.

Cry of agony arose and broke harshly and anxiously.
Despair, at the end of its strength, grasped at nothing.
He reared, trembling in fear of the heaviness –
Until the command forced him to his knees.

But as he rose the firelight
of the chosen one shone round his head. And descending
He carried the torch into the night.

The millions bowed to him in silence,
Delivered. The heavens flamed with the pale flame of morning.
The sun rose. And with it rose the Reich.[66]

Herbert Böhme, later leader of the Reich's professional association for poetry, extends this need for suffering and sacrifice to the whole people. In *Confessions of a Young German* (1935), he declares: 'We believe in the vocation of our people, and in the living sacrifice of our dead for the immortal greatness of our work, the Germans' desire, the eternal *Reich*.'[67] And again:

> This faith means nothing other than: Germany.
> Germany, understood celestially, a people in all its infinity, that is the *Reich*.[68]

Heidegger calls the German students to the same attitude: 'May the courage to sacrifice [yourselves] for the salvation of the essence and the exaltation of the innermost power of our people in its state grow in you unceasingly.'[69]

Heidegger's eschatology between Romanticism and Nazism

Böhme, Schumann and Heidegger project a predominantly spiritual vision of the German people and *Reich* that is typical of many intellectuals who saw in the Nazi Party the potential heir of a great German tradition.[70] But this vision is at odds with the increasingly dominant definition of the *Volk* as, in Hitler's words, 'a substance of flesh and blood'[71] demanding a 'political faith'.[72] 'It requires all the energy of a young, missionary-style idea', writes Hitler in *Mein Kampf*, 'to hoick our people, wresting them from the coils of this international serpent [Bolshevism] and arresting the contamination of our blood from within'. 'The powers of the nation thus released', he reassures his readers with messianic confidence, 'may then be used for the safeguarding of our peoplehood, which may, until time everlasting, prevent a repetition of recent catastrophes'.[73]

The key work of this religio-racial approach to nationalism is Alfred Rosenberg's programmatic *Myth of the Twentieth Century* (1930), which propounds a 'religion of blood', replete with a metaphysics of race, to supersede Christianity.[74] Rosenberg commends some of the values of Christianity, but thinks that its fatal flaw was to disregard the 'law of blood': 'the stream of blood-red, real life, which rushes through the veins of all true peoples and every culture' and alone makes the creation and maintenance of values possible. In Christianity and all forms of 'humanism', 'blood

was de-souled into a chemical formula and so "explained"'.[75] The
study of history in the context of racial theory, by contrast, reveals

> that today we are faced with a final decision. Either we will,
> through the renewed experience and cultivation of the ancient
> blood, together with a heightened will to fight, rise to a purifying
> achievement, or even the last Germanic-occidental values of
> civilisation and national breeding will sink into the dirty floods
> of people of the world cities, will be stunted on the blistering,
> infertile asphalt of a bestializing inhumanity, or will drain away
> as infectious germs in the form of self-bastardizing emigrants to
> South America, China, Dutch India, Africa.[76]

Heidegger never accedes to this primary identification of the *Volk*
by blood. Rather, he maintains the identification by spirit (*Geist*)
familiar from Romantic nationalism, and continues to regard
Germany not as isolated but as part of 'the West', built on Greek
political foundations. All this is apparent even in that most notorious
of his testimonies to National Socialism, his inaugural lecture upon
election to the rectorship of the University of Freiburg in 1933, 'The
Self-Assertion of the German University' (more commonly known
as the Rectoral Address or *Rektoratsrede*).[77]

The Rectoral Address is forceful in its assertion of the necessity
of university reform, but also notoriously ambiguous in its specific
vision for such reform. Scholars have typically emphasized those
rhetorical features which the speech shares with or owes to National
Socialist rhetoric or policy; but a closer look shows a much more
multivalent use of terminology, which can be read with equal
plausibility as an illustration of Nazi ideology, of a Platonist vision
of philosophy, or of anti-modernist rhetoric. Thus, for example,
Heidegger's tri-partite scheme of national 'service' – knowledge,
work and defence – neatly (if somewhat unnervingly) folds
National Socialist ideas into Plato's ideal Republic, administered by
philosopher kings, workers and soldiers.

What emerges clearly, however, is a conception of the people
and its calling very different from that peddled by Rosenberg and
Hitler. Heidegger describes his acceptance of the rectorship as 'the
commitment to the spiritual [or intellectual] leadership of this
institution of higher learning'. But this spiritual leadership requires
that 'the leaders, first and foremost and at any time, are themselves

led – led by the relentlessness of that spiritual [or intellectual] mission which forces the destiny of the German people into the shape of its history'.[78] The current revolution, accordingly, is for Heidegger only a preliminary step towards a second, spiritual (or intellectual) revolution. To Elisabeth Blochmann, he writes shortly after assuming the rectorship that the political upheavals of the moment are always in danger of remaining an 'adhesion to the superficial', but have the potential of becoming the 'way of a first awakening', *provided that* 'we are preparing ourselves for a second and deeper one'.[79] This second, spiritual awakening requires that 'we, as a historical-spiritual people, still and once again will ourselves'.[80] The present, he emphasizes to Blochmann, can only be understood from out of the future.[81]

The way to achieve this spiritual or intellectual mission, according to Heidegger, is to concentrate one's life in the service of a higher law (given to the people by its own Spirit), rather than to 'drift through life' oblivious of that law. This does not resemble typical Nazi rhetoric, but does reflect Hegelian and Fichtean nationalist visions. Within his own work, the contrast echoes Heidegger's 1920s' rhetoric of authenticity and inauthenticity; but it is perhaps even more reminiscent, because it is communally oriented, of his earliest, anti-Modernist writings. In 1910, criticizing the contemporary demand for 'free scientific enquiry and free thought',[82] Heidegger had countered that for such freedom, 'intellectual emancipation from the lower drives is necessary'. Such emancipation, however, 'requires continuing, innermost contact with the richest and deepest source of religious-moral authority', the Church.[83] In the Rectoral Address, this authority is shifted from the church to the *Volk*:

> To give oneself the law is the highest freedom. The much-lauded "academic freedom" will be expelled from the German university; for this freedom was not genuine because it was only negative. It primarily meant lack of concern, arbitrariness of intentions and inclinations, lack of restraint in what was done and left undone. The concept of the freedom of the German student is now brought back to its truth. In future, the bond and service of German students will unfold from this truth.[84]

The striking similarities between Heidegger's earliest, conservatively Catholic polemics and this nationalist text raise tricky questions: On the one hand, they beg interpretation; on the other, they resist being pressed into the service of straightforward claims either that Heidegger has de-Christianized originally Christian concerns, or that he merely tends to channel a psychological pre-disposition to biddability or asceticism through whatever system of authority he followed at the time.

In this quandary, it is perhaps more interesting to mark the particular shifts than to venture a global interpretation. Two are especially salient. The first is the shift from church to people. German nationalism was carried, both during the nineteenth century and during World War I, by Protestants. By contrast, Heidegger, like many Catholics, retreated to an ultramontanist position during the *Kulturkampf*, and identified with Rome more than with the nation. It is clear that his investment in the German *Volk* could therefore come only after significant changes associated (though not in direct theological ways) with his conversion to Protestantism.[85]

The second is the striking renunciation of *substantive* demands or parameters. In the early anti-Modernist writings, Heidegger repeatedly emphasizes the truth stewarded by the Church and demanding assent. In the Rectoral Address, by contrast, struggle and discipline are necessitated by the very questionableness of existence. Heidegger reminds his students that they are bound 'to the spiritual mission of the German people'. This spiritual mission, however, has no substantive directive, only a performative one: 'This people works at its fate by . . . continually fighting for [*erkämpfen*] its spiritual world anew. Thus exposed to the most extreme questionableness of its own existence, this people wills to be a spiritual people.' And again: 'The very questionableness of being forces the people to work and fight and forces it into its state [*Staat*], to which the professions belong.'[86] This attitude is already in evidence in 1930, when Heidegger declares to the students who have gathered for a torch procession in celebration of his rejection of the offer of a professorship in Berlin: '[I]n our present time, we have no footing in any objective, universally binding knowledge or power; the only foothold [*Halt*] that remains to us is our bearing [*Haltung*].'[87] This connection between *Kampf* and the questionableness of existence – the lack of a clear *telos*, the unanswerability, in any traditional sense, of the question of Being – is clearly dependent on a prior rejection of Christianity as capable of answering the questions of existence.

Turn to Hölderlin

One of the central figures of Heidegger's personal development in this domain was the Romantic poet Friedrich Hölderlin, whose poems had been a 'new' and 'wholly original' reading experience for Heidegger during his service in World War I,[88] and now became a central resource for formulating the eschatology of the 'coming god' that defined Heidegger's movement via Nazism to his later thought. The development of his Hölderlin interpretation can be traced through a long sequence of public lectures and university lecture series on the poet spanning the years 1934–46 and beyond.

Under National Socialist rule, Hölderlin was officially presented as a proto-fascist and 'cultural prophet' of the *Volksgemeinschaft*, preparing the people for struggle.[89] Numerous academics at the time sought to substantiate this connection, among them Max Kommerell, Paul Böckmann and Kurt Hildebrand.[90] Werner Bartscher's 1942 study *Hölderlin und die Deutsche Nation* praises Böckmann's and Hildebrandt's works in particular, in vocabulary characteristic of the newly slanted Hölderlin interpretation: 'Hildebrandt's inspiring work . . . offers a grandiose and often new picture of this heroic poet as an ingenious leader [*Führender*], a spearhead for the German world view.' Hildebrandt's work, he concludes, can therefore be called a 'political-scholarly deed, because it demonstrates the fertile relationship between the ingenious German poet and his people'.[91]

Popular editions and biographies of Hölderlin were produced by leading publishing houses. For the youth, the *Reichsjugend-führung* distributed 16,000 copies of a collection entitled *Command and Fulfilment* among their branches. The Hitler Youth recited Hölderlin's poetry at their celebrations.[92] A number of 'Hölderlin Breviaries' were published and distributed to members of the *Wehrmacht*.[93] 1943 was proclaimed a 'Hölderlin Year', celebrating the poet 'as one whose spirit would lead the fatherland to victory'.[94] On 7 June of that year, Josef Goebbels as guest of honour attended the founding of the *Hölderlin-Gesellschaft* (Hölderlin Society).

Heidegger's Hölderlin lectures at Freiburg – first his 1934/35 lecture course on Hölderlin's poems 'Germania' and 'The Rhine', then his 1936 lecture 'Hölderlin and the Essence of Poetry' – seem at first sight to fit neatly into this renewed valorization. In his 1934–35 lecture course, Heidegger presents the poet as announcing precisely what Heidegger himself understands the rise of the Nazi Party to be, namely a new history for the West, dominated by German: 'The hour of our [German] history has struck.'[95]

However, the dominant and constant element of Heidegger's reading of Hölderlin is not a political programme but an eschatological vision: a vision which becomes increasingly more apophatic as Heidegger's disillusion with Nazism grows. In 1934/35 as well as his 1936 lecture 'Hölderlin and the Essence of Poetry', Heidegger interprets the new age announced by the poet – the 'hour of German history' – explicitly as an apocalyptic one: 'It is the age of the gods that have fled *and* of the god that is coming.'[96] Hölderlin is rightly hailed as a prophet because he no longer looks back to the West as originally identified with the Greeks and their gods, but 'anticipates' a new historical time, a new beginning for the West to be identified with the Germans and the god to come.

In the 1940s, Heidegger no longer argues that the eschatology articulated by Hölderlin has been (or is about to be) realized. But what he has given up is only the identification of Hölderlin's coming god with the Third Reich, not the eschatological orientation as such. Thus, in the preface added to the published version of his 1934/35 lectures on Hölderlin's hymns 'Germania' and 'The Rhine', Heidegger deliberately shifts the historical framework of the lectures:

> One reads Hölderlin "historically" and mistakes the one essential thing, that his still time-space-less work has already overcome our historical posturing and founded the beginning of a different history – that history which begins with the struggle [*Kampf*] for a decision about the arrival or flight of the god.[97]

This quote supports the view that Heidegger's Hölderlin-interpretation in the early years of the Nazi era was not merely a way of rationalizing his political attitude, but that, on the contrary, his support for the Nazis was rooted in a pre-existing, quasi-theological taste for eschatology which survived even the breakdown of Heidegger's conviction that that eschatology was realized in National Socialism. The next chapter will follow out this thought trajectory more thoroughly.

Notes

1 Some well-known examples include Víctor Farías, *Heidegger and Nazism* (Philadelphia: Temple University Press, 1989), and Emmanuel Faye, *Heidegger: l'introduction du nazisme dans la philosophie* (Paris: Albin Michel, 2005).

2 The most significant German publications of the last few years, in this field, are Holger Zaborowski's masterful and painstaking 800-page assessment, *Eine Frage von Irre und Schuld?: Martin Heidegger und der Nationalsozialismus* (Frankfurt: Fischer Verlag, 2010), and the two research volumes which inform it: *Heidegger und der Nationalsozialismus I: Dokumente* (= HJB 4) and *Heidegger und der Nationalsozialismus II: Interpretationen* (= HJB 5), both eds. Alfred Denker and Holger Zaborowski (Freiburg: Karl Alber Verlag, 2010).

3 See, among many similar letters, Jaspers to Heidegger, 24 December 1931, in *Heidegger/Jaspers*, p. 147; Heidegger to Bultmann, 15 January 1930, in *Bultmann/Heidegger*, p. 123; Heidegger to Blochmann, 12 April 1933, in *Heidegger/Blochmann*, p. 62; as well as the account of Heidegger's and Jaspers's decade-long discussions of these questions in Alfred Denker, 'Die Neubelebung der Philosophie in dürftiger Zeit: Martin Heidegger und Karl Jaspers (1919–1933)', in Holger Zaborowski and Stephan Loos (eds.), *Leben, Tod und Entscheidung: Studien zur Geistesgeschichte der Weimarer Republik* (Berlin: Duncker und Humblot, 2003). Heidegger's efforts towards university reform – particularly greater autonomy of the Philosophy Faculty and the university from extraneous and academically apathetic state interference – is also documented in the Minutes of the Philosophy Faculty Board meetings of 1928–33. See e.g. UAF (= University Archive Freiburg) MSS A10/108 (2 November 1929), B3/797 (26 November 1929), and B3/798 (20 December 1932); as well as Sylvia Paletschek, 'Entwicklungslinien aus der Perspektive der Fakultätssitzungen', in Eckhard Wirbelauer (ed.), *Die Freiburger Philosophische Fakultät 1920–1960: Mitglieder, Strukturen, Vernetzungen* (Freiburg: Karl Alber, 2006), pp. 58–107; pp. 69–71.

The larger intellectual debate surrounding university reform in the early 1930s is well reflected in the 1931/32 series 'Gibt es noch eine Universität?' ('Is there still such a thing as a university?') which appeared in the newspaper *Frankfurter Zeitung*, and included contributions by Karl Jaspers, Paul Tillich, Ernst Bloch, Theodor Haecker and others; now collected in *Gibt es noch eine Universität? Zwist am Abgrund - eine Debatte in der Frankfurter Zeitung 1931/32*, ed. Dieter Thomä (Konstanz: Konstanz University Press, 2012).

4   See e.g. Heidegger to Bultmann, 24 January 1931, in *Bultmann/ Heidegger*, pp. 151–3.

5   See e.g. Heidegger to Elfride Heidegger, 20 June 1932, in *Heidegger/ Elfride Heidegger*, pp. 179–81; p. 180; Heidegger to Jaspers, 20 April 1933, in *Heidegger/Jaspers*, p. 152. See also Reinhard Bollmus, *Das Amt Rosenberg und seine Gegner. Studies zum Machtkampf im nationalsozialistischen Herrschaftssystem* (Stuttgart: Oldenbourg, 1970), p. 242f.

6   The dominant National Socialist view largely follows Fichte and Paul de Lagarde. Fichte's term for Paul's corrupting influence (appropriated by Paul de Lagarde and, after him, National Socialist religious thinkers such as Dietrich Eckart) is 'Ausartung des Christentums'; quoted in Klaus Scholder, *Die Kirchen und das Dritte Reich* (Berlin: Propyläen, 1985), vol. 1, p. 103. For many, again following Fichte, this was related to Paul's allegedly 'Judaizing' influence: 'For Fichte', Scholder summarizes, 'Christianity, Jesus, truth and the Germans belong together just as much as Judaism, Paul, and error'; Scholder, *Die Kirchen und das Dritte Reich*, vol. 1, p. 103. On Eckart's appropriation of Fichte, see particularly Claus-Ekkehard Bärsch, *Die politische Religion des Nationalsozialismus* (Munich: Fink, 2nd edn, 2002), esp. 71ff.

7   'Rede des Gauobmanns der Glaubensbewegung "Deutsche Christen" in Gross-Berlin Dr. Krause gehalten im Sportpalast am 13. November 1933' (pamphlet) (Berlin: Verlag Unsere Volkskirche, 1933); quoted in Scholder, *Die Kirchen und das Dritte Reich*, vol. 1, p. 704.

8   Scholder, *Die Kirchen und das Dritte Reich*, vol. 1, p. 704.

9   Ibid., p. 705.

10 Ibid.

11 Adolf Hitler, Speech on 2 November 1932 in Berlin, as quoted in 'Das dichterische Wort im Werk Adolf Hitlers', *Wille und Macht*, Special Issue (20 April 1938); quoted in Klaus Vondung, *Die Apokalypse in Deutschland* (Munich: Deutscher Taschenbuch-Verlag, 1988), p. 208. The argument for a shift from a nationalism of 'spirit' to one of 'blood' is made rudimentarily in that book.

12 See *Sein und Zeit* (1927), GA 2, §§72–77.

13 Much stronger readings than my own of the continuity between §§72–77 of *Being and Time* and Heidegger's Nazi involvement can be found, e.g., in Johannes Fritsche, *Historical Destiny and National Socialism in Heidegger's Being and Time* (Berkeley: University of California Press, 1999), and Tom Rockmore, *On Heidegger's Nazism and Philosophy* (Berkeley: University of California Press, 1991).

14 The following paragraphs, summarizing German apocalyptic thought in the nineteenth and early twentieth centuries, are indebted to Vondung's collection and presentation of sources. Where a source is quoted after Vondung, it is marked 'cited in Vondung, page number'; where a source has been suggested by Vondung but treated independently, it is marked 'see also Vondung, page number'. A summary of apocalypticism in Germany can also be found in Judith Wolfe, 'Messianism', in Nick Adams, George Pattison and Graham Ward (eds.), *Oxford Handbook of Theology and Modern European Thought* (Oxford: Oxford University Press, 2013), pp. 301–23.

15 Among the most prominent are Johann Gottlieb Fichte, Friedrich Schlegel, Heinrich von Kleist, Max von Schenkendorf, Ernst Moritz Arndt, Theodor Körner and Ludwig Achim von Arnim. See Oskar Richter, *Die Lieblingsvorstellungen der Dichter des deutschen Befreiungskrieges* (Leipzig: Seele, 1909); cited in Vondung, *Apokalypse*, p. 155.

16 The standard survey of this topic is still Norman Cohn, *The Pursuit of the Millennium* (Oxford: Oxford University Press, 2nd edn, 1970).

17 Ernst Moritz Arndt, *Geist der Zeit*, vol. 2; in E. Schirmer (ed.), *Ernst Moritz Arndt's Sämtliche Werke* (Magdeburg: Anst, 1908), vol. 9, p. 83; cited in Vondung, *Apokalypse*, p. 158.

18 Proponents of such interpretations of the Napoleonic Wars included Johann Heinrich Jung-Stilling and King Gustav IV Adolf of Sweden.

19 Ernst Moritz Arndt, *Geist der Zeit*, vol. 2; in Schirmer (ed.), *Arndt's Sämtliche Werke*, vol. 9, p. 128; cited in Vondung, *Apokalypse*, p. 26.

20 Arndt excerpted Jung-Stilling's millenarian tract *Die Siegesgeschichte der christlichen Religion in einer gemeinnützigen Erklärung der Offenbarung Johannis* in or before 1809; see Vondung, *Apokalypse*, p. 159.

21 Arndt, *Geist der Zeit*, vol. 3; in Schirmer (ed.), *Arndt's Sämtliche Werke*, vol. 10, p. 111, pp. 127–8; cited in Vondung, *Apokalypse*, p. 160.

22 Ibid., pp. 303, 305; cited in Vondung, *Apokalypse*, p. 160.

23 Edith Ennen, 'Ernst Moritz Arndt: 1769–1860', in *Bonner Gelehrte: Beiträge zur Geschichte der Wissenschaften in Bonn* (Bonn: H. Bouvrier & Co Verlag, 1968), pp. 9–35; pp. 15–16. The 'third epoch' of Christianity is a reference to Joachim of Fiore's (1135–1202) apocalyptic periodization of history, in which the ages or 'kingdoms' of the Father (Old Testament) and of the Son (New Testament and Church) will be followed by an eschatological age of the Holy Spirit. This periodization later also inspired Arthur Moeller van den Bruck's coinage of the term 'The Third Reich'; see below.

24   Johann Gottlieb Fichte, 'Erste Rede', *Reden an die deutsche Nation* (1808); in Fritz Medicus (ed.), *Werke: Auswahl in sechs Bänden* (Leipzig: Felix Meiner, 1911–22), vol. 5, pp. 388–9. The German ideal of national (for the sake of global) education is rooted in the eighteenth century, where it finds epitomic expression in Gotthold Ephraim Lessing's *Die Erziehung des Menschengeschlechts* (1777); cf. Rainer Piepmeier, 'Erziehung des Menschengeschlechts', in Joachim Ritter and Karlfried Gründer (eds.), *Historisches Wörterbuch der Philosophie* (Basel: Schwabe, 1971–2005), vol. 2, pp. 735–9.

25   Fichte, 'Vierte Rede', *Werke*, vol. 5, p. 426.

26   Herder, 'Publicum', *Werke*, vol. 17, p. 287.

27   Fichte, 'Vierte Rede', Werke, vol. 5, pp. 422–5.

28   Fichte, 'Siebte Rede', *Werke*, vol. 5, p. 470.

29   Fichte, 'Vierte Rede', *Werke*, vol. 5, p. 423.

30   Ibid., p. 436.

31   Ibid., p. 438.

32   Fichte, 'Vierzehnte Rede', *Werke*, vol. 5, p. 607.

33   Ibid.

34   Ibid.

35   A deliberate echo, of course, of Jesus' proclamation of Isa. 61 in Lk. 4.16-21; Fichte, 'Erste Rede', *Werke*, vol. 5, p. 390.

36   Fichte, 'Vierzehnte Rede', *Werke*, vol. 5, p. 609.

37   Ibid. Cf. also Fichte's claim that the German Spirit would effect a 're-creation of the human race' (*Werke*, 568), and Max von Schenkendorf's proclamation, 'In Germany shall flower/the salvation of all the world' (Schenkendorf, *Gedichte* [Stuttgart: J. G. Cotta, 1815], p. 6); cited in Vondung, *Apokalypse*, p. 189.

38   G. W. F. Hegel, *Grundlinien der Philosophie des Rechts*, §342; translated as *Philosophy of Right* (trans. T. M. Knox; Oxford: Oxford University Press, 1942), p. 216. In this and subsequent quotations from Hegel, translations are silently emended.

39   Hegel, *Rechtsphilosophie*, §352 (pp. 218–19).

40   'Weltgeschichte ist das Weltgericht der Völker'; Arndt, *Werke. Auswahl in zwölf Teilen*, eds. August Leffson and Wilhelm Steffens (Berlin: Bong, n.d.), vol. 12, pp. 127–8; cited in Vondung, *Apokalypse*, p. 139 (my italics).

41   Arndt, *Werke*, vol. 12, pp. 127–8; cited in Vondung, *Apokalypse*, p. 139.

42   Arndt, *Hoffnungsrede vom Jahre 1810*, ed. Erich Gülzow (Leipzig: Greifswald, 1921), p. 55; cited in Vondung, *Apokalypse*, p. 175.

43 See esp. Heidegger's 1943 manuscript notes on 'Bread and Wine', published in GA 75, 45–56; and his 1946 private lecture 'Wherefore Poets?', published in GA 5, 269–320. No fewer than two passages from 'Bread and Wine' are also represented among the small catena of verses Heidegger chose to be read out at his funeral, published in GA 16, 749–51.

44 Heidegger, *Hölderlins Hymnen 'Germanien' und 'Der Rhein'* (lecture series WS 1934/35), published as GA 39; here pp. 18 and 62–3; cf. Kathleen Wright, 'Heidegger and the Authorization of Hölderlin's Poetry', in Karsten Harries and Christoph Jamme (eds.), *Martin Heidegger: Politics, Art, Technology* (New York: Holmes and Meier, 1994), pp. 164–74; p. 171.

45 Hegel, *Rechtsphilosophie*, §358 (ET 221).

46 Ibid., §360 (ET 222).

47 Fichte and Arndt enjoyed almost unprecedented popularity in Bismarck's Germany. Fichte's *Addresses to the German Nation*, reports Vondung, appeared in at least 15 single editions between 1870 and 1914, as well as in two Collected Works editions and numerous anthologies. Arndt's Collected or Selected Works were published in six editions between 1895 and 1914, and single books appeared in numerous other editions; see Vondung, *Apokalypse*, p. 197.

48 Gogarten, 'Volk und Schöpfung', *Protestantenblatt* 48 (1915), col. 55; cited in Vondung, *Apokalypse*, p. 191.

49 Plenge, *Der Krieg und die Volkswirtschaft* (Münster: Borgmeyer, 1915), p. 200; cited in Vondung, *Apokalypse*, p. 191.

50 König, *Sechs Kriegspredigten* (Jena: Diederichs, 1915), p. 6; cited in Vondung, *Apokalypse*, p. 191.

51 Eucken, *Die weltgeschichtliche Bedeutung des deutschen Geistes* (Stuttgart: Deutsche Verlags-Anstalt, 1914), p. 22; see also Vondung, *Apokalypse*, p. 207.

52 'Geistesmacht ist auch unser Heer und unsere Flotte'; Lasson, 'Deutsche Art und deutsche Bildung', being pamphlet 4 of *Deutsche Reden in schwerer Zeit* (Berlin: Carl Heymanns Verlag, 1914); see also Vondung, *Apokalypse*, p. 204.

53 König, *Neue Kriegspredigten* (Jena: Diederichs, 1914), p. 15; cited in Vondung, *Apokalypse*, p. 204.

54 '. . .[u]m endlich den endlichen Endsieg zu kriegen, und dann also endlich unendlich zu siegen'; Karl Kraus, *Die letzten Tage der Menschheit*, ed. E. Früh (Frankfurt: Suhrkamp, 1992), p. 278.

55 The seminal work introducing the subject is Eric Voegelin, *Die politischen Religionen*, ed. Peter J. Opitz (Munich: Fink, 1993

[1938]). Contemporary analyses and discussions include Claus-Ekkehard Bärsch, *Die politische Religion des Nationalsozialismus* (Munich: Fink, 2nd edn, 2002 [1998]); Axel Dunker, *'Den Pessimismus organisieren': Eschatologische Kategorien in der Literatur zum Dritten Reich* (Bielefeld: Aisthesis, 1994); Michael Ley and Julius H. Schoeps (eds.), *Der Nationalsozialismus als politische Religion* (Bodenheim: Philo Verlagsgesellschaft, 1997); Anna Neumaier, *Apokalyptik als Redeform des Nationalsozialismus: eine Diskursanalyse früher Reden Hitlers* (Bremen: Institut für Kulturwissenschaftliche Deutschlandstudien, 2010); Vondung, *Die Apokalypse in Deutschland*. See also Klaus Schreiner, 'Messianism in the Political Culture of the Weimar Republic', *Towards the Millennium*, eds. Peter Schäfer and Mark Cohen (Leiden: Brill, 1998), pp. 311–62; and Wolfe, 'Messianism', esp. 310–15.

56 See note 23 above.

57 Arthur Moeller van den Bruck, *Das dritte Reich* (Hamburg: Hanseatische Verlagsanstalt, 1923), pp. 13–14; all quotations are from the authorized English translation, *Germany's Third Empire* (trans. and ed. E. O. Lorimer; London: Allen & Unwin, 1934). For a more thorough discussion of the apocalyptic origins of the Nazi use of the term, see Bärsch, *Die politische Religion des Nationalsozialismus*, B.I.1-2.

58 Quoted in Wolfgang Wippermann, 'Drittes Reich', in Wolfgang Benz et al. (eds.), *Enzyklopädie des Nationalsozialismus* (Stuttgart: dtv, 5th edn, 2007), pp. 479–80; p. 480 (no original source cited).

59 Rosenberg, *Der entscheidende Weltkampf: Rede des Reichsleiters Alfred Rosenberg auf dem Parteikongreß in Nürnberg 1936* (Munich: M. Müller & Sohn, 1936), p. 2. For a more thorough discussion of the Jew as the Antichrist in the National Socialist 'political religion', see Bärsch, *Die politische Religion des Nationalsozialismus*, B.I.2.c and B.I.3.c.

60 Entry of 26 June 1926, *Das Tagebuch von Joseph Goebbels, 1925/26*, ed. Helmut Heiber (Stuttgart: Deutsche Verlags-Anstalt, n.d.), p. 85.

61 Adolf Hitler, *Mein Kampf* (Munich: Franz Eher Verlag, 855th edn, 1943 [vol. 1: 1925, vol. 2: 1927]), pp. 69–70. For an analysis of religious and apocalyptic features of *Mein Kampf*, see Gerhard Kurz, 'Braune Apokalypse', in Jürgen Brokoff and Joachim Jacob (eds.), *Apokalypse und Erinnerung in der deutsch-jüdischen Kultur des frühen 20. Jahrhunderts* (Göttingen: Vandenhoeck & Ruprecht, 2002), pp. 131–46; p. 134. Scholder analyses the apparent identification of Hitler with Jesus in *Die Kirchen und das Dritte Reich*, vol. 1, 128ff.

62 Bruck, *The Third Reich*, pp. 242–3.

63 Klaus Vondung, 'National Socialism as a Political Religion: Potentials and Limits of an Analytical Concept', *Totalitarian Movements and Political Religions* 6, 1 (2005), pp. 87–95; p. 88.

64 Vondung, 'National Socialism as a Political Religion', p. 92.

65 Schumann joined the National Socialist German Students' League in 1930; he served in the Ministry of Culture and Education (*Kultusministerium*) from 1933, and in the *Reichskultursenat* from 1935. In 1936, he won the national book prize instituted by Goebbels.

66 Schumann, *Die Lieder vom Reich* (Munich: Albert Langen, Georg Mueller, 1936), p. 20.

67 Boehme, 'Bekenntnis', in *idem*, *Bekenntnisse eines jungen Deutschen* (Munich: Franz Eher, 1935), p. 28.

68 Boehme, 'Deutsches Bekennen', in *Bekenntnisse*, pp. 29–34; p. 32.

69 Heidegger, 'Aufruf an die deutschen Studenten', *Freiburger Studentenzeitung* 8, 1 (3 November 1933); rpt. in GA 16, 184–5; p. 184.

70 How common this hope was up to 1932, even among intellectuals who came to fiercely criticize the Nazi regime, is exemplified in a letter from Bultmann to Heidegger in December 1932, in which he regrets the consolidation of the national socialist *movement* into a political *party*, conceding that the 'actual movement was, and perhaps still is, something great [*etwas Großes*], with its instinct for the ultimate [*für das Letzte*], its feeling of solidarity, and its discipline'; Bultmann to Heidegger, 14 December 1932, in *Bultmann/Heidegger*, pp. 187–8.

71 Speech on 2 November 1932 in Berlin, as quoted in 'Das dichterische Wort im Werk Adolf Hitlers', *Wille und Macht*, Special Issue (20 April 1938).

72 Hitler, *Mein Kampf*, p. 414.

73 Ibid., pp. 751–2.

74 Rosenberg, *Der Mythus des 20. Jahrhunderts: Eine Wertung der seelisch-geistigen Gestaltenkämpfe unserer Zeit* (Munich: Hoheneichen-Verlag, 33rd edn, 1934 [1930]), p. 23.

75 Rosenberg, *Mythus*, p. 22.

76 Ibid., p. 82.

77 Although the Rectoral Address is the most notorious of Heidegger's National Socialist documents, we do in fact see a brief slide into

almost complete subservience to Nazi ideology in his university-internal speeches and publications of the months June 1933 to April 1934. It is worth mentioning, however, that these internal communications are outliers, and only appear for a brief period.

78　Heidegger, 'Die Selbstbehauptung der deutschen Universität' (Rektoratsrede vom 27. Mai 1933), in GA 16, 107–17; p. 107.

79　Heidegger to Blochmann, 30 March 1933, in *Heidegger/Blochmann*, p. 60. See also the similar recollection by Georg Picht, a student of Heidegger in 1933–34: Georg Picht, 'Die Macht des Denkens', in Günther Neske (ed.), *Erinnerung an Martin Heidegger* (Pfullingen: Neske, 1977), pp. 197–206; p. 198.

80　Heidegger, 'Rektoratsrede' (1933), GA 16, 117.

81　Heidegger to Blochmann, 30 March 1933, in *Heidegger/Blochmann*, p. 60.

82　Heidegger, 'Per mortem ad vitam' (1910), GA 16, 3.

83　Heidegger, 'Autorität und Freiheit' (1910), GA 16, 7.

84　Heidegger, 'Rektoratsrede' (1933), GA 16, 113.

85　This also makes clear why Víctor Farías's immensely influential claim that Heidegger's early championing of Abraham a Santa Clara was a proto-Nazi gesture motivated by his sympathy with Santa Clara's anti-Semitism, is at once understandable and a gross oversimplification (see his *Heidegger and Nazism*, ch. 3).

86　Heidegger, 'Rektoratsrede' (1933), GA 16, 114.

87　Heidegger, '[Studenten ehren Professor Heidegger]' (1930), in GA 16, 755–8; p. 758.

88　Heidegger to Elfride Heidegger, 30 August 1918, in *Heidegger/Elfride Heidegger*, p. 77.

89　Among the numerous accounts of the Nazi appropriation of Hölderlin, see esp. Donna Hoffmeister, 'Hölderlin-Biography, 1924–1982: Transformations of a Literary Life', *Seminar* 21, 3 (1983), pp. 207–31; Claudia Albert (ed.), *Deutsche Klassiker im Nationalsozialismus: Schiller, Kleist, Hölderlin* (Stuttgart: J. B. Metzler, 1994); Ralf Schnell, *Dichtung in finsteren Zeiten: Deutsche Literatur und Faschismus* (Reinbek: Rowohlt, 2002); and Richard Unger, 'Hölderlin and His German Readers', in *idem*, *Friedrich Hölderlin* (Boston: Twayne, 1984), pp. 127–33.

90　See e.g. Max Kommerell, *Der Dichter als Führer in der deutschen Klassik* (Frankfurt: Klostermann, 1928); Paul Böckmann, *Hölderlin und seine Götter* (Munich: C. H. Beck, 1935); Kurt Hildebrandt, *Hölderlin, Philosophie und Dichtung* (Berlin: W. Kohlhammer, 1939).

91 Bartscher, *Hölderlin und die Deutsche Nation* (Berlin: Junker und Dünnhaupt, 1942), pp. 221–2.

92 See Bartscher, *Hölderlin*, pp. 222–3.

93 See Unger, *Hölderlin*, p. 131.

94 Ibid.

95 Heidegger, *Hölderlins Hymnen 'Germanien' und 'Der Rhein'* (1934/35), GA 39, 5.

96 Heidegger, 'Hölderlin und das Wesen der Dichtung' (1936), published in GA 4, 33–48; p. 47.

97 Heidegger, *Hölderlins Hymnen 'Germanien' und 'Der Rhein'* (1934/35), GA 39, 1 ('Vorbemerkung').

6

The later Heidegger
(1935 and beyond)

We have seen that Heidegger's path from the mid-1920s onwards was characterized by a persistent sense that existence is a *question*, but shifting opinions as to whether or not this question is in principle and in practice capable of being *answered*. In *Being and Time*, the realization that life is a question that can never be answered, or a possibility that can never be fulfilled, is the basic condition of an authentic existence. In the early 1930s, the life of the nation supplants that of the individual as the focus of Heidegger's attention, and the plane on which the question of existence plays out is no longer that of a lifetime but that of a national destiny. For a brief year, Heidegger thinks that an *answer* might be in sight: not in the form of a predetermined goal, but in the simple act of answering.[1] The questionableness of existence becomes a call to *act*, to 'still and once again will ourselves'. The *Führer* is the embodiment of this will to act, this choice for one's self; it is in this way that 'the Führer himself and alone *is* the present and future German reality and its law' (the very law, we will remember from Heidegger's rectorial address, which it is 'the highest freedom' 'to give oneself').

However, this active, militant attitude is soon exhausted by the realities of political life, and Heidegger's premature resignation from the rectorship marks the beginning of a retreat not only from any active involvement in the Nazi party but also from any hope that its rise might provide an answer to the question of existence – indeed that any such answer can be enforced or enacted at all. Rather, Heidegger turns to find in Hölderlin's vision of the present age as one in which we suffer the absence of the gods who dwelt in ancient Greece and Palestine, and are called to wait for the coming or return of the 'last god', a different and more compelling version of a national existence which is, at its deepest, a question.

This vision is different from Heidegger's early thought in focusing on the life of a people rather than the individual life, and in holding out at least the in-principle possibility of an answer rather than insisting on the structural unanswerability of the question of existence. But it is also different from Heidegger's brief alignment with National Socialism in rejecting any idea that the question of the meaning of our existence could be answered by a sheer act of will or self-choice. The answer – embodied in Heidegger's notoriously elusive 'coming god' – can only come from without. The task of the philosopher is to expose any surrogate contentedness and to witness steadfastly to the absence of the 'coming god', keeping open a space of knowing unknowing into which that god might descend. Heidegger arrives, at the last, at a radically apophatic eschatology.

This chapter falls into two parts: biographical and thematic. The first charts Heidegger's turbulent and shifting relationship to Christianity as it is reflected in his letters, lectures and activities of the period, using some recently released archival material from Freiburg. The second discusses the two complementary sides of Heidegger's later vision, both of which relate more or less directly to theology: his critique of metaphysics as onto-theology, and his call to an ascetic, quasi-mystical discipline of thought capable of waiting for the advent of the 'last god'.

Heidegger and Christianity

Heidegger's relationship to Christianity remained turbulent and fraught throughout his life. The 1910s saw his 'conversion' from anti-modernist Catholicism to Protestantism. The 1920s marked a journey from self-definition as a 'Christian theo*logian*', via the development of an explicitly a-theistic methodology serving as a *praeparatio evangelica*, to a substantive commitment to philosophy (rather than faith) as sole necessary mediator of an authentic existence. However, the upheavals of the 1930s and the continual development of his own thinking destabilized this position, too.

A period of intense personal struggle with the faith of his youth, sometimes accompanied by vehemently anti-Christian polemics in the public sphere, resolved, in the 1940s and 1950s, into an acceptance that his theological origins had set him on the path of thinking, and into a systematic attempt to think through the implications of the new-found realization that 'origin always remains future'.

Anti-Christian polemics

Heidegger's growing commitment, in the late 1920s, to philosophy over and against theology was reinforced by, and in turn encouraged, an increasingly exclusive focus on the 'degenerate' form of Christianity which he had criticized from the beginning. His developing understanding of the history of Being confirmed Heidegger in the Overbeckian conviction that Christianity's earliest experience no longer remained an option for it, and was consequently no viable model for the present.[2] Accordingly, the philosopher's dominant perspective on Christian faith and theology was increasingly less historical and more systematic: 'Faith' and 'theology', in the late 1920s and early 1930s, became co-terminous with systematic theology in its urge for *answers*. Thus, in his 1927 lecture 'Phenomenology and Theology', Heidegger called faith the 'mortal enemy' of philosophy[3]; and in 1928, he insisted that 'in the *philosophical* problem of existence there is necessarily . . . an absolute opposition to all Christianity'.[4] This 'systemic' focus went hand in hand with a renewed orientation towards Catholicism rather than Protestantism as most genuinely representative of Christianity – an orientation that Heidegger retained for the rest of his life.[5]

The intellectual opposition formulated in the late 1920s continued without significant change in the 1930s. Thus, in 1935, Heidegger insisted in his lecture series Introduction to Metaphysics that to believe in the Bible as divine revelation is to make oneself incapable of genuinely asking the basic philosophical question, 'Why are there beings rather than nothing?', because one's very starting point is a particular (apparent) answer to that question. From a Christian standpoint, he claimed, it would be mere 'foolishness' (with all the implications of Ps. 14) to raise the question anew; to do so sincerely, rather than merely as an intellectual exercise, would mean 'giving oneself up as a believer'. But precisely 'this foolishness', Heidegger continues (now with overtones of 1 Cor. 1), 'constitutes philosophy'.[6] It is because of this fundamental opposition that 'Christian philosophy is a square circle and a misunderstanding'.[7]

But although the substance of Heidegger's critique of Christianity remained constant throughout the late 1920s and early 1930s, his tone changed. After his return from Protestant Marburg to Catholic Freiburg in 1928, his intellectual opposition to Christianity acquired an increasingly vehement and acrimonious quality, sometimes culminating in open hostility at the university. In a letter to his friend Elisabeth Blochmann shortly after his arrival in Freiburg, Heidegger expressed his 'abhorrence' with 'present-day Catholicism' (as well as institutionalized Protestantism).[8] This abhorrence became the dominant tone of his public attitude to Christianity in the 1930s, expressed both in his lectures and in his severe assessment of a number of (later well-known) Catholic doctoral and post-doctoral researchers, including J. B. Lotz, Max Müller and Gustav Siewerth. This 'discrimination' has led theologians to speak of Heidegger 'having become personally atheistic'[9] in the 1930s, a fact often linked to his (alleged) ideological Nazism.[10] But a more careful consideration of the substance and university-political context of Heidegger's utterances and actions shows that this assessment has to be significantly moderated.

One of the most important factors of Heidegger's increasing acrimony, usually overlooked by scholars, is the institutional context of his work in the 1930s. The Philosophy Faculty of the University of Freiburg, where Heidegger had studied since 1911, taught as a non-stipendiary lecturer (*Privatdozent*) from 1916 to 1923, and returned as Husserl's successor in 1928, had been established in the fifteenth century to provide a preliminary, general education to students of the University wishing to continue to one of the professional faculties: medicine, law, or theology. The faculty retained this generalist character, holding courses not only in philosophy, but also in philology, social sciences (especially history) and fine art. (The Board protested with partial success when enjoined to establish a lectureship in the history and theory of physical education in 1929.[11]) While some courses were offered as free-standing honours degrees, others were supplementary to honours courses in different subjects and faculties.

It was in its role of providing supplementary courses in history and philosophy for theologians, most of whom were candidates for the priesthood, that the Philosophy Faculty was reluctantly drawn into the intellectual and political upheavals and ambitions of the Roman Catholic Church described in Chapter 1. The modernist crisis brought much debate and friction in the faculty, particularly as a result of the 1907 encyclical *Pascendi* and the 1910 Oath against Modernism. The 1907 encyclical ruled that candidates for the priesthood must not attend courses at state institutions which they could also attend at confessional institutions – meaning, for example, that students like the young Heidegger (before his switch of subjects) were not allowed to attend lectures on the Early Church in the Philosophy Faculty if lectures on a similar subject were offered in the Theology Faculty.[12] The anti-modernist oath obliged all 'professors in philosophical-theological seminaries' to repudiate central innovations of modern scholarship, including the historical-critical method and post-Kantian epistemology. As we saw in Chapter 1, the anti-modernist oath and the papal commendation of Thomism as the sole authoritative philosophy were milestones on the young Heidegger's path from Catholicism to an 'undogmatic Protestantism'.[13]

A particular nexus of interaction between the Philosophy Faculty and the Roman Catholic authorities was one of the faculty's two professorial chairs in philosophy (usually referred to as 'Philosophy (II)'). While the primary chair in philosophy ('Philosophy (I)') had, in the nineteenth century, acquired a close association with neo-Kantianism – when Heidegger acceded to it in 1928, his recent predecessors had been Wilhelm Windelband, Alois Riehl, Heinrich Rickert and Edmund Husserl – this secondary chair was traditionally devoted to 'Christian philosophy'. It had been transferred from the Theology Faculty in 1901,[14] and was dedicated, in compliance with the papally backed neo-Scholastic revival, to the advancement of Scholastic philosophy. Heidegger's post-doctoral work (*Habilitation*) on Scotist philosophy was designed to make him a suitable candidate for the post, and it was his 1916 failure to win it which precipitated the young philosopher's open shift of allegiance to Protestant scholarship.

In 1932, this personal and institutional conflict came to a head when the Concordat between Baden and the Holy See placed the Philosophy Faculty's chairs in Christian philosophy and medieval history under the direct control of the Roman Catholic authorities, stipulating that they be held by 'personages suitable for the impeccable education of students of theology'.[15] The Faculty Board, on which Heidegger served, strongly protested the establishment of these 'Concordat Chairs', but was ignored by the Senate.[16] Years of friction followed. In 1941, after the death of its incumbent, the Faculty (no doubt aided by an anti-Christian regime) temporarily abolished the Concordat Chair in Christian Philosophy, re-dedicating it to psychology; to what extent Heidegger was involved in this effort is unclear.[17] The chair reverted to its confessional status in 1946, with Max Müller as its first post-war incumbent.

Heidegger, who had devoted much of his intellectual energy since the early 1920s both to university reform in general and to a rigorous defence of the essential separation of theology and philosophy as disciplines, did not suffer these impositions easily. His double failure – to bring academic reform to the university and to assert his vision of philosophy even in his own faculty – made him particularly hostile to all perceived encroachments of 'Christian philosophers' on his academic field.[18] Outbursts of frustration mark his lectures of the time. In 1935, the third edition of an extremely successful book of Christian anthropology by the Roman Catholic theologian Theodor Haecker appeared, entitled *Was ist der Mensch?* (*What is Man?*).[19] Heidegger, who was familiar with the book, complained in his metaphysics lectures:

> There may now be books with the title, "What is Man?". But the question is only written in letters on the cover. There is no actual questioning; not because the author happened to forget it amidst all that book-writing, but because he already has an answer – the kind of answer that stipulates that one mustn't even ask. To personally believe the dogma of the Catholic Church is an entirely individual matter, and not under discussion here. But to write on the cover of one's book the question "What is Man?" despite *not* asking, because one is *unwilling* and *unable* to ask, is to forfeit any right to be taken seriously.[20]

The same animus surfaced in his academic service, especially his assessment of Catholic philosophy candidates. As Chair in Philosophy (I), Heidegger habitually served as second examiner for doctoral and post-doctoral (qualifying) theses submitted to the Chair in Philosophy (II), Martin Honecker. Heidegger's examiner's reports for the qualifying theses of Gustav Siewerth and Max Müller, both submitted in 1937, reflect his frustration with the consequences of church control over academic posts. Of Siewerth's work, he wrote sardonically that a text so laden with presuppositions could only be justified by the Concordat, and concluded by declaring himself 'incapable' of assessing its merits as philosophy (since it wasn't that).[21] Of Müller's work on Thomas Aquinas, he noted that 'though the author talks a lot about "problems", these remain confined to a dogmatic domain which is itself not at all problematized, and within which the decisive questions of philosophy are not raised because they cannot be raised'. Heidegger concluded with double-edged praise that as far as academic suitability was concerned, 'it must be said that the candidate is exceptionally well-qualified for a Catholic professorship'.[22]

Coming to terms with the faith of his youth

However, these public expressions of distaste for Christian pseudo-philosophy not only reflected Heidegger's institutional frustrations, but also concealed a long and difficult personal struggle. 'Heidegger is an immensely deep, but torn and tormented man', Max Müller reflected in 1947, 'who cannot tear the fishhook of God . . . from his flesh, though this hook is often a torment to him. This may explain why he hates the church as often and as passionately as he loves it'. The second half of the 1930s, marked by the multiple failures of its first half, were a period of particularly intense struggle, whose eventual outcome became determinative of the path of Heidegger's later thought as a whole.

After the end of the summer semester of 1935, in which he had delivered his lectures on metaphysics, Heidegger wrote to Karl Jaspers, congratulating the friend on his steady productivity and adding with shame about his own work:

As for myself, I'm fumbling about laboriously. Only in the last few months have I found my way back to the work broken off in the winter of 1932/3 (sabbatical term); but it's paltry babble, and anyway, really overcoming the two thorns [in my flesh] – the struggle with the faith of my youth and the failure of the rectorship – is just about enough to be dealing with.[23]

In Heidegger's own reflections on his path thus far and on the possible future of his work, this effort to 'overcome' the Christianity of his youth was now a consistent theme, and served him as a lens on his past as well as a goal for the present. Thus, he remembered his Marburg period in a private manuscript composed in 1937/38 as having 'brought a more intimate experience of a Protestant Christianity – but always already as that which must be fundamentally overcome, though not destroyed'.[24]

What exactly he meant by 'overcoming' was a question Heidegger himself was only just trying to work out. In the same 1937/38 manuscript reflecting on 'My Path So Far', Heidegger tries to capture the shape of his conflict with Christianity, which, he realizes, has 'affected the whole path of my questioning like subterranean, seismic shocks'.

> And who should fail to recognize that my entire path so far has been accompanied by a silent engagement with Christianity: an engagement that has never taken the form of an explicitly raised "problem", but was rather *at once* the preservation of my ownmost provenance – the childhood house, home, and youth – and a painful emancipation from it.[25]

What made this struggle so difficult was that it could not be rationally analysed or discussed, because it did not revolve primarily around issues of doctrine. Rather (in the enigmatic image that was to become determinative of Heidegger's later thought), it centred 'only on the single question: whether the god is fleeing from us or not, and whether we ourselves are still experiencing this genuinely, i.e. creatively'.[26] A systematic look at this 'god' has to await the next section.

In his 1935 letter to Jaspers, Heidegger is eager to put the Christian faith of his youth behind him. Yet already, the Pauline image of the 'thorn in the flesh' (alluding to 2 Cor. 12) hints at a different conclusion. By 1937/38, Heidegger adopted a different narrative of his relationship to Christianity – one of equilibrium in conflict. 'Struggle' or 'confrontation' (*Auseinandersetzung*), he concluded, was not merely a passing phase but remained, and must remain, the enduring quality of his relationship to Christianity. The reason for this lay in Christianity's originary role both biographically and historically, that is, both for his own path and for the history of the West, which could not simply be escaped. This originary role, however, was counterbalanced by Christianity's wrong-headedness in positing premature answers rather than bearing lack and uncertainty – a development that must be resisted or 'overcome'.[27] What Heidegger came to see was a need not merely to analyse but to experience this dialectic. Only one who is 'deeply rooted' is able 'actually to experience the uprootedness' that this conflict brings[28]; and precisely this dialectic of rootedness and overcoming is the virtue required of the thinker who neither clings to the past nor overhastily anticipates the future, but witnesses to the absence of the 'last god' as he genuinely waits for that god's 'arrival or return'.[29]

In the 1940s and 1950s, the claim of 'origin' became a central locus of Heidegger's life and thought, both intellectually and (as we will see in the next chapter) practically. In 1953/54, he famously remarked, 'Without my theological beginning I would not have embarked on the path of thinking. And our beginning always remains our future.'[30]

> Interlocutor: They say that you changed your standpoint [after *Being and Time*].
>
> Heidegger: I left an earlier standpoint, not in order to exchange it for another, but because the previous standpoint, too, was only a sojourn on the way. What endures, in thinking, is the path. And paths of thought bear the mystery that we can walk them forward as well as backward – indeed, that only the way back leads us forward.[31]

By the end of his life, Heidegger turned away from his earlier conviction of the obvious superiority of philosophy over theology. When he decided to publish his 1927 lecture 'Phenomenology and Theology' in 1970, he significantly reframed his earlier endeavour. Rather than reiterating the difference between philosophy as ontological and theology as merely ontic science, the new preface places them side by side, expressing the hope that this publication may 'encourage a renewed consideration of all that is question-worthy about the Christianness of Christianity and its theology, as well as what is question-worthy about philosophy and especially also about the thoughts presented here'.[32] Neither philosophy nor theology is capable of providing its own answers.

Heidegger's later thought
in the vicinity of theology

Heidegger's personal relationship to Christianity anticipates many of the movements of his later thought as a whole. This thought comprises a critical and a constructive movement, converging, respectively, on his accounts of technology and onto-theology,[33] and his deliberations on poetry, letting-be and 'the last god'.[34] In his critical movement, Heidegger comes to see the entire history of metaphysics from Plato and Aristotle onwards as a systematic neglect of Being. Following their first great metaphysicians, Europeans forgot or repudiated their original receptivity to the self-revelation of the world, instead erecting frameworks of representation and (causal) explanation that progressively remade the world in the image of its beholders. Modern science and technology, with their open aim of subduing nature and often fellow human beings, are merely the culmination of this age-old pursuit of metaphysics. Against this systematic neglect, Heidegger calls to a new mindfulness of Being. This requires not so much deliberate *action* – since a proactive 'framing' of the world is precisely what has distorted it – as an attentive letting-be, a spiritual discipline that allows the self to become a 'clearing' on which the light of Being may fall and show forth beings as they are. It is important for the later Heidegger that it is never in one's own power whether this coming-into-view will occur: revelation and communion must always come from without. The human calling is merely to hold oneself in readiness for them.

Both of the movements characterizing Heidegger's thought after the so-called 'turn' raise immediate associations with theology on the one hand and Christian spiritual practice on the other. It is no wonder that many theologians have found the later Heidegger an intriguing conversation partner (or, in many cases, teacher). Neither should it be a surprise that other theologians have detected in Heidegger's a-Christian quasi-mysticism a vitiation of religious practice and content that ought to be exposed rather than emulated. Some of these contrasting theological responses will be discussed in the next chapter. The aim of the remainder of this chapter is merely to draw the outlines of Heidegger's later work as he understands it, making some factual remarks about theological references and sources as appropriate.

Onto-theology and its overcoming

Heidegger's critique of metaphysics or ontology begins with a critical analysis of the history of its foundational term *logos* (Greek) or *ratio* (Latin). Metaphysics, he explains, can only get off the ground insofar as the world is 'logical' or 'rational': insofar as it can be organized into ordered parts forming an ordered whole. Heidegger regards G. W. Leibniz's seminal series of arguments as archetypal of this approach to the world:

> 1. Reason (*ratio*) is in nature, which is why something exists rather than nothing. This is consequent upon the great principle that nothing happens without reason, just as there has to be a reason why one thing rather than another exists.[35]

It is essential for metaphysics that this 'reason' be both ontological and epistemological – that it be both 'cause' (of existence) and 'grounds' (for knowledge). In fact, for Leibniz, the possibility of the second, that is, rational knowledge and exposition, is a consequence of the first, that is, the nature of the world as an ordered whole of cause and effect:

> 2. This reason must reside in something really existing, or in a real cause. For nothing can be a cause unless it is a real reason, and the truths of possibility and necessity . . . cannot effect anything unless these possibilities are grounded in something actually existing.[36]

It is for this reason that metaphysics and theology, as Heidegger avers, are 'one': Metaphysics, as Leibniz conceives it, cannot operate without positing God as the first cause or reason. Leibniz's series of arguments culminates in the third, theological claim:

> 3. This being, however, must be necessary, otherwise one would have to seek a cause outside of it, by reason of which it exists

rather than not existing, as per the default hypothesis. This [necessary] being is the ultimate reason for all things, and is customarily referred to by one word: GOD.[37]

As Heidegger puts it:

This highest and first cause is called *to theion*, the divine, by Plato and, accordingly, Aristotle. Ever since the interpretation of that-which-is as *idea*, thought about the being of that-which-is has been metaphysical, and metaphysics has been theological. Theology here means the interpretation of the "cause" of that-which-is as God, and the transfer of being onto this cause, which contains being in itself and releases it from out of itself, because it is the being-est [i.e. the most fully existing] of all that is.[38]

This construal assigns several interrelated roles to God. First, God is the *summum ens*, the highest or fullest being. Because being, within this paradigm, is presence, God as its highest instance is therefore also radically available or present.[39] Secondly, God is the *causa prima*, the first cause. This identification, according to Heidegger, goes hand in hand with a narrowing of the meaning of 'cause' to efficient causality.[40] Thirdly, God is, in these capacities, also the *summum bonum*, the summative value and guarantor of value.[41]

Heidegger regards this threefold understanding of God as pernicious both as a philosophical and as a theological construct. His philosophical critique centres on the fact that the construal of 'God' as *summum ens* and *causa prima* amounts merely to the hypostatization of a limited and limiting (Aristotelian) conception of being.[42] By being quite literally deified, a conception of being as presence and cause is authorized and perpetuated, thus obstructing genuine thought about being in its constitutive *difference*: 'Theologians', Heidegger complains, 'talk about the being-est of all beings [*das Seiendste alles Seienden*], so that it never occurs to them to think about being [*Sein*] itself'.[43] Talk about God thereby contributes to the forgetfulness of being which Heidegger diagnoses as the predicament of the Western thought from Aristotle to the present. This affects our view of the world as well as of what it is to be human:

Being is experienced as ground. This ground is interpreted as *ratio*, accountability. Man is the accounting [or calculating] animal. All this manifests itself in many versions yet consistently throughout the whole history of occidental thought. This thought has . . . led the world to the present age, the atomic age. In the face of this simple and yet, for Europe, uncanny circumstance, we ask:

Does the above definition of man as the rational animal exhaust the essence of man? Is the last word that can be said about being: being is ground? Or do the essence of man, his belonging to being, and the essence of being itself not rather remain still and ever more startlingly worthy of thought? May we, should this be the case, relinquish this thought-worthy for the sake of the fury of purely calculating thought and its gigantic successes? Or are we rather called to find ways in which thought may follow the thought-worthy, rather than thinking past it, bewitched by calculating thought?

That is the question. It is the world question of thought. Our answer to it will decide what is to become of Earth and the existence of man on this Earth.[44]

Heidegger's *theological* critique of the metaphysical concept of God centres on the fact that God is here inherently confined within human thought and representation, and is therefore always already a dead God, an abstraction. (In this sense, the declaration of Nietzsche's 'madman' that 'God is dead' is merely the summation, not the negation, of metaphysical thought.[45]) 'To this God', Heidegger remarks pointedly, 'man can neither pray nor sacrifice. Man cannot fall to his knees in awe before the *causa sui*, nor can he make music or dance before this God'.[46] This is true not only of God as *summum ens* (highest being) and *causa prima* (first cause), but also as highest value: 'God, thought as value, and be it the highest, is no God.'[47]

The structural similarities between Heidegger's philosophical and theological critiques of metaphysics are reflected in their similar outcomes: within philosophy, the call to a renewed mindfulness of being; within theology, the gesture towards a God before whom one can 'dance and make music'. Despite these similarities, however, Heidegger strongly rejects a conflation of 'God' and 'being':

Being and God are not identical, and I would never attempt to think the essence of God via being. Some of you know, perhaps, that I started in theology and have retained an old love for it and am reasonably well-versed in it. If I were yet to write a theology – and sometimes the thought tempts me – the term "being" would not appear in it.[48]

This repudiation of identity naturally raises the question how the relation or relative position of 'God' and 'being' is to be conceptualized. Heidegger remains ambivalent about this question. In his *Letter on Humanism*, he reiterates a defining conviction of his early religious thought, namely that the term 'god' can only be constituted from out of experience. Already in 1918, he had argued that God cannot be understood in the manner of a 'rationalist metaphysics' as an 'absolute', a 'highest measure' or 'measure *per se*'; rather, the sense of the term 'God' must be determined by experience (specifically, the quintessential experience of perpetual ascent).[49] In 1946, he reiterates in more poetic language: 'Only from out of the truth of being can the essence of the holy be thought. Only from out of the essence of the holy can the essence of divinity be thought. Only in the light of the essence of divinity can we think and say what the word "God" shall name.'[50] Later, Heidegger repeats this general guideline without a concretization of its content. In a discussion with students of Zurich University following a presentation of his lecture '... Poetically Man Dwells ...' in November 1951, he adds to his rejection of an identification of God and being the specification that 'being can never be thought as the ground and essence of God', but that 'the experience of God and his revealedness (insofar as it encounters man) occurs in the dimension of being. This doesn't mean, of course, that being could function as a possible predicate of God. Entirely new distinctions and delimitations are necessary here'.[51]

However, these apparent calls to believers or theologians to rethink 'God' from out of 'being' are counterweighted by the repeated insistence that theologians and philosophers are (at least in their professional capacities) radically incapable of saying anything at all about each other's subjects. God – the 'unapproachable',[52] the 'tremendous' or 'uncanny' (*das Un-geheuere*)[53] – is not within the purview of the 'thinker of being', Heidegger insists.[54] Conversely, 'faith does not need the thinking of being';[55] it 'has nothing to do with the understanding of being [*Seinsverständnis*] as such'.[56] Heidegger's own understanding, as well as its legitimate theological reception, remain matters of debate in theology then and now.

An apophatic eschatology

As already suggested above, Heidegger's critique of metaphysics calls for a different engagement with the world altogether. This more genuine approach, 'overcoming' the enframing tendencies of metaphysical thought, begins not from quasi-objective judgements, but from situated moods or attunements. Approaching the world through mood or attunement testifies to the fact that humans are not disembodied 'eyes' objectively assessing everything, but are addressed and affected by the self-revelation of people, things and larger realities around them. Accordingly, the language appropriate to Heidegger's post-metaphysical approach is not primarily conceptual and denotative, but evocative and poetic, calling or recalling its hearers to an *experience* of the world in which they are always already immersed, rather than circumscribing aspects of the world by fixed concepts.

As in his early work, Heidegger is interested not merely or primarily in incidental, localized moods, but also in more dominant moods characteristic of the age as such. One of the dominant moods that characterize the present age, or ought to characterize it, is god-forsakenness. This god-forsakenness is not a result of the demise of Christianity, and does not equate to atheism. Rather, traditional (metaphysical) Christianity is as much a symptom of it as modern atheism. In fact, the mood of god-forsakenness, for Heidegger, bridges the dichotomy between theism and atheism, which is premised on an absolutization of presence or absence. God-forsakenness, by contrast, incorporates both presence and absence:

> The lack of God and of the divine is absence. However, absence is not nothing; rather, it is the only just to-be-appropriated presence of the hidden fullness of that which was – and which thus, in having been, is gathered in existence: the divine in the Greek world, the prophetic-Jewish world, the preaching of Christ. This no-longer is in itself a not-yet of the veiled advent of its [i.e. the divine's] inexhaustible being [*Wesen*].[57]

In this situation, both traditional Christianity and fashionable atheism pose the risk of furnishing an illusion of *knowledge* and thus control, and so of masking the real situation, which calls for existential involvement. The antidote to such illusions is not the erection of an alternative conceptual framework that would allow the reader to gain conceptual control of the current situation; after all, any such proposition would merely perpetuate the oblivion – the failure to recognize one's own destitution – which characterizes the age. What is needed, rather, is the traduction of a narrative within which the reader can find himself, or the evocation of a mood into which the reader can enter. This is precisely what Heidegger finds in poets such as Rilke and Hölderlin, and what he himself seeks to emulate in writing about them:

> In Hölderlin's experience of history, the appearance and sacrificial death of Christ ushers in the end of the day of the gods. Evening descends. After the "three together", Heracles, Dionysius and Christ, have left the world, the evening of the world age turns into night. The night of the world spreads its darkness. The world age is determined by the tarrying of God, by the "absence of God". . . . This night of the world is a destitute time because it grows increasingly more destitute: Already it is no longer capable of recognizing the absence of god as an absence.[58]

Heidegger's style here is not denotative but performative. His act of writing is both itself a performance of the task of 'a poet in destitute times' – 'to watch, singing, for [or over] the traces of the gods who have fled'[59] – and an attempted liberation of the reader for the same task.

This performative understanding of philosophy not as a system of thought but as the 'formal indication' of a way of living marks, among other things, a return to Heidegger's earliest reading of Pauline eschatology. What Heidegger had valued in Paul's eschatological discourse in the years 1920/21 was Paul's rejection of any 'metaphysical' speculation about the exact time of Christ's return, in favour of a configuration of eschatology as a call to a subjective experience of time 'without order and fixed spots, which cannot be grasped by any objective notion of time',[60] and is thus marked by an insurmountable sense of affliction or 'watchfulness'.[61] But if Paul provided a model for Heidegger's own developing hermeneutics of facticity in 1920/21, he also functioned as a foil for the rigorous demands of phenomenology. As in his reading of Augustine, Heidegger felt compelled to reject the (apparently purely dogmatic) assertion of a future *parousia* of Christ in favour of a purely this-worldly eschatology: an orientation towards an unknown and uncontrollable future whose end would be not the wish-fulfilment of a beatific vision, but one's own dissolution.

In his late work, by contrast, Heidegger arrives at a contrary insistence precisely on the need for openness to a god who must come from without, or doom humankind by remaining absent. This is at its most explicit in his famous interview with the journal *Spiegel* in 1966, published shortly after his death in 1976, which takes its title from just this insistence:

> Philosophy will not be able to bring about an immediate change in the current state of the world. This is true not only of philosophy, but of all merely human thought and desire. Only a god can now save us. I see the only possibility of rescue in preparing, through thought and poetry, a readiness for the appearance of this god or for the absence of this god in our downfall; so that we will not, to put it crudely, "croak", but, if we go down, go down in the face of the absent god.

> [Philosophy and the individual can do nothing more than] prepare this readiness to hold themselves open for the arrival or non-appearance of the god. Even the experience of non-appearance is not nothing, but a liberation of man from what I have called, in *Being and Time*, his addiction to that-which-is.[62]

The *Spiegel* reporter somewhat incredulously replies: 'But this would actually necessitate the famous impulse from without, from a god or whomever. Thinking alone would be impotent.' But Heidegger remains firm, if enigmatic.

This is not, of course, a return to Christianity. Even on an understanding of Christianity as vitiated rather than essentially constituted by an onto-theological understanding of God and the world, Heidegger's radical apophaticism regarding the nature of the God to come is at basic odds with the Christian orientation by and towards a revelation of God that has already occurred. This raises again the theological question that had already dominated the mid-1920s: whether this apophaticism may be seen as preparatory for an acceptance of the gospel, or whether it is in competition with it. Heidegger's friendships with theologians, which are the subject of the next chapter, were marked by a continual explicit and implicit debate about this question.

Notes

1 It is no wonder that Nietzsche became important to Heidegger in this period; see his lecture and seminar series of 1936–39: *Nietzsche: Der Wille zur Macht als Kunst* (lecture series WS 1936/37), included by Heidegger in revised form in *Nietzsche I* (now GA 6.1), and published posthumously in its original lecture form as GA 43; *Nietzsches metaphysische Grundstellung im abendländischen Denken: Die ewige Wiederkehr des Gleichen* (lecture series SS 1937), included by Heidegger in revised form in *Nietzsche I*, and published posthumously in its original lecture form as GA 44; 'Nietzsches metaphysische Grundstellung (Sein und Schein)' (seminar series SS 1937), published posthumously as GA 87; 'Nietzsches zweite Unzeitgemäße Betrachtung' (seminar series WS 1938/39), published posthumously as GA 46; and *Nietzsches Lehre vom Willen zur Macht als Erkenntnis* (lecture series SS 1939), included by Heidegger in revised form in *Nietzsche I*, and published posthumously in its original lecture form as GA 47. See also *Nietzsche: Der europäische Nihilismus* (lecture series SS 1940), included by Heidegger in revised form in *Nietzsche II* (now GA 6.2), and published posthumously in its original lecture form as GA 48; and 'Nietzsches Metaphysik' (lecture series planned for WS 1941/42, but not held), included by Heidegger in revised form in *Nietzsche II*, and published posthumously in its original manuscript form as GA 50. Of particular theological interest is the essay 'Nietzsches Wort "Gott ist tot"' (1943), in GA 5, 209–67.

2 See Franz Overbeck, *Über die Christlichkeit unserer heutigen Theologie* (Leipzig: C. G. Naumann, 1873), *passim*, and *Christentum und Kultur*, p. 7. See esp. Heidegger to Blochmann, 8 August 1928, in *Heidegger/Blochmann*, p. 32.

3 GA 9, 66.

4 Heidegger to Julius Stenzel, 14 April 1928, quoted in Ott, *Heidegger*, p. 159.

5 This is corroborated in 1947 by Heidegger's erstwhile student and life-long friend Max Müller; see Max Müller to Alois Naber SJ, 2 February 1947, in *Heidegger/Müller*, pp. 71–81; p. 74.

6   In his 1949 introduction to the 5th edition of 'What is Meta-
    physics?' (published in English as a separate essay under the title
    'The Way Back into the Ground of Metaphysics'), Heidegger
    suggests sardonically, and with typical double-edgedness, that
    Christian theology 'just for once' try to take seriously Paul's
    words in 1 Cor. 1.20 and recognize the 'foolishness of philosophy';
    GA 9, 379.

7   GA 40, 9.

8   Heidegger to Blochmann, 8 August 1928, in *Heidegger/Blochmann*,
    p. 32. What Heidegger means by an institutionalized Protestantism
    that approximates Roman Catholicism is reflected in his letter to
    Rudolf Bultmann dated 24 January 1931, in *Bultmann/Heidegger*,
    pp. 149–53.

9   John Caputo, 'Heidegger and Theology', in Charles Guignon (ed.),
    Cambridge Companion to Heidegger (Cambridge: Cambridge
    University Press, 2nd edn, 2006), pp. 326–44; p. 333.

10 See e.g. Ott, *Heidegger*, pp. 259–64.

11 See University Archive Freiburg (UAF) MS B3/797, 350 (Faculty
    Board minutes of 14 May 1929); Paletschek, 'Fakultätssitzungen',
    p. 69.

12 Reported in Schaber, 'Herkunft', *HJB* 1, 174–5.

13 See Edmund Husserl to Rudolf Otto, 5 March 1919, in Husserl,
    Briefwechsel, vol. 6, p. 207.

14 See Paletschek, 'Fakultätssitzungen', p. 102, and UAF B38/131
    (ministerial letter of 31 January 1901).

15 'Concordat between the Holy See and the Free State of Baden',
    Addendum to Article IX, in *Badisches Gesetz- und Verordnungsblatt*
    1933, p. 19.

16 See Paletschek, 'Fakultätssitzungen', 70, documenting the minutes of
    the Philosophy Faculty Board meeting of 20 December 1932 (UAF
    B3/798, 32). It is worth noting that a year earlier, Rudolf Bultmann
    had threatened to resign his Chair at Marburg in protest against the
    Preussen Concordat with the Protestant Church, which consolidated
    similar church control. His contingency plan of moving to Freiburg
    and obtain a licence to lecture (*Habilitation*) in philosophy was
    gently dismissed by his friend Heidegger. See *Bultmann/Heidegger*,
    pp. 145–53, and Chapter 7 below.

17 Ott and Caputo write as if the abolition of the Chair was more or
    less single-handedly Heidegger's doing; but there is no evidence
    for this claim. See Ott, *Heidegger*, p. 265; Caputo, 'Heidegger and
    Theology', p. 333.

148 HEIDEGGER AND THEOLOGY

18 See Heidegger's letter to Karl Jaspers of 1 July 1935, quoted below, in which he speaks of the 'faith of his youth' and the 'failure of the rectorship' as two thorns in his flesh (*Heidegger/Jaspers*, p. 157).

19 Leipzig: J. Hegner, 3rd edn, 1935 [1933]. See also Ott, *Heidegger*, pp. 255–9.

20 GA 40, 151 (original emphases). Heidegger later called this outburst an unnecessary insult ('*Ausfall*'); see Heidegger to Müller, 18 April 1954, in *Heidegger/Müller*, pp. 36–8; p. 37.

21 University Archive Freiburg; quoted in Ott, p. 262.

22 'Martin Heideggers Gutachten zur Habilitation Max Müllers' (1937), published in *Heidegger/Müller*, pp. 68–70; p. 70. A fuller account of Heidegger's relationship to Max Müller, including his role in the university's withholding of Müller's *venia legendi*, can be found in Chapter 7 below.

23 Heidegger to Jaspers, 1 July 1935, in *Heidegger/Jaspers*, p. 157.

24 Heidegger, 'Mein bisheriger Weg' (1937/38); published posthumously in GA 66, 411–28; p. 415.

25 Heidegger, 'Mein bisheriger Weg' (1937/38), GA 66, 415.

26 Ibid.

27 See Heidegger, 'Mein bisheriger Weg' (1937/38), GA 66, 416. Heidegger here seems to regard a similar error as characteristic of Nazism.

28 Heidegger, 'Mein bisheriger Weg' (1937/38), GA 66, 416.

29 Heidegger, 'Wozu Dichter?' (1946), in GA 5, 269–320; p. 270.

30 Heidegger, 'Aus einem Gespräch von der Sprache' (1953/54), in GA 12, 79–146; p. 91.

31 Ibid., GA 12, 94.

32 'Vorwort zu *Phänomenologie und Theologie*' (1970); in GA 9, 45–6; p. 45.

33 See esp. Heidegger, 'Überwindung der Metaphysik' (1936), in GA 7, 67–98; *Nietzsche I* and *II* (1936–39 and 1939–46), now GA 6.1 and 6.2; 'Nietzsches Wort "Gott ist tot"' (1943), in GA 5, 209–67; 'Die Frage nach der Technik' (1953), in GA 7, 5–36; *Identität und Differenz* (1955–57), now GA 11; 'Der Satz vom Grund' (public lecture 1956), in GA 10, 189–211; 'Die onto-theo-logische Verfassung der Metaphysik' (1957), in GA 11, 51–80.

34 See esp. Heidegger, 'Der Ursprung des Kunstwerkes' (1936), in GA 5, 1–74; *Beiträge zur Philosophie (Vom Ereignis)* (1936–38), now GA 65; *Besinnung* (1938–39), now GA 66; *Erläuterungen zu*

Hölderlins Dichtung (1936–68), now GA 4; 'Wozu Dichter?' (1946),
in GA 5, 269–320; 'Das Ding' (1950), in GA 7, 165–87; *Unterwegs
zur Sprache* (1950–59), now GA 12; 'Bauen Wohnen Denken' (1951),
in GA 7, 145–64; '. . . dichterisch wohnet der Mensch . . .' (public
lecture, presented twice in 1951), in GA 7, 189–208; 'Was heißt
Denken?' (1952), in GA 7, 127–43.

35 G. W. Leibniz, 'Philosophische Abhandlungen', in C. I. Gerhardt
(ed.), *Die philosophischen Schriften von Gottfried Wilhelm Leibniz*,
(Hildesheim: Georg Olms, 1978), vol. 7, pp. 251–344; p. 289. Quoted
in Heidegger, *Die Metaphysik des deutschen Idealismus* (lecture series
SS 1941), published as GA 49; here p. 200. See also Heidegger, *Der
Satz vom Grund* (lecture series WS 1955/56), now GA 10.

36 Leibniz, 'Philosophische Abhandlungen', p. 289.

37 Ibid.

38 Heidegger, 'Platons Lehre von der Wahrheit' (1931/32, 1940), in
GA 9, 203–38; pp. 235–6.

39 Heidegger, 'Die onto-theo-logische Verfassung der Metaphysik'
(1957), GA 11, 75.

40 See *Nietzsche II* (1939–46), now GA 6.2, 375ff; 'Wissenschaft und
Besinnung' (1953), GA 7, 37–65; p. 43.

41 See Heidegger, 'Aufzeichnungen aus der Werkstatt' (1959), in GA
13, 151–4; p. 153; 'Brief über den Humanismus' (1946), in GA 9,
313–64; p. 349. See also Rainer Thurnher, 'Heideggers Distanzierung
von der metaphysisch geprägten Theologie und Gottesvorstellung',
in Norbert Fischer and Friedrich-Wilhelm von Herrmann (eds.), *Die
Gottesfrage im Denken Martin Heideggers* (Hamburg: Felix Meiner,
2011), pp. 175–93; pp. 181–2.

42 See e.g. Heidegger, 'Die Frage nach der Technik' (1953), GA 7, 27.

43 Heidegger, 'Nietzsches Wort "Gott ist tot"' (1943), GA 5, 260. See
also 'Vom Wesen der Wahrheit' (1930, 1943), in GA 9, 177–202;
pp. 180–2.

44 Heidegger, 'Der Satz vom Grund' (1956), GA 10, 189.

45 See Heidegger, 'Nietzsches Wort "Gott ist tot"' (1943), GA 5, 259–60.

46 Heidegger, 'Die onto-theo-logische Verfassung der Metaphysik' (1957),
GA 11, 77. See also *Beiträge zur Philosophie* (1936–38), GA 65, 437.

47 Heidegger, 'Aufzeichnungen aus der Werkstatt' (1959), GA 13, 154.

48 'Gespräch mit Martin Heidegger am 6. November 1951', in GA
15, 425–39; p. 436. See also 'Die onto-theo-logische Verfassung der
Metaphysik' (1957), GA 11, 63 and 77.

49	Heidegger, 'Das Absolute' (1918), in GA 60, 325.

50	Heidegger, 'Brief über den Humanismus' (1946), GA 9, 351.

51	'Gespräch mit Martin Heidegger' (1951), GA 15, 436.

52	Heidegger, 'Vorwort zu *Phänomenologie und Theologie*' (1970), in GA 9, 45–6; p. 46.

53	Heidegger, 'Brief über den Humanismus' (1946), GA 9, 356 (see also pp. 330–1, 338, 351); *Der Satz vom Grund* (lecture series WS 1955/56), in GA 10, 11–188; p. 21. See also *Nietzsche II*, GA 6.2, 21.

54	'Gespräch mit Martin Heidegger' (1951), GA 15, 436.

55	Ibid. See also Heidegger to Müller, 18 April 1954, in *Heidegger/ Müller*, p. 37.

56	Heidegger to Müller, 12 June 1965, in *Heidegger/Müller*, pp. 51–3; p. 52.

57	Heidegger to Hartmut Buchner, 18 June 1950, published as 'Brief an einen jungen Studenten' in GA 7, 184–7; p. 185. See also Heidegger, 'Was heißt Denken?' (1952), GA 7, 132; Heidegger, 'Hölderlins Erde und Himmel' (1959), in GA 4, 152–81; pp. 169–70 and 178.

58	Heidegger, 'Wozu Dichter?' (1946), GA 5, 269.

59	Ibid., 251.

60	Heidegger, *Einleitung in die Phänomenologie der Religion* (1920/21), GA 60, 98.

61	Ibid, 104.

62	'"Nur noch ein Gott kann uns retten": *Spiegel*-Gespräch mit Martin Heidegger am 23. September 1966', *Der Spiegel* 30, 23 (31 May 1976), pp. 193–219; rpt. in Günther Neske and Emil Kettering (eds.), *Antwort: Martin Heidegger im Gespräch* (Pfullingen: Neske, 1988), pp. 81–114; pp. 100–1.

7

Heidegger among
theologians

Heidegger's theological legacy matches his theological debts in breadth and complexity. If his early influence on theology was mediated primarily by those who worked and studied with him, he quickly rose to the rare status of a classic of twentieth-century philosophy, whom theologians – whether critical or sympathetic – avoided at their peril. Although almost equally widespread in German-, French- and English-speaking countries, the theological reception of Heidegger's work has taken rather different forms in these countries and languages. In Germany, largely through the mediation of Rudolf Bultmann, Heidegger is known among theologians mainly for his early work and its influence on theological existentialism and hermeneutics. In France, his theological influence is most strongly visible in the so-called theological turn of French phenomenology, which draws on elements of his early phenomenology as well as of his later critique of metaphysics. Among English-speaking theologians, interest concentrates above all on Heidegger's critique of metaphysics and of technology, as interpreted by John Caputo, Merold Westphal, George Pattison and others.

This and the next chapter hope to provide orientation in a large and growing field of scholarship by offering helpful background information, drawing rough intellectual maps and suggesting some generative lines of enquiry. The current, short chapter begins this task by documenting Heidegger's friendships and significant acquaintances with theologians, both Protestant and Catholic. Among the former, the most important is Rudolf Bultmann, whose life-long friendship with Heidegger can now be traced in their recently published correspondence, spanning the years 1925–76, when both men died.[1] This correspondence, along with those of Barth, Brunner, Gogarten and Eduard Thurneysen, also makes possible an assessment of Heidegger's fraught interactions with dialectical theology, the movement of which Bultmann was, during the most intense period of their friendship, a leading proponent. A brief sketch of these interactions is intended to provide a biographical background for some of the theological analysis in the next chapter, and to encourage further research and analysis.[2] Among Catholic theologians, those closest to Heidegger were, on the one hand, teachers and religious he knew from home, and on the other, colleagues and students in Freiburg, particularly Max Müller and Bernhard Welte. These companionships have often been neglected or seriously distorted in the secondary literature; but letters and reminiscences, gathered in tireless work (above all) by Alfred Denker and Holger Zaborowski, bring to life an otherwise unfamiliar aspect of Heidegger's interactions with theologians, which make an important addition to our image of Heidegger as man and thinker.

Rudolf Bultmann and dialectical theology

As is commonly known, Heidegger and Bultmann met upon Heidegger's 1923 appointment to an associate professorship (*Extraordinariat*) in philosophy at Marburg, and struck up a close friendship that lasted until their deaths in 1976. They also developed a productive working relationship. Bultmann – then in the excited rush of the new turn against liberal theology which he spearheaded with Barth, Thurneysen, Gogarten and Brunner in the movement soon called dialectical theology – tried for many years to integrate Heidegger into his circle. But his association with Heidegger, rather than a boost to the movement, became instead a catalyst for the differences that led Barth, Brunner, Gogarten and Bultmann, in the aftermath of the publication of *Being and Time*, to disperse.

Bultmann's own relationship to Heidegger, as documented in the letters and memoirs of both men, had a warm but intellectually ambivalent quality. In its foreground stood their shared work at the Marburg Faculty, often as a joint front against dominant trends,[3] and their constructive joint reading of Christian sources. They occasionally participated in each other's courses, particularly Bultmann's New Testament seminars[4] and Heidegger's lectures on time and on logic.[5] More importantly, from 1924 until Heidegger's call to Freiburg in 1928, Heidegger and Bultmann read the Gospel of John together most Saturday afternoons with profit and enjoyment, and throughout that time, Heidegger persistently encouraged Bultmann's efforts to finish his great commentary on the book.[6] Methodologically, they shared the conviction, expressed by Bultmann to Barth in 1925, that Bultmann's task was 'to show the relation or identity of historical (exegetical) and systematic theology . . . and so also the identity of *critical* exegesis and systematic theology'.[7] But while Bultmann regarded this task as one aspect of a theological project that also comprised a philosophical side, Heidegger saw it as an independent undertaking, and dismissed Bultmann's involvement in more philosophical endeavours almost entirely. When Erik Peterson's searing critique of Barth and Bultmann, '*What is Theology?*', appeared in 1925, Bultmann wrote to Barth that he would draft a response and also try to 'mobilize Heidegger', in order to 'place phenomenology in the right spot' in the debate.[8] But Heidegger declined to get involved, and Bultmann was reduced to emphasizing on sending the galleys of his rejoinder to Gogarten that they had at least been 'looked through by Heidegger'.[9]

By 1927, Heidegger made his preferences more vocal, writing to Bultmann that 'your commentary must push theology back into concrete problems and make clear that something like "dialectical theology" is a mere spectre'.[10] Dismissing Barth as a 'lightweight' without enough sense even to grasp the philosophical issues at stake,[11] he expected Bultmann's agreement in describing their work as clearly segregated:

> We can only get things moving if we work radically from the most extreme positions. You from the theological side, positively-ontically . . . , I from the philosophical side, ontologically-critically – where the ontic in the sense of the positivity of the Christian [position] remains unthematic and question-marked.[12]

Bultmann responded evasively, and continued to try to draw Heidegger into his wider theological interests, an attempt culminating in his nomination of Heidegger as philosophy editor for *Theologische Rundschau*, a theological journal Bultmann was involved in relaunching in 1928. Heidegger declined with a renewed emphasis on the separation of theology and philosophy: 'The more I think about these things . . . the more it seems to me that all explicit philosophical discussion ought to disappear from theology, and all power of thought be redirected to a historical engagement with the New Testament, "historical" in an essential sense.' The fact that Heidegger is nevertheless listed on the masthead of *Theologische Rundschau* volumes 1–16 ('new series', 1929–44) is a result partly of accident and partly of Bultmann's tenacity, but not of Heidegger's practical involvement. Bultmann had already sent the first volume to print with Heidegger's name on the title page when Heidegger's negative answer came, and thought that it would be 'fatal' after that to be forced to strike it from the second volume. He attempted to persuade Heidegger to collaborate after all, arguing that his negative appraisal of theology in 'Phenomenology and Theology' did not, after all, impair his ability to be an expert advisor, and that he need not do more than contribute a few articles, something which, Bultmann prodded, Heidegger was 'keeping in view anyway'. But in practice, Heidegger never did contribute to the journal.[13]

The other theologians associated with dialectical theology responded to Heidegger much more critically. Karl Barth, keenly aware of the fundamental difference between Heidegger's anthropocentric and his own theocentric approaches, was careful to frame that difference not as a competition but as evidence that philosophy and theology operated on different paradigms with little mutual input. Unwilling to be pulled into a discussion he saw neither as his calling nor as his strength, he kept his distance from Heidegger from the beginning.[14] In September 1925 (as Barth recalls in 1964), Bultmann first broached the subject of Heidegger over 'coffee and streusel cake' by bringing 'a large manuscript' of his notes on Heidegger's lectures and proceeding enthusiastically to read them out – though with little effect on the impassive colleague.[15] In July 1927, Barth declined Bultmann's invitation to a weekend in Marburg to meet Heidegger and attend his lecture on 'history and time' with mock self-irony: 'As a lumbering Swiss, I'm not so quick off the mark that I could grasp fast enough what Heidegger, whom I don't even know, wants' so as to be a useful discussion partner.[16] Bultmann urged that the belatedness of Barth's acquaintance with Heidegger made its 'necessity' all the 'more urgent', but Barth did not come.[17] Repeated invitations to lecture in Marburg himself were similarly persistently declined. 'Marburg is rampant with puristic adherence to Bultmann and Heidegger', Barth commentated spikily to Thurneysen in 1928. 'They keep wanting to lure me there to lecture, and I keep refusing with the explanation that I don't want anything to do with such know-it-alls.'[18] In 1930, Bultmann organized a symposium on natural theology to bring together Barth, Gogarten and Heidegger, but Barth cancelled on short notice. Bultmann, deeply disappointed, assumed that this was due to Barth's 'persistent refusal to engage with Heidegger',[19] and Barth himself confirmed his speculation by writing to Bultmann the following year that he regarded his adherence to Heidegger as a return to the 'slave house of Egypt'.[20]

Bultmann's attempts to bring together Heidegger and Gogarten were only marginally more successful. In December 1923, Bultmann wrote eagerly to Gogarten that a visit to Marburg would be most welcome, not least because it seemed 'important' that he meet Heidegger, 'who is familiar with your work and, as far as I can see, close to you'.[21] Gogarten seems not to have come[22]; a renewed invitation for winter 1924 met with similar polite refusals.[23] Bultmann's hope for reciprocal sympathy nevertheless continued through 1927, when he hastened to recommend to Gogarten upon publication of *Being and Time* that he volunteer to review the book for their journal *Zwischen den Zeiten* – partly to avoid a review by Heinrich Barth.[24] But Gogarten did not respond to the request, and the review eventually published was, after all, by Karl Barth's eager brother.[25] A meeting between Gogarten and Heidegger did take place in 1927 at the first of a series of symposia of (later so-called) 'Old Marburgians', but generated no warmth. The further symposium in 1930 to which Barth, too, had been unsuccessfully invited met with a short-notice cancellation by Gogarten, who had apparently confused the dates and double-booked the weekend.[26]

Emil Brunner engaged Heidegger more actively and directly. Unlike Barth, he accepted an invitation to lecture to the Marburg Theology Faculty in January 1925, choosing as his subject a proposal to ground theology in a natural perception of divine law, which reduces man to a nothingness from which he can only be raised by God's revelation in the form of forgiveness.[27] Heidegger sharply criticized the lecture, and a lengthy exchange of opinions among Brunner,

Barth, Bultmann and Gogarten followed. Bultmann immediately reported to Barth that 'Brunner spoke here yesterday. . . . Very weak, almost embarrassing. Horribly battered by Heidegger.'[28] Brunner, in turn, complained to Barth that phenomenology and a turn to metaphysics had taken over Marburg, which must be regarded 'not [as] neutral ground, but [as] enemy territory', attempting, just like 'Catholic-mystical' thinking, to 'turn into knowledge and vision what only belongs to faith'.[29] Barth, countering with a critique of Brunner's own attempt to establish any kind of foundation for theology, nevertheless agreed with his assessment of Marburg. As much as six years later, he remembered with indignation the 'patronising-policing' attitude of Bultmann's students that had plagued Brunner and soured Barth's own lecture when he finally gave one, two years after Heidegger's departure.[30]

Neither Barth nor Heidegger seems to have revised their opinions of each other in later life. In 1932, Heidegger wrote to Bultmann that he found Barth's foreword to the newly published second edition of *Church Dogmatics* I so vainglorious that he had no desire to read the book itself,[31] and there is no evidence that he engaged with any part of Barth's *magnum opus*. Barth, conversely, remained consistently silent about Heidegger, excepting only a brief discussion of 'What is Metaphysics?' (1929) as illustrative of a certain modern attitude in an excursus on 'God and Nothingness' in *Church Dogmatics* III.[32] In a 1965 interview, he commented parenthetically that Heidegger seems to have 'arrived at a kind of mystical atheism', but no substantial engagement with Heidegger's later development is in evidence.[33]

Although Bultmann and Heidegger remained friends until their deaths in 1976, Bultmann, too, never seriously engaged with the work Heidegger did after the achievements of the Marburg period (i.e. *Being and Time*, 'Phenomenology and Theology', and 'What is Metaphysics?'). Bultmann himself was painfully aware of the growing intellectual rift between them. For Christmas 1931, Heidegger made him a gift of Nietzsche's *Letters to Friends*, which opens with a poem that laments the 'turning' of old friends and exhorts the speaker to welcome new friendships.[34] Bultmann had promised a long letter for the Christmas vacation,[35] but it was not until a year later that he brought himself to write it.[36] When he did, he expressed his grief at the perceived personal message in the previous year's Christmas gift: 'I take it that you think our paths are

diverging more than we could foresee during our Marburg time.'
Bultmann emphasizes his own 'willingness to hold on to [their]
community', but confesses that he has 'no real sense of the path
your work has taken' since the departure to Freiburg.[37] Heidegger
answers warmly but evasively, emphasizing the personal nature of
their friendship, which 'luckily doesn't depend on the definition of
the relation between theology and philosophy'.[38]

This dynamic – Bultmann's often diffident wish for continuing
intellectual community, and Heidegger's deflections, mostly designed
to avoid having to give unfavourable judgements of his friend's
philosophical efforts – continues to characterize their correspondence.
A striking example is the correspondence engendered by Prussia's
1930 Concordat with the Lutheran Church. Bultmann regarded
the Concordat's proposed stipulation to make all appointments
at theological faculties dependent on ecclesial evaluations of the
candidates' suitability as an unacceptable 'Catholicization of the
Church' and a threat to the academic freedom needed for serious
theological work. Along with four colleagues, he threatened to
resign his post and leave the church should it come into force.
Bultmann's contingency plan, of which he informed Heidegger
hoping he could count on his support, was to move to Freiburg to
retrain in philosophy. Heidegger hurried to distract his friend from
the idea, and ignored repeated attempts by Bultmann to bring it up
again.[39] Though Bultmann made one or two attempts to interpret
Heidegger's later philosophy, both were relatively inept, and only
met with silence from Heidegger.[40] In 1968, Barth commented
sardonically that 'Bultmann is still preaching the Ur-Heidegger'.[41]
Still, their friendship lived in the undiminished warmth of memory
until the year of their deaths – memories whose strength is attested
in a 1950 letter from Heidegger to a Freiburg colleague, in which he
confesses that 'my time in Marburg was in [some] respects the most
fruitful of my whole academic activity'.[42]

Catholic companions

Although the majority of the theological friends and interlocutors
Heidegger acquired as an adult were Protestant, his attachment to
his hometown Messkirch, and his contact with Catholic friends,
acquaintances and mentors he had known there, remained intact,

and resumed increasing importance after his forced retirement. Towards the end of his life, it appears, his ties to the Catholic churches, writers and companions of his youth were closer than the Protestant ties of adulthood, and it is perhaps no surprise that many Catholics who remembered and still remember him were and are unaware of any decisive turn away from the Catholic Church.[43]

Characteristic of these ties is Heidegger's relationship to the nearby Benedictine abbey St Martin in Beuron.[44] As a child, Martin sometimes walked the pilgrims' path to the abbey with his mother, and as a student and scholar, he often stayed for several days or weeks during vacations and worked in its library.[45] On these visits, he formed lifelong friendships with some of the monks, particularly Anselm Manser OSB (1876–1951). Heidegger also participated fully in the life of the abbey while there, observing their strict rhythms and attending services. 'Since Friday I'm back in my old cell and have already acclimatized to the closed and quiet life of the monks', he wrote to Blochmann in autumn 1931 – lamenting only that he could not wear a habit. And after a joined visit, he reassured her that although 'contemporary Catholicism . . . must remain abhorrent to us', 'Beuron' and what it represented would 'unfold as the seed of something essential'.[46] After several long stays and two guest lectures (on Augustine and Plato) in 1930–31, Heidegger stayed away from the abbey until 1949, but began to visit again frequently in older age.[47]

This resumption of old contacts and memories is typical of Heidegger's later years. After his retirement, he returned to Catholic influences and acquaintances whom he had largely neglected during the years in Freiburg, when his relationship to Catholicism was strained by his political involvement, and by persistent conflicts with a Catholic institutional power experienced as intrusive and anti-philosophical. Sometimes, these re-acquaintances had practical occasions: Early in the denazification trials of 1945 and 1946, for example, Heidegger sought help from Conrad Gröber, a fellow native of Messkirch and erstwhile rector of Heidegger's school in Constance, who had become Archbishop of Freiburg in 1932.[48] Others were matters of reminiscence and gratitude: In the 1950s and 60s, Heidegger spoke repeatedly and fondly of the lasting influence of his Catholic professor Carl Braig (a native of nearby Kanzach), and remembered many local personages – including, once again, Abraham a Sancta Clara – in commemorative speeches given in Messkirch and throughout the region.[49] In the 1950s, years after Conrad Gröber's death, Heidegger also repeatedly spoke of the erstwhile rector's formative influence,[50] and faithfully sent his regards to Gröber's sister Maria in Messkirch until her death.[51]

At this time, Heidegger also relaxed the tense distance he had kept during the Nazi years from former Catholic students and post-docs, some of whom now became lifelong friends. In the 1930s, the (later prominent) Catholic theologians J. B. Lotz, Karl Rahner, Max Müller and Gustav Siewerth had attended Heidegger's lectures or seminars while conducting research under his Catholic colleague Honecker, but found no friend in the philosopher.[52] After his retirement, Heidegger entered into warm and sustained exchanges with some of them, particularly Max Müller and his Freiburg friend and colleague Bernhard Welte. Far more distant was his relationship to that most famous, and most outspokenly Heideggerian, of his erstwhile students, Karl Rahner, with whom he very rarely interacted. Although Rahner spoke in the warmest terms about Heidegger as a 'teacher', he also conceded that he 'had only very few personal contacts' with him over their 30-year acquaintance.[53] Heidegger, in turn, stated in a 1945 submission to the denazification committee that 'for a number of semesters the Jesuit Fathers Prof. Lotz, Rahner, Huidobro were members of my advanced seminar' and 'often in our house', but made no claim to a personal mentorship, even though such a claim would have been advantageous in his denazification trials.[54] Later, Heidegger only very rarely mentioned 'Father Rahner' in passing in letters to Müller (in April 1964 and May 1967), and once asked Müller to pass on a brief response to a letter Rahner had sent Heidegger (in October 1964).[55] Whether Heidegger ever read *Spirit in the World*, Rahner's most 'Heideggerian' work, is not clear. He did not read its successor volume, *Hearers of the Word* (published 1941) until after his forced retirement in 1946, when he commented on it critically but not unkindly.[56]

Heidegger's warmest and most sustained relationships with Catholic theologians were with Max Müller (1906–94) and Bernhard Welte (1906–83), both of whom completed their doctoral and post-doctoral studies in Freiburg and went on to teach there: Müller as Honecker's successor, Welte as professor of philosophical theology in the Theology Faculty. Both men – themselves lifelong friends – made a Christian engagement with Heidegger's thought in its continuing development the centre of their life's work, and remained in a continual, mutually challenging dialogue with Heidegger about that thought and its relationship to faith and theology.[57]

Both Müller and Welte were significant thinkers in their own right and immensely influential within German theology, though largely neglected in English-speaking Heidegger scholarship. Ironically, the main reason for this neglect is also the reason Heidegger particularly valued them: Neither tried to distil from Heidegger a particular substantive view, but to engage the ever-new challenges and impulses that his 'paths of thinking' posed for a living, ever-developing approach to philosophy and life. This was the attitude which Heidegger himself tried to instil in students in his seminars. Georg Picht, a former student, recalls a fellow student's presentation of a script full of Heideggerian phrases, rudely interrupted by Heidegger with the comment: 'I will not have my students Heideggering. We proceed to the subject matter.'[58] To Müller, the older colleague repeatedly insisted that 'there mustn't emerge a Heidegger scholasticism'.[59] Conversely, he often expressed his gratitude and sincere appreciation to both Müller and Welte for their attentive and independent '*Mitdenken*' (thinking-with). It was this conversational mode of philosophical exchange which, for Heidegger, marked authentic intellectual friendship and so also philosophical growth.[60]

Particularly in Müller's case, this friendship testified to a sincere intellectual regard on both parts, which overcame not insignificant biographical obstacles. Heidegger had supported Müller as a doctoral student in the late 1920s, but was sceptical of his increasingly strong Catholic commitments.[61] In the mid-1930s, while completing his habilitation, Müller was also writing entries on political subjects for the prominent conservative Catholic encyclopaedia *Der grosse Herder* (4th, fully revised edition, 1931–35), a publication that came under intense scrutiny by the Nazis and was prohibited in 1937.[62] Despite anonymous authorship, Müller's collaboration on the project was discovered by the Freiburg philologist Wolfgang Aly, a notoriously militant Nazi, and reported to the university senate with the aim of preventing Müller's habilitation, which was due to be completed in 1937.[63] The senate sought a secondary report from Heidegger, who wrote very favourably but conceded that Müller was 'negatively inclined towards the state'. Müller pleaded with Heidegger to take out the sentence, but Heidegger declined, pointing out that refusal to answer an explicit question would be 'just as negative' for Müller (and would presumably subject Heidegger himself to increased scrutiny). Shortly after, in 1938, Müller was indeed (after seven years of work and excellent marks on his qualifying thesis and examined lectures) refused a licence to lecture 'for ideological-political reasons', and could not teach at the university until 1945.[64] He began lecturing at the Freiburg seminary instead, ceasing all contact with Heidegger until Heidegger sought its renewal in 1945.[65]

The case bespeaks Heidegger's strong ambivalence vis-à-vis his student or younger colleague.[66] As mentioned in Chapter 6, he was deeply opposed to the perceived tendency to commandeer philosophy for dogmatic Catholic purposes in which Müller's qualifying thesis participated – an opposition reflected in his critical, though formally supportive, examiner's report. At the same time, Heidegger recognized real philosophical talent in Müller, both before the habilitation debacle, when he fostered Müller as a student,[67] and later. In 1945–46, when the former Chair in Christian Philosophy (re-dedicated to psychology during the war) was being reinstated, Heidegger strongly advocated Müller's appointment as Honecker's successor.[68] Müller, in whom intellectual admiration for Heidegger as a thinker seems to have been and remained the dominant sentiment, in turn set aside the disappointment of 1938. From 1946 to 1950, he was a tireless and proactive advocate for Heidegger in the painfully prolonged faculty discussions about the future of the philosopher, who was at the time suspended from his duties (and, partly thanks to Müller, was granted full emeritus status in 1951). Over the decades of Heidegger's retirement, the two scholars corresponded with solicitude and warmth, both personally and academically. In Müller's encomium at the 1959 conferral of honorary citizenship of Messkirch on Heidegger, he singled out the achievement for which the older philosopher himself would no doubt most have liked to be known: 'The operative fact was a lived life, which experienced . . . mystery as mystery and succeeded in putting that experience into words. . . . For this life, our collective thanks.'[69]

Heidegger's relationship with Bernhard Welte was much less turbulent. Welte had never studied under Heidegger, but was decisively influenced by his work, and made its relevance for theology one of the central questions of his own career as professor of philosophical theology at Freiburg. Heidegger's reciprocal, warm respect for the younger colleague's 'thinking-with' found expression in numerous letters and other tokens of appreciation, including several poems. One – on the pre-eminence of gratitude even over poetry and thought – was written in thanks for Welte's last seminar as professor of philosophical theology, which had treated the question of a metaphysical God in light of Heidegger's later writings:[70] 'May gratitude remain, [which is] more endowing than poetry, more founding than thought. Those who reach gratitude are brought back by it to the presence of the unapproachable to which we – all mortals – belong [or: are dedicated] from the beginning.'[71] Five months before his death, Heidegger asked Welte to deliver the eulogy at his funeral, which took place on 28 May 1976 at St Martin's Church in Messkirch.[72]

Notes

1 Rudolf Bultmann and Martin Heidegger, *Briefwechsel 1925–1975*, eds. Andreas Großmann and Christof Landmesser (Frankfurt: Klostermann, 2009).

2 This is aided by the publications of Bultmann's correspondences with Barth, Gogarten and Heidegger, and Barth's correspondences with Brunner and Thurneysen. See Karl Barth and Eduard Thurneysen, *Briefwechsel 1913–1935* (3 vols; Zürich: Theologischer Verlag, 1973–2000); Karl Barth and Rudolf Bultmann, *Briefwechsel 1911–1966*, ed. Bernd Jaspert (Zurich: Theologischer Verlag, 2nd revised and expanded edn, 1994); Karl Barth and Emil Brunner, *Briefwechsel 1911–1966*, ed. Eberhard Busch (Zürich: Theologischer Verlag, 2000); Rudolf Bultmann and Friedrich Gogarten, *Briefwechsel 1921–1967*, ed. Hermann Götz Göckeritz (Tübingen: Mohr Siebeck, 2002).

3 See e.g. their exchanges between 13 and 29 March 1927, in *Bultmann/Heidegger,* pp. 5–26.

4 See e.g. Bultmann to Gogarten, 22 December 1923, in *Bultmann/ Gogarten,* p. 53.

5   Bultmann attended at least Heidegger's lectures on the concept of time (SS 1925) and on logic (WS 1925/26), now published as GA 20 and GA 21. See Bultmann to Gogarten, 21 November 1925, in *Bultmann/Gogarten*, p. 97. See also Barth's reminiscence of Bultmann reporting on Heidegger's 1925 lectures on the concept of time in 'Gespräch mit Tübinger "Stiftlern" (2 March 1964)', in Barth, *Gespräche 1964–1968*, ed. Eberhard Busch (Zurich: TVZ, 1996), pp. 31–129; pp. 122–3.

6   Bultmann first mentioned the joint reading to Gogarten on 19 October 1924; *Bultmann/Gogarten*, p. 62. Encouragement by Heidegger is found in nearly every letter he writes Bultmann during this time. Bultmann's commentary finally appeared in 1941 as *Das Evangelium des Johannes*, Meyer's Kritisch-Exegetischer Kommentar (KEK) 2 (Göttingen: Vandenhoeck & Ruprecht, 21st edn, 1986).

7   Bultmann to Barth, 3 February 1925, in *Barth/Bultmann*, pp. 44–5.

8   Bultmann to Barth, 19 July 1925, in Erik Peterson, *Theologie und Theologen: Briefwechsel mit Karl Barth u.a., Reflexionen und Erinnerungen*, ed. Barbara Nichtweiß (Würzburg: Echter, 2009), p. 222.

9   Bultmann to Gogarten, 21 November 1925, in *Bultmann/Gogarten*, p. 96. Peterson's essay appeared in pamphlet form as 'Was ist Theologie?' (Bonn: Cohen, 1925); rpt. in Peterson, *Theologische Traktate* (Würzburg: Echter, 1994 [1951]), pp. 1–22. Bultmann's response appeared as 'Die Frage der "dialektischen" Theologie: Eine Auseinandersetzung mit Peterson', in *Zwischen den Zeiten* 4 (1926), pp. 40–59.

10 Letter dated 14 March 1927, in *Bultmann/Heidegger*, pp. 19–22; p. 22.

11 'Für die schwelenden Probleme ist Barth sogar ein zu leicht wiegender Gegner – so leicht, daß er auf Grund [Krügers] Aufsatzes nicht einmal merken wird, worauf es ankommt'; Heidegger to Bultmann, 29 March 1927, in *Bultmann/Heidegger*, pp. 24–6; p. 25. The essay in question is by Gerhard Krüger, a student of Heidegger. It was sent in advance copy to Heidegger and published the same year as 'Dialektische Methode und theologische Exegese: Logische Bemerkungen zu Barth's "Römerbrief"', in *Zwischen den Zeiten* 5 (1927), pp. 116–57.

12 Heidegger to Bultmann, 29 March 1927, in *Bultmann/Heidegger*, pp. 24–6; p. 25.

13 See Heidegger to Bultmann, 23 October 1928 (in *Bultmann/Heidegger*, pp. 62–9; pp. 62–4); Bultmann to Heidegger, 29 October 1928 (in *Bultmann/Heidegger*, pp. 69–78; p. 70); and Heidegger to Bultmann, 9 April 1929 (in *Bultmann/Heidegger*, pp. 105–11; p. 108).

14 Barth to Brunner, 13 March 1925, in *Barth/Brunner,* pp. 114–18;
    pp. 114–15.

15 'Gespräch mit Tübinger "Stiftlern"', in Barth, *Gespräche 1964–1968,*
    pp. 122–3.

16 Barth to Bultmann, 15 July 1927, in *Barth/Bultmann* 36. See also
    Bultmann to Barth, 4 July 1927, in *Barth/Bultmann,* pp. 35–6.

17 Bultmann to Barth, 18 July 1927, in *Barth/Bultmann,* pp. 36–7.

18 Barth to Thurneysen, 12 March 1928, in *Barth/Thurneysen* II.
    562–7; p. 565.

19 Bultmann to Ernst Fuchs, 17 November 1930, in *Bultmann/
    Gogarten,* pp. 183–4, n. 11. See also Bultmann's exchange on the
    subject with Barth in *Barth/Bultmann,* pp. 102–18.

20 Barth to Bultmann, 27 May 1931, in *Barth/Bultmann,* pp. 114–18;
    p. 117. The occasion is Bultmann's newly published 'Die
    Geschichtlichkeit des Daseins und der Glaube: Antwort an Gerhardt
    Kuhlmann', *Zeitschrift für Theologie und Kirche* 11 (1930),
    pp. 229–64. Barth repeats his accusation in a letter of 20 June 1931,
    in *Barth/Bultmann,* pp. 122–7; p. 127.

21 Bultmann to Gogarten, 22 December 1923, in *Bultmann/Gogarten,*
    pp. 54–6; p. 56.

22 See Bultmann to Gogarten, 16 March 1924, in *Bultmann/Gogarten,*
    pp. 56–7; p. 56.

23 See Bultmann to Gogarten, 19 October 1924 (in *Bultmann/Gogarten,*
    pp. 58–63; p. 63), and Gogarten to Bultmann, 3 November 1924 (in
    Bultmann/Gogarten, pp. 63–6; p. 64).

24 See Bultmann to Gogarten, 15 May 1927, in *Bultmann/Gogarten,*
    p. 108.

25 'Ontologie und Idealismus: Eine Auseinandersetzung von Heinrich
    Barth mit Martin Heidegger', *Zwischen den Zeiten* 7 (1929),
    pp. 511–40.

26 See Bultmann to Ernst Fuchs, 17 November 1930, in *Bultmann/
    Gogarten,* pp. 183–4, n. 11. For an example of the later Gogarten's
    more positive reception of Heidegger via Bultmann, see Gogarten,
    Demythologizing and History (London: SCM, 1955 [1953]).

27 The lecture, held on 23 January 1925, was subsequently published
    with corrections as 'Gesetz und Offenbarung: Eine theologische
    Grundlegung', *Theologische Blätter* 4 (1925), cols. 53–8.

28 Bultmann to Barth, 24 January 1925, in *Barth/Bultmann,* p. 40.
    See also his 10 March letter to Gogarten in *Bultmann/Gogarten,*
    pp. 71–4; p. 73.

29 Brunner to Barth, 10 March 1925, in *Barth/Brunner*, pp. 107–13; pp. 109–10. Brunner had reported immediately after the lecture: 'I fared badly in Marburg. I was so tired that I didn't have the wherewithal to respond to Heidegger's somewhat loutish elbowing. So I kept silent and lost the battle. It was partly my fault for trying to pack much too much into the lecture and coming out with very unguarded formulations. What surprised me a bit was that Bultmann didn't say anything'; Brunner to Barth, 28 January 1925, in *Barth/ Brunner*, pp. 105–7; p. 106.

30 Barth to Bultmann, 21 June 1931, in *Barth/Bultmann*, pp. 124–6.

31 Heidegger to Bultmann, 3 November 1932, in *Bultmann/Heidegger*, p. 181.

32 *Church Dogmatics* III. 3. §50 (1949/50).

33 'Interview with H.-Ch. Tauxe', first published in *Gazette de Lausanne* (20 April 1965), rpt. in Barth, *Gespräche 1964–1968*, pp. 197–202; p. 198.

34 See *Bultmann/Heidegger*, p. 184. The volume in question is Friedrich Nietzsche, *Freundesbriefe*, ed. Richard Oehler (Gesellschaft der Freunde des Nietzsche-Archivs, 1931). The prefatory poem is entitled 'Aus hohen Bergen'; it is reprinted in *Bultmann/Heidegger*, pp. 273–5.

35 Bultmann to Heidegger, 13 December 1931; *Bultmann/Heidegger*, pp. 174–5; p. 175.

36 In the summer, Bultmann apologized that he still hadn't written the promised longer letter, and in November, Heidegger noted that he was still waiting for it; see *Bultmann/Heidegger*, pp. 176 and 180.

37 Bultmann to Heidegger, 11 December 1932; *Bultmann/Heidegger*, pp. 182–9; pp. 184–5.

38 Heidegger to Bultmann, 16 December 1932; *Bultmann/Heidegger*, pp. 189–92; pp. 189–90.

39 See *Bultmann/Heidegger* 145–59. Heidegger's own opposition to a similar Concordat with the Catholic Church in Baden is related in Chapter 6.

40 See esp. Heidegger's non-responsiveness to Bultmann's attempted interpretation of his later work in a 1963 piece entitled 'Reflections on Heidegger's Path' (*Bultmann/Heidegger*, pp. 305–17), and their correspondence after the publication of *Phenomenology & Theology* in 1970 (*Bultmann/Heidegger*, pp. 237–45).

41 'Gespräch mit Wuppertaler Studenten (1 July 1968)', in Barth, *Gespräche 1964–1968*, pp. 472–521; p. 504.

42 Heidegger to Müller, 11 November 1950, in *Heidegger/Müller*, pp. 26–7; p. 27.

43 See e.g. the conversations with Messkirch neighbours and acquaintances recorded in Alfred Denker and Elsbeth Büchin, *Martin Heidegger und seine Heimat* (Stuttgart: Klett-Cotta, 2005), pp. 239–42. My own conversations with relevant men and women confirm this impression.

44 On Heidegger's relationship to Beuron, see Johannes Schaber OSB, 'Te lucis ante terminum: Martin Heidegger und das benediktinische Mönchtum', in *Edith Stein Jahrbuch 8: Das Mönchtum* (Würzburg: Echter Verlag, 2002), pp. 281–94; Schaber, 'Phänomenologie und Mönchtum: Max Scheler, Martin Heidegger, Edith Stein und die Erzabtei Beuron', in Zaborowski and Loos (eds.), *Leben, Tod und Entscheidung*, pp. 71–100; and Alfred Denker, 'Ein Samenkorn für etwas Wesentliches: Martin Heidegger und die Erzabtei Beuron', in *Erbe und Auftrag* 79, 2 (2003), pp. 91–106.

45 See e.g. *Heidegger/Blochmann*, pp. 31–2, 34, 39–40, 43–6.

46 Heidegger to Blochmann, 12 September 1929, in *Heidegger/Blochmann*, p. 33. St Martin in Beuron was a significant spiritual centre for many others as well. Among Heidegger's intellectual circle, Edith Stein visited fifteen times during the years 1927–33, and Max Scheler, too, maintained ties to the abbey. See Schaber, 'Phänomenologie und Mönchtum'.

47 See Denker and Büchin, *Heidegger und seine Heimat*, pp. 30–3 and 240.

48 Heidegger wrote to Gruber's secretary, Bernhard Welte, on 29 December 1945, requesting a meeting with the Archbishop 'within the next few days', in *Heidegger/Welte*, p. 11. Welte later told his friend Max Müller that Heidegger had come to seek the Archbishop's help; see 'Ein Gespräch mit Max Müller' (1985), in *Heidegger/Müller*, pp. 110–42; p. 139.

49 See Denker and Büchin, *Heidegger und seine Heimat*, pp. 144–71; 'Schriftenverzeichnis', *HJB* 1, 542–77.

50 See e.g. 'Antrittsrede' (1957), GA 1, 56; Heidegger to Welte, 3 October 1959, in *Heidegger/Welte*, pp. 15–17; p. 16.

51 Greetings to Maria Gröber – who, after her brother's death in 1948, joined the household of the archbishop's former secretary Bernhard Welte – are included in every letter Heidegger sent Welte between 1946 and 1959; see *Heidegger/Welte*, pp. 11–17.

52 See Chapter 6.

53 Karl Rahner, [Untitled], in Richard Wisser (ed.), *Martin Heidegger in Gespräch* (Freiburg: Alber, 1970), pp. 48–9; p. 48.

54 Heidegger, 'Das Rektorat 1933/34: Tatsachen und Gedanken' (1945), in GA 16, 372–94; p. 392.

55 See *Heidegger/Müller,* pp. 46–7 and 57.

56 Heidegger to Welte, 12 May 1946, in *Heidegger/Welte,* pp. 11–12; p. 12.

57 See the two volumes of correspondence: *Martin Heidegger/Bernhard Welte: Briefe und Begegnungen,* eds. Alfred Denker and Holger Zaborowski (Stuttgart: Klett-Cotta Verlag, 2003), and *Martin Heidegger/Max Müller: Briefe und andere Dokumente,* eds. Holger Zaborowski and A. Bösl (Freiburg: Karl Alber Verlag, 2004).

58 'Hier wird nicht geheideggert. Wir gehen zur Sache über'; Georg Picht, 'Die Macht des Denkens', in Günther Neske (ed.), *Erinnerung an Martin Heidegger* (Pfullingen: Neske, 1977), pp. 197–206; p. 202.

59 E.g. in Heidegger to Müller, 11 December 1964, in *Heidegger/Müller,* pp. 47–8; p. 48.

60 It should be no surprise that this model of philosophy as 'friendship' has been largely submerged in the reception of Heidegger, but is a central concern of some of Heidegger's indirect heirs, especially Stanley Cavell. See e.g. Cavell, *Conditions Handsome and Unhandsome: The Constitution of Emersonian Perfectionism* (Chicago: University of Chicago Press, 1990); Cavell, *Cities of Words: Pedagogical Letters on a Register of the Moral Life* (Cambridge, MA: Harvard University Press, 2004), esp. ch. 19.

61 See 'Gespräch mit Max Müller' (1985), in *Heidegger/Müller,* p. 138.

62 Verlag Herder, founded in 1801, was and remains a leading conservative Catholic publishing house in Freiburg.

63 See Georg Aly, 'Habilitation Max Müller', MS in the Archive of the Faculty of Philosophy, Freiburg; quoted in 'Gespräch mit Max Müller' (1985), in *Heidegger/Müller,* 131n. 46.

64 'Gespräch mit Max Müller' (1985), in *Heidegger/Müller,* pp. 131–2.

65 See 'Gespräch mit Max Müller' (1985), in *Heidegger/Müller,* p. 132. An earlier episode, also occasionally mis-told, may be worth a marginal mention here: In 1933, Müller was appointed student representative by the Philosophy Faculty, but was removed from post by the then-rector Heidegger several months later as 'politically unsuitable' ('Gespräch mit Max Müller', in *Heidegger/Müller,* p. 120). It is worth noting, in this connection, that Heidegger subsequently forced Müller's successor to step down for excessive Nazi fervor (as remembered by Georg Picht, 'Die Macht des Denkens', in Neske (ed.), *Erinnerung an Martin Heidegger,* 198–9); his vision of the post was clearly not politically one-sided.

66 The case Müller, usually reported without mention of Müller's authorial activity and Georg Aly's role, is routinely cited as an

example of Heidegger's 'disgusting' Nazism and 'secret denunciations' of politically other-minded students and colleagues (see e.g. Thomas Sheehan, 'Heidegger and the Nazis', *New York Review of Books* 35, 10 [16 June 1988], pp. 38–47; pp. 40–2; Víctor Farías, *Heidegger and Nazism* [Philadelphia: Temple University Press, 1989]). This is not supported by the evidence.

67 For details, see 'Gespräch mit Max Müller' (1985), in *Heidegger/ Müller*, pp. 112–13.

68 See Müller to Alois Naber SJ, 2 February 1947, in *Heidegger/Müller*, p. 71. See also Chapter 6 above.

69 'Ansprache Max Müllers in Meßkirch anläßlich der Verleihung der Ehrenbürgerurkunde an Martin Heidegger am 27. September 1959', in *Heidegger/Müller*, pp. 93–7; p. 97.

70 See Heidegger's and Welte's letters of 1973 and 1974, in *Heidegger/ Welte*, pp. 33–40.

71 'Stiftender als Dichten/Gründender als Denken,/bleibe der Dank./ Die in's Danken gelangen/bringt er zurück vor/die Gegenwart des Unzugangbaren/der wir – die Sterblichen alle –/vom Anfang her/geeignet sind'; Heidegger to Welte, c. 26 September 1974, in *Heidegger/Welte*, p. 40.

72 Welte's eulogy is published in Neske (ed.), *Erinnerung an Martin Heidegger*, pp. 249–52, and reprinted in *Heidegger/Welte*, pp. 124–7.

8

Heidegger in theology

This chapter falls into two parts: The first analyses early criticisms by Protestants on the one hand and Catholics on the other, with the aim of providing a genealogy for central theological contestations that continue to the present day. The second offers a schematic map of theological appropriations of Heidegger's philosophy, divided into the heuristic categories 'Existential Theology' (represented here by Rudolf Bultmann, Paul Tillich and John Macquarrie), 'Phenomenology and Thomism' (represented here by Karl Rahner and Edith Stein), and 'Post-Metaphysical Theology' (represented here in English by John Caputo and Merold Westphal, and in French by Jean-Luc Marion). I situate each of these vis-à-vis Heidegger's own development of thought (as described in the preceding chapters), provide references to important work having been or being done in the area, and then usually follow out a particular argument or strand of engagement, with the aim of showing some of the continuing potential of the relevant form of reception and whetting the reader's appetite for further work. Heidegger's influence on theology far exceeds the direct reception of his thought, of course; important indirect strands of influence not discussed here include theological hermeneutics, theories of language and transcendental theology. Nevertheless, what is offered here should be enough for the student to be getting on with.

Although this chapter limits itself to broadly Christian theological engagements with Heidegger, it is worth noting that Heidegger was also interested in the potential links of his later philosophy to Asian religions, particularly Buddhism, and that these links have been a topic of constructive and reflective academic work since his own lifetime.[1] Heidegger was in contact with members of the Kyoto

School while teaching in Freiburg, for example Keiji Nishitani, who studied with Heidegger in 1937–39.[2] Around 1946, Heidegger attempted a translation of the Daoist classic the *Daodeching*, in collaboration with the Chinese scholar Paul Shih-yi Hsiao.[3] In his lecture series 'What is Thinking?' of 1951–52, he first spoke of the 'inevitable dialogue with the East Asian world'[4] – a dialogue he initiated in the 1953/54 'conversation on language' with Tomio Tezuka, a Japanese scholar of German.[5] In Heidegger's opinion, however, this rapprochement could not be hurried: 'For the process of the encounter between Occident and Orient', he is recorded as having said, 'I budget 300 years.'[6]

Theological contestations:
A brief genealogy

Before turning to the positive reception of Heidegger's thought in twentieth-century theology, it is instructive, perhaps indispensable, to get a sense of the critical reception of his work among theologians of his own generation. The critical debate was at its liveliest after the publication of *Being and Time*, which, as well as being his acknowledged *magnum opus*, was also the immediate (though long-delayed) successor to what had until then been Heidegger's only work: a monograph on a medieval theological text. Theological colleagues and readers justifiably expected a successor volume which would be, if not outright theological, at least directly relevant to theology. Consequently, *Being and Time* received more attention from theological journals than the publication of any of Heidegger's later works, and sparked debates among theologians which illustrate and define what remain some of the main pressure points of a theological engagement with Heidegger.

In 1931, Gerhardt Kuhlmann, in trying to define the task of Protestant theology vis-à-vis Heidegger's ontology, dismisses the Catholic position as *a priori* useless for the Protestant, because it is incapable of even acknowledging the problem:

> For Catholicism, the relation between philosophy and theology presents no problem. For Catholic theology is essentially natural theology. The God of the Catholic doctrine of revelation is

exactly and assuredly the God whom natural man can know as his Creator, indeed because of his *imago dei*-quality *must* know as his Creator unless he maliciously closes himself off from a true understanding of his Being. . . . Catholic theology degrades philosophy to mere conceptual analysis and logical statistics, and then takes it into its service as a "handmaid". This is not merely its right, but its obligation. For Catholic dogma proclaims the identity of the Christian Saviour-God with the Creator-God of natural reason.[7]

This is a deft sketch of the rift between the Catholic and the Protestant response to Heidegger in the late 1920s and early 1930s. The Catholic response is premised on repudiating altogether the epistemological question that motivates the philosopher, namely how the question of Being is to be raised. Instead, Catholics welcome Heidegger's 'retrogression' to the traditional primacy of Being as the subject of philosophy, construing his analyses as metaphysical claims that stand to be either refuted or harnessed for the superior enterprise of Roman Catholic metaphysics. This construction is at once problematic and thought-provoking. On the one hand, it falls short of the problematization of metaphysics that is at the heart of Heidegger's (as of Kierkegaard's and Barth's) work.[8] But on the other, it raises the counter-question whether it really is (as Heidegger wishes) possible to extract oneself from metaphysical commitment. The Catholic claim is precisely that Heidegger's deconstruction of metaphysics is itself based on a dogmatically assumed 'metaphysics of immanence'. Disagreement among Catholic commentators arises in their assessment of whether this metaphysics lends itself to supplementation or correction, or whether it can only be combatted outright.

The Protestant reaction to Heidegger, by contrast, is marked by a shared question and sharply diverging answers. For his Protestant critics, as for Heidegger himself, the question how to know what it is to be human is central. What Bultmann, Brunner, Barth and their colleagues argue about is the question whether the challenge implicit in Heidegger's project of a fundamental description of man must be met, or whether to fight on the turf staked out by the philosopher is already to cede victory. Bultmann and Brunner feel strongly that Heidegger's challenge cannot be ignored without risking forfeiture of theology's claim to be relevant, indeed necessary, to both knowing and forming human existence in its full depth. Barth, on the other hand, is convinced that because only revelation can disclose anything of import about man, philosophy is precisely irrelevant, and to engage it at all is already to have distorted both subject and object of any enquiry into what it is to be human.

The Barthian critique

I have already mentioned the debate between Barth and Brunner sparked by Brunner's somewhat disastrous 1925 guest lecture in Marburg. Brunner had proposed to ground theology in a natural perception of divine law, which reduces man to a nothingness from which he can only be raised by God's revelation in the form of forgiveness. When Brunner later complained to Barth of a hostile reception by Heidegger, Barth countered that Brunner's own attempt at establishing a quasi-Kantian foundation for theology, however radically theo-centric, made him vulnerable to attack:

> The truly and effectively recognized law[, because it cannot be perceived outside revelation,] stands in indissoluble correlation with the gospel and vice versa. You say so yourself. But if this is so, then any "theological groundwork" will be flimsy, inasmuch as it has to operate with a concept of law seemingly in common to theology and philosophy. Philosophy *as such* may be capable of "noticing" something of the "law" in its theological sense, but not of *saying* anything about it – and that's what would count.[9]

In this statement and Heidegger's own contention that 'philosophical questioning strictly "knows" nothing of sin',[10] there is the tantalizing hint of a rapprochement between the thought of the two men which, in some sense, unites them against Brunner. Indeed, Heidegger himself noticed this resemblance, and encouraged Barth's and Thurneysen's insistence on a thoroughly *theo*logical rather than any philosophical grounding of theology throughout the 1920s and early 1930s. In 1923, responding to a guest lecture by Thurneysen in Marburg, Heidegger recalled him to theology's task of 'calling to faith in faith'.[11] In 1927, he acknowledged Barth's exemplary acceptance of that task by noting, in *Being and Time*, that theology was 'slowly beginning once more to understand

Luther's insight that its dogmatic system rests on a "foundation" that is not rooted in . . . faithful questioning [or: questioning that arises out of faith], and whose concepts therefore are not merely inadequate to theology's field of problems, but obscure and distort it'.[12] In 1931, Heidegger even counselled his friend Bultmann to 'work with Barth's indifference vis-à-vis philosophy, but with the understanding *for* it which you have acquired'.[13]

However, the resemblance is ultimately superficial, and so easily misleads. On Heidegger's part, the separation of theology and philosophy implies a decidedly inferior role for theology. Although he concedes that the Christian experience of sin 'has its own testimony, which is fundamentally inaccessible to any philosophical experience',[14] he also insists that 'faith and "worldview," provided they wish to make any claims to *conceptual* understanding in talking about [man's sinfulness], will have to take recourse to the existential structures [Heidegger has] uncovered'.[15] But the second comment threatens to obviate the first, as Heidegger himself admits in a footnote: 'Strictly speaking, one cannot even say whether the ontology of Dasein in itself leaves open the possibility [of sin], inasmuch as philosophical questioning strictly "knows" nothing of sin.'[16]

Barth, in turn, wholly rejects the distinction between ontic and ontological levels of existence and discourse within which Heidegger situates his statement. Barth shares with Brunner the assumption of an ontological rift (here in the traditional rather than the Heideggerian sense of 'ontological') between ungraced and graced existence. But whereas Brunner wants to bridge this gap by a natural recognition of sinfulness and consequent appeal for grace, Barth regards the sinful state as one of complete anosognosia: the unsaved cannot know God or themselves even to the extent of discerning their sinfulness and God's judgement over them.[17] Ultimately, the structural similarities between Barth and Heidegger conceal a profound disagreement about the underlying causes of philosophy's and theology's radical separation, which – the attempts of some followers of Barth notwithstanding – make a meaningful integration impossible. This is, it seems to me, as true of their later developments as of their early work. Some of Barth's students, most influentially Heinrich Ott (1929–2013), have sought to demonstrate the convergence of Barth's thought and the later, post-metaphysical Heidegger.[18] Thus, for example, Ott interprets salvation history as a Heideggerian history of being, and the covenantal call and response of God and man as a Heideggerian clearing in which man is addressed by being. The inadequacies of such an account as an interpretation of Heidegger are touched on below.[19] Its claims to be a consistent development of Barth were dismissed by Barth himself in 1962,[20] and have been a subject of debate ever since.[21] Ott remains influential; but the challenges to a Heideggerian theology posed by Barth seem to me as open as when he first raised them.

The neo-Thomist critique

The thinkers who most shaped the earliest Roman Catholic responses to Heidegger were theologians with neo-Scholastic sympathies and varying degrees of phenomenological training: Erich Przywara (1889–1972), Edith Stein (1891–1942), Romano Guardini (1886–1968), and, from the periphery of the movement, Hans Urs von Balthasar (1905–88). Their responses were shaped by certain expectations established (intentionally or unintentionally) by Heidegger himself. His last published work, 11 years earlier, had been a quasi-neo-Scholastic treatise on Duns Scotus (or rather, Thomas of Erfurt). His new work signalled a radical return, within secular modern philosophy, to Scholastic or scholastically derived language, particularly 'being' and 'essence'. To the neo-Scholastics, consequently, Heidegger's project presented itself as a key for re-establishing the philosophical primacy of Being repudiated by Kant. Their main critique, accordingly, was that this project frustrated its own potential through a wilful obfuscation of the Scholastic categories it employed, amounting to a dogmatic and/or incoherent denial of the transcendence of (divine) Being and of the analogical nature of human existence and discourse.[22]

Erich Przywara, a leading editor of the Jesuit journal *Stimmen der Zeit*, was at the forefront of a larger endeavour to harness the insights of Husserlian, Schelerian and Heideggerian phenomenology for a renewal of neo-Scholasticism. He was influenced by his encounters with Edith Stein, and himself exercised a decisive influence on Hans Urs von Balthasar, particularly through his *magnum opus, Analogia entis*.[23] In his essay 'Three Directions of Phenomenology' (1928), Przywara succinctly expresses the neo-Scholastics' ambivalence regarding Heidegger's project:

The work [*Being and Time*] seems, on the one hand, a most incisive "regression towards tradition", since, in sharpest opposition to the entirety of modern philosophy, it traces knowledge (theoretical reason) and action and obligation (practical reason) back to the concept of Being and thereby establishes the Aristotelian-Thomist doctrine of Being as foundational *prima philosophia* (see pp. 1ff, 436). And yet it frames the concept of Being in such a way that, perhaps more axiomatically than anywhere else in modern philosophy, the immanent [lit.: inner-worldly] is closed and locked in on itself, since Being as Being is in its essence "in the world". At the same time, the transcendent [lit.: super-worldly] falls away by itself or must at least be traced back to the immanent. (cf. pp. 180, 313, 427)[24]

Catholic critics develop this basic position variously. Alfred Delp SJ, in his extremely influential *Tragic Existence: On the Philosophy of Martin Heidegger* (1931) – the first book-length study of Heidegger's existential ontology – accuses the philosopher of aspiring to a 'self-divinization of man' by distorting the Scholastic use of *analogia*.[25] Following Aquinas, Delp regards human existence as explicable only by an *analogia attributionis*: an analogical use of the term 'being' in reference to God (*analogans*) and man (*analogatum*), warranted by the fact that man's being is causally dependent on God's being, which is the first and proper referent of the term. In J. A. Quenstedt's formulation of Aquinas, made famous by Barth: '*Deus substantia est absoluta et independenter, creatura vero dependenter et per participationem.*'[26] In other words, man exists by participation, and his finite being therefore intrinsically points beyond itself to the infinite being of God. Heidegger, Delp argues, presents a skewed *analogia attributionis* in which not God but Nothingness functions as the analogans of man's being.[27] What Delp finds interesting here is that Heidegger derives not a weary nihilism but a tragic heroism from this fact – a heroism that requires but also contradicts man's constitutive 'immersion in Nothingness'.[28] 'The resolution, the heroism of [man in the face of] nothing', Delp maintains, 'is nothing other than a denial of the finitude that has just been asserted with such pathos'.[29] Heidegger's narrative is an intoxicating but ultimately incoherent myth.[30]

   Przywara is more optimistic: Rather than requiring debunking, Heidegger's work, in his estimation, invites supplementation by the theologian. Przywara takes Heidegger's 'misprision' of Aquinas to consist not in a misidentification of the analogans of man's being, but in denying the contingency of human existence altogether. Heidegger's ontology, he argues, posits an absolutized existence as the 'essence' of Dasein; in other words, it claims the exclusively divine identity of existence and essence for the creature, rejecting the ontological difference which characterizes all created beings in Patristic and Scholastic thought.[31] But, Przywara goes on, 'Heidegger's ontology . . . is forced back into the Patristic-Scholastic doctrine . . . by the course of its own investigation': The Scholastic difference between Being and essence merely resurfaces in Heidegger's 'doctrine of the difference between being there [*Dasein*] and being thus [*Sosein*]'.[32] This, Przywara argues, inescapably opens his analysis to a theological dimension: 'Phenomenology here transcends itself towards the essential doctrine of Scholasticism: the existential openness [*seinshafte Aufgebrochenheit*] of the creature towards God lodged in the inner difference between being thus and being there', that is, between essence and existence.[33]

At first sight, Delp and Przywara's criticisms seem to demonstrate merely that Scholastic ontology is a Procrustean bed unfit for Heidegger's existential analytic. Rather than trying to tune into Heidegger's methodological and terminological innovations, they simply transpose his terms back into a metaphysical system that Heidegger seeks to expose as inadequate. It is clear, for example, that Heidegger does not in fact try to deny an ontological difference; indeed, his work is premised on it. Rather, he seeks to problematize what we can know and how we can speak of Being from our inescapably localized and temporal perspective. The dictum 'The "essence" of Dasein lies in its existence'[34] is deliberately unsettling: an 'outrageous send-up'[35] of the Scholastic definition of God as the necessary being, rather than merely the transposition of a definition of God onto man. Delp's pre-critical assimilation of Heideggerian to Scholastic terms is similarly inadequate (as Edith Stein already notes).[36] And yet for all that, their counter-question whether Heidegger really can extract himself from metaphysical commitment as easily as he would like commands attention.

Like the Barthian critique, the neo-Scholastic critique is a continuing and developing theological stance. A number of recent writers in the Scholastic tradition (particularly its more analytical wing) have continued Delp's and Przywara's lines of questioning without much change.[37] But significantly more complex and hard-hitting versions of the charge that Heidegger cannot extricate himself from metaphysical commitment have been developed, first and foremost by theologians associated with Radical Orthodoxy.[38] This continues to be a fertile field of enquiry.

Theological appropriations: A map

If the last section aimed to provide genealogies for some of the main ways of *contesting* Heidegger to this day, this section aims to offer a conceptual map of theological *receptions* of his work. Since Heidegger himself consistently resisted a theological reading of his texts, the various ways in which his work has been appropriated by theologians usually depend, however deferential and sympathetic they are, on selective disagreements either with the philosopher's self-understanding or with his interpretation of particular theological texts or theses.

In his work up to the 'turn' of the 1930s, there are two main junctures at which the theologian might contest Heidegger. The first is Heidegger's adoption, in the late 1910s and early 1920s, of a 'Protestant' understanding of God as radically external. In his mature theological thought of that time, Heidegger equates the (Patristic/Catholic) idea of God as dwelling within the believer with the arrogation of a simple continuity between the human and the divine realm (a 'theology of glory'), or of the possibility of a God's-eye view of man (a *philosophia perennis*). But this equation is not necessarily justified, and some theologians are at pains to distinguish between the (often hubristic) neo-Scholastic claim to a natural knowledge of the divine on the one hand, and the Thomist claim of a God who is 'more intimate [to man] than anything' on the other. Such are the theologians who advocate what I will call a 'phenomenological Thomism' – most significantly Edith Stein, Karl Rahner and Max Müller.

The second juncture is Heidegger's step, in the mid-1920s, from regarding a self-confessedly a-theistic phenomenological description of human existence as a *praeparatio evangelica* to regarding it as a competing medium of 'salvation', contesting the claim of Christian faith to be a necessary condition for an authentic human life. 'Existentialist theologians' such as Rudolf Bultmann, Paul Tillich and John Macquarrie embrace Heidegger's early, 'existentialist' description of human life as fraught with anxiety in the face of our 'thrownness' and uncertain future, but reject (in one way or another) Heidegger's claim that it is in *accepting* the inescapable, undelegable possibility of death that humans find 'authenticity', and instead hold out Christianity as a salvation from that fate.

In Heidegger's work after the 'turn', sympathetic theologians detect an absence rather than a criticism of the 'true' Christian God. How and whether his non-religious mysticism is to be re-Christianized is therefore the main burden of their discussions.

Existential theology

'Existential (or existentialist) theology' was long the primary theological appropriation of Heidegger, also drawing significantly on Søren Kierkegaard, Karl Jaspers and others. Although fiercely criticized by the subsequent generation of theological Heidegger readers for participating in Sartre's existentialist misreading of the early Heidegger, it has remained extremely influential and is not, I would argue, to be dismissed as easily as Heideggerian theologians of the 1950s and 1960s would have liked. The main proponents of an existentialist theological reading of Heidegger are Rudolf Bultmann and Paul Tillich (1886–1965) in Germany, and John Macquarrie (1919–2007) in Britain. Tillich encountered Heidegger while he was associate professor in Systematic Theology at Marburg from 1924 to 1925 (when he became professor of Religious Studies in Dresden). Macquarrie was Lady Margaret Professor of Divinity in Oxford, and co-translator of the (still canonical) English translation of *Being and Time*.[39]

'Existential (or existentialist) theology' consciously restricts itself to Heidegger's early work, either disregarding his later thought altogether (as Bultmann does), or explicitly sequestering the early work from the later (as Tillich and, to a lesser extent, Macquarrie do). It is noteworthy but not necessarily decisive that Heidegger himself repudiates the existentialist interpretation of his early thought by Jean-Paul Sartre and others in his 1947 *Letter on Humanism* (titled in response to Sartre's 1946 tract 'Existentialism is a Humanism'). That Heidegger's scepticism is not decisive has two reasons, one general and one specific to a theological reception. First, despite

Heidegger's emphasis on 'paths, not works',[40] *Being and Time* is a systematically coherent text, and its incompleteness permits other philosophically legitimate interpretations and continuations than those at which Heidegger himself arrived.[41] Tillich emphasizes this 'independent philosophical standing' of *Being and Time*, 'whatever Heidegger may say about it in criticism and retraction',[42] and Macquarrie suggests the inadequacy of the later work as a completion of the early 'existentialist' thought, even if one accepts that Heidegger always intended to go beyond a philosophy of existence.[43] Secondly, existentialist theology agrees with Heidegger's insistence, contra Sartre, that a narrow 'existential' focus on the human individual is inadequate, and must be set within the context of a broader ontological outlook. In this sense, it circumvents or even anticipates one of the *Letter*'s central criticisms against existentialism. This is not to say that theological existentialism does not run counter to, and at times explicitly repudiates, Heidegger's own understanding of his early work. But it is an interpretation that merits genuine philosophical-theological discussion, rather than being dismissible as a simple misunderstanding.

The basic premise of an existentialist theology is that to be *salvation*, Christian faith must be relevant to the human condition: it must address a vital and universal need or question. Furthermore, this need or question cannot be merely abstract or theoretical, but must be *existential*, that is, immediately and inescapably affecting every existence. But if this is so, then it should at least in principle be possible for a non-Christian philosopher or psychologist to identify and describe this need, even if he or she cannot propose an adequate answer. In fact, a philosopher or psychologist might be better equipped to do so than a theologian, whose training and vantage point often occlude non-Christian existence. Just such a description of the existential structure of human existence – the human condition to which Christianity addresses itself or within whose parameters it has relevance for humans – is what Bultmann, Tillich, Macquarrie and others find in Heidegger's existential analytic.

In this context, there are two basic ways in which Heidegger's 'existential analytic' can be understood. Either (as Heidegger himself proposes) it is a purely formal analysis of the abiding structures or parameters of human existence, which define a Christian and a non-Christian life alike; or it is a snapshot of sinful existence, that is, a description of the plight to which the new life of faith is the solution. Macquarrie takes the former view:

> What the theologian understands by fallenness is a concrete *existentiell* situation. This understanding is to be validated and clarified by relating it to man's ontological structure, and by showing that it does lie within the horizons of what is genuinely possible for man. But these horizons are delineated by the existential analytic, which reveals, among other phenomena, this existential concept of fallenness.[44]

Tillich, by contrast, advocates the latter. For him, the distinguishing mark of all existentialist philosophy is its description of existence – contra the optimistic essentialism of Hegel – as estrangement: in other words, it articulates a question to which it does not have an answer.[45]

But both interpretations face a range of challenges. One of these, particularly relevant to Macquarrie's construal, is the question of precedence: If (as many would argue) Heidegger's existential analysis is not prior to and independent of theological concepts, but itself derived from the New Testament and Christian tradition, then it cannot be trusted to provide the validation the theologian seeks. But perhaps more damningly, as Gerhard Kuhlmann notes as early as 1929, both interpretations ultimately undermine themselves. In the first case, the Christian terms introduced by the theologian are merely mythologizations of philosophical ones, and so at best superfluous; in the second, the theologian must disregard the most basic guiding intentions of the philosopher he is trying to appropriate, and is therefore *prima facie* untrustworthy in his construal of that thought.[46]

Tillich and Macquarrie have partial responses to these challenges which are worth engaging. For the purpose of this chapter, however, it seems more fruitful to analyse Bultmann's account in more depth: not only because of his intimate acquaintance with Heidegger or because his corpus is, of the three, the most influential, even defining, for twentieth-century theology, but also because his thought bears unexpected resemblances to that of independent, contemporary thinkers, and so merits renewed consideration.[47]

Bultmann's earliest scriptural exegesis influenced by Heidegger is somewhat inauspicious. His first major article, 'The Eschatology

of the Gospel of John' (1928), runs counter not merely to one of
the problems identified by Kuhlmann, but worse, conflates the two
possible ways of interpreting Heidegger's existentialia, and so bears
the combined weight of both criticisms. However, as we shall see,
Bultmann develops, under the pressure of Kuhlmann's criticisms,
a position that is both more critical and more substantial than his
original contribution. In his essay 'The Historicity of Dasein and
Faith' (1930) he proposes a substantial reconfiguration of the
relationship between 'ontic' and 'ontological' levels of enquiry, and
therefore also of theology and phenomenology.

In a series of publications between 1926 and 1929, culminating in
'The Eschatology of the Gospel of John' (1928), Bultmann develops
a theological reading of Johannine eschatology as an existential
dynamic that eschews the dramatic, other-worldly apocalypticism
of other New Testament texts in favour of an 'eschatological now'
which opens up – every moment anew – the future as possibility: as
the advent of the genuinely new.[48] Bultmann's account deliberately
relies on Heidegger's existential analytic as a conceptual and
ontological framework, drawing particularly on the terminology
of being-in-the-world and of authenticity and inauthenticity.
Briefly following out his use of those terms gives a good sense of
the force, but also of the challenges of an existentialist theology à
la Heidegger.

Bultmann sets his analysis within a phenomenological framework by identifying the Johannine *kosmos*[49] with Heidegger's
Welt ('world' or 'worldhood'), of which humans are always
already part. However, he immediately superimposes on what he
presents as a phenomenological description of man's constitutive
being-in-the-world a theological dimension whose methodological
basis is not at all clear:

Man does not *face* the world, he *is* world; i.e. the world is not
an object present at hand "in itself", which man confronts in
theoretical contemplation. (Rather, such contemplation would
itself be part of the world, itself be "world".) But being [part
of the] world means first of all being created; and that man *is*
world – that is, created – includes, according to the Prologue [of
John's Gospel], that man is capable of *understanding* himself in
this his creatureliness.[50]

Bultmann never theorizes or justifies his use of the Johannine Prologue to inflect Heidegger's understanding of worldhood. This failure to clarify the relation between two very different kinds of sources – phenomenological analysis and Biblical declaration – introduces a problematic ambiguity which becomes evident in the following two steps of his argument.

In a first step, Bultmann makes his emphasis on the *creatureliness* of the world into the lynchpin of an interpretation of the disjunctive force of John's gospel as a Heideggerian tension between authenticity and inauthenticity. 'Precisely because it is created', he writes, the world 'has the possibility of misunderstanding itself, of setting itself against God'.[51] At the same time, 'in the possibility of knowing oneself a creature, the world has always already had the possibility of accepting the Word'.[52] This 'Word' – the proclamation of the gospel – in this scheme only 'activates' or 'actualizes' antecedent existential possibilities: By bringing man face-to-face with his Creator, the Word elicits either an acknowledgement of his own creatureliness or its denial.

In a second step, Bultmann tries to resolve this existential possibility into the Christian concepts of sin and salvation: for the denial of creatureliness, when it is maintained in the face of a direct revelation, is no longer mere misunderstanding but downright sin.[53] At this point, Bultmann reverts to a specifically Biblical use of the term 'world' which he never explicitly delineates against its phenomenological sense: 'In the face of revelation, which calls the world in its worldhood into question, it is sin to cleave to worldhood.'[54] Conversely, for those who believe, 'the world is, in some sense, at an end'.[55] Here, the term 'world' negatively describes an obstinately immanent realm that bars itself against the irruption of the Word and thereby forfeits any genuine possibility of change or growth. But if 'worldhood' is an existential feature of Dasein, which may be engaged authentically or inauthentically, then 'worldhood' cannot at the same time be an existentiell condition that can be avoided by accepting a particular proclamation, or contracted by its rejection.

Gerhard Kuhlmann, in the intervention already mentioned above, argues that Bultmann risks incoherence by conflating the two alternative ways in which a theologian wishing to appropriate Heidegger might interpret the philosopher's 'existentialia': either as purely formal analyses, which span Christian and non-Christian existence alike; or as specific descriptions of sinful existence, which cannot encompass the new life of faith. What is worse, Kuhlmann continues, both approaches are ultimately self-subversive (as discussed above). Bultmann's case, even if it were coherent, would collapse under the combined weight of their problems. Even on a more sympathetic reading than Kuhlmann's, Bultmann requires, at the least, an account of *why* the theologian is justified in introducing a theological dimension to his phenomenological narrative.

Kuhlmann's critique elicits from Bultmann a response that is both more critical and more substantial than his original account. In his rejoinder, 'The Historicity of Dasein and Faith' (1930), Bultmann reiterates his conviction that the theologian, in order to speak scientifically (*wissenschaftlich*), must draw on the phenomenological work of the philosopher.[56] 'If the Christian event that takes place in faith and "rebirth" is not a magical transformation that lifts the believer right out of human existence', Bultmann argues, then the theologian can and must come to grips with the existential structures that are receptive to redemption.[57]

The question that necessarily follows is whether an atheist philosopher, who knows nothing of redeemed human existence, is equipped to identify these enduring existential structures. Bultmann's answer is ambivalent. He initially responds by way of an analogy of Christian faith with friendship that 'a friendless man who consciously or unconsciously longs for friendship *knows* what "friendship" is' every bit as well as a man who has experienced it.[58] A lived friendship adds no conceptual knowledge about the phenomenon 'friendship', but only an ever new 'qualification' of my own life – 'in work, joy, struggle and pain' – by the concrete relationship.[59] In the same way, Bultmann polemically argues, 'no believer can say more precisely or fully what "revelation" is than any unbeliever', because every being that knows death is also capable of knowing, and longing for, 'revelation and life, grace and forgiveness'.[60]

This is a problematic but also intriguing statement, both as an independent argument and as an interpretation of Heidegger. Its problems are obvious. First, Bultmann's claim that the friendless man knows all there is to know about friendship does not carry the force he intends; for that man's knowledge is likely to rest on the cultural and personal testimony of those who *have* experienced friendship (including such seminal figures as Cicero and Augustine) rather than on pure intuition. Bultmann's analogous claim about revelation is liable to the same problem. Furthermore, his claim about the unbeliever's knowledge of revelation sits uneasily as an interpretation of Heidegger, since far from projecting a longing for life, grace and forgiveness, authentic existence, for Heidegger, is premised precisely on an unflinching acceptance of the ultimacy of death and the irremovability of guilt.

Nevertheless, Bultmann's discussion of knowledge is worth probing a little more fully. The claim that the friend gains not conceptual knowledge but a 'qualification of life' can be read both as a reiteration of a Kierkegaardian dismissal of the rational content of Christian faith in favour of its existential dynamic,[61] and as an anticipation of Stanley Cavell's later distinction between knowledge and 'acknowledgment'.[62] The relevance of this distinction to a theological response to Heidegger is not to be underestimated. Heidegger's ontological account of being-with, because it seeks to uncover the existential structures within each individual that make phenomena such as community possible in the first place, bars itself by that very principle from making an ontologically significant distinction between the capability for relationship and its achievement. Real others are bracketed from the analysis; the ontological concept of *being-with* is called upon to explicate, univocally, both the attainment and the failure of actual community.

A related problem in Heidegger is that being-with (*Mitsein*) as an existential structure of Dasein is always in tension with (if not outright contradiction to) being-unto-death. The inescapable solitariness of death as the ultimate criterion of authenticity implies a deep rift within Dasein: Even if a form of authentic community can be found by and among 'self-owning' (*eigentlich*) individuals, it will be rooted in mutual recognition of the ultimate isolation of each.[63] While such distance can take salutary forms in practice, its necessity nevertheless queries Heidegger's claim of the existential, that is, constitutive, relationality of Dasein. These are the pressure points that Bultmann addresses in the remainder of his essay, through a juxtaposition of Heidegger's 'being-unto-death' and Friedrich Gogarten's 'being-towards-the-other' (love).

While for Heidegger, it is being-unto-death that defines the historicity of human existence, for Gogarten, history – in the sense of 'something happening' – takes place only 'when a Thou faces an I and is acknowledged [*anerkannt*] in its claims by the I'. These two analyses, Bultmann argues, are not in direct conflict, but reflect the two thinkers' different disciplinary spheres: 'Heidegger speaks as an ontologist and therefore has neither the occasion nor the right to speak of love. Gogarten, on the other hand, speaks as a theologian of the ontic; and it is in this sphere alone that love, in the radical sense in which he understands it, is to be found.'[64] In other words, fundamental ontology can only ever speak of internal human structures ('existentialia'); it cannot, by its nature, include in its analysis any actual relationships. But it is precisely such actual relationships which, for Gogarten (and Bultmann following him) alone make possible the authentic actualization of human historicity.

Bultmann expresses this idea and its implications in a paragraph of dense theological-philosophical prose:

> Love is only possible in Christ. What does that mean? To answer this, we must recall that on the one hand, love is not the concrete purpose of a resolution which Dasein can simply take, but is rather the "how" of resolution, which first reveals its purpose; on the other hand, love is not (like historicity) a characteristic of Dasein as such (an existentiale) but rather an ontic determination of resolution. Since these things are the case, I can only appropriate my own factic thereness [Da] as someone who loves if I am already loved, i.e. already immersed in love, and if the fact that I always already loved is promised me by the proclamation of Christ and appropriated in faith.[65]

In other words, authentic resolution (of the kind that grasps its own historicity) is only possible when motivated by love. But loving is only possible if one is already loved, and it is this 'already' which is revealed and received in faith. What is more, it is only from this standpoint of knowing oneself to have always already been loved by God that one is capable of seeing natural existence (the 'world' of Bultmann's earlier article) as always already graced, 'as creation'.[66]

This means that the theologian cannot ultimately accept the philosopher's analysis as final. For from the perspective gained by faith, the resolution to face death in solitude must appear not authentic but inauthentic, because death is *not* in fact solitary: It is always shared with Christ. And yet this cannot be known in advance of the proclamation of the gospel. This perspective also entails a critique of Heidegger's central term 'possibility'. For ultimately, Bultmann argues, Heidegger's analysis neutralizes this term by disallowing anything genuinely *new* ever to happen to Dasein. Possibility must indeed, as Heidegger implicitly argues in Part II of *Being and Time*, be defined eschatologically: but eschatology must be allowed to retain its irruptive character, its promise of the advent of something new and unanticipated.

This brings Bultmann surprisingly close to Thomas Aquinas' contention that 'man by his nature is ordained to beatitude' – that is, communion with God – 'as his end', but that he is ordained to *attain* this end 'not by his own strength, but by the help of grace'.[67] The strict separation here between capability and attainment is not arbitrary, but entailed by the kind of vocation of which the Christian faith speaks, namely a vocation to transcend both self and death. The self cannot effect this transcendence of its own boundaries by its own resources; rather, it is the Incarnation – God's human birth, death and resurrection from the dead – that enables humans to participate in God's life. Death, once final, is now transformed from within into a means of sharing in the action and life of Christ, and so of moving towards that life with God which is the innermost human calling.

Phenomenology and Thomism

If Bultmann's justification for (re-)introducing a theological dimension into Heidegger's phenomenological analyses is an experiential one – namely the event of something fundamentally new breaking in on one's existence in-the-world–, that of Thomists such as Karl Rahner or Edith Stein is metaphysical. Bultmann implicitly contests Heidegger's analysis of *possibility*, arguing that it dogmatically excludes the advent of something genuinely new, namely God, or at least underestimates to what extent such an advent may change our understanding even of ontological structures. But this contestation depends on sharing a prior decision of Heidegger's, made at the earliest stage of his phenomenology of religion: namely to define God as radically external to the human being (and so arriving as something fundamentally new). This externalization is part and parcel of Heidegger's formative rejection of the (seemingly blasphemous) claim to ontological and rational continuity with the divine in favour of an acceptance of existential finitude as the main mark of humanity; in other words, his Lutheran turn from a 'theology of glory' to a 'theology of the cross'. Once completed, this turn has important implications for the role of the philosopher: it is precisely because grace and God irrupt into the human sphere from without that a phenomenological analysis can and must bracket God from its delineation of 'natural' human existence. However, as we saw in Chapter 3, this reasoning, dovetailing with Heidegger's developing distinction between the ontic and the ontological, ultimately led the philosopher to relegate any theological account to a secondary, 'ontic' level conceptually dependent on a phenomenological description. Both Barth and Bultmann (at his best) contest that distinction.

By contrast, Rahner, Stein and other Roman Catholic scholars who embrace both Thomism and phenomenology contest Heidegger's earlier decision to describe God as radically external to the individual. Instead, they return to Augustine's and Thomas Aquinas' profession of a God 'innermost in each thing' – descriptions within which to *be*, for the human being, is nothing other than to be continually preserved in being by God, 'as light is caused in the air by the sun as long as the air remains illuminated'.[68] Two consistent emphases of these thinkers, therefore, are first, that it is not in fact possible to give a coherent and complete phenomenological description of man without noting a constitutive openness to something greater than him; and secondly, that a profession of such a God is not identical with (or necessarily results in) a triumphalist neo-Scholasticism.

'Phenomenological Thomism' differs from the metaphysical critiques of Heidegger advanced by Przywara, Delp and their neo-Scholastic heirs in viewing the phenomenological method as irreplaceable by metaphysical speculation in the endeavour to describe the human relation to God, world and self. This view gives rise to two tasks: the constructive project of a phenomenological-theological description of man's constitutive openness to the divine, and the critical project of demonstrating that phenomenology risks distortion or incoherence by denying such openness. A complementary task, pursued at the intersection of phenomenological Thomism and post-metaphysical theology by writers like Max Müller and John Caputo, is to analyse whether and how Thomas Aquinas circumvents or 'overcomes' Heidegger's critique of onto-theology.[69]

Karl Rahner (1904–84) famously said that he had had 'many schoolmasters', but 'only one teacher', namely Heidegger.[70] Rahner had been sent to Freiburg in 1934 by the Society of Jesus to earn a doctorate in philosophy, so that he might be able to teach the subject at the Jesuit seminary in Pullach (now the Munich School of Philosophy). During his two years in Freiburg, he attended Heidegger's lectures and seminars, including his Introduction to Metaphysics,[71] though he does not seem to have had much personal contact with Heidegger. Rahner's doctoral thesis was, like those of his fellow Jesuits, supervised and examined by Martin Honecker, who set as Rahner's topic an exegesis of *Summa Theologiae* 1.84.7, an article on the metaphysics of knowledge.[72] The resulting thesis – later revised and published as *Spirit in the World* – was failed by Honecker, and Rahner was recalled to the Jesuit seminary at Innsbruck, where he earned a doctorate in theology the following year.[73] Honecker's negative assessment of Rahner's thesis is often attributed to its Heideggerian influence,[74] but this claim is hard to assess. The only available documentation (Honecker's report to Rahner being lost) is Rahner's letter to his provincial concerning the outcome, in which Rahner reports that Honecker commended his 'ingenious and interesting' interpretation, but thought his exegesis and results vitiated by an unwarranted importation of modern considerations and concepts.[75] Although *Spirit in the World* does at times smack of Heideggerian pastiche, it relates itself to a range of modern thinkers, and Honecker is much more likely to be objecting to Rahner's tendency to eisegesis in general than to his Heideggerianism in particular.[76]

Spirit in the World (1939), organized around a discussion of Aquinas' metaphysics of knowledge, undertakes the constructive task of giving a phenomenological-theological description of man's constitutive openness to the divine. At the outset, Rahner contends that 'metaphysics is not the discovery of something one did not know beforehand; rather, it is the bringing-to-itself of the understanding that man always already has of himself by virtue of being human'.[77] This self-understanding always includes a pre-thematic apprehension of the horizon within which every individual thing appears, something which Rahner calls, in an odd Heideggerian-Thomist coinage, 'pre-apprehension (or "anticipation") of Being' (*Vorgriff auf esse*). This characteristic of the agent intellect is one particular manifestation of what Rahner later describes (in a no less awkward metaphysization of Heidegger) as the 'supernatural existential' (*übernatürliches Existential*) – the supposed existential orientation of all humans towards faith and grace which results from their creation in Christ, but is recognizable only from the standpoint of achieved salvation.[78] Rahner's theological inflections of Heidegger are well worth engaging with; however, they are also fraught with problems not only as interpretations of Heidegger, but also with regard both to their internal coherence and to the exact relationship between their early philosophical and their later theological iterations.[79]

I would therefore here like to look at a different (and less well-known) Thomist engagement with Heidegger, namely that of Edith Stein. Stein (1891–1942) had known Heidegger personally since 1916 through their respective work with Husserl. To her friend and colleague Roman Ingarden, she recounted a memorable 'religion-philosophical walk' in 1918 with Husserl and 'little Heidegger',[80] and continued to report on Heidegger's development in subsequent years, noting in particular the 'decisive' differences between him and Husserl.[81] She read *Being and Time* soon after it was published, and immediately commented to Roman Ingarden that the book made it obvious that Heidegger was 'something great, and runs rings round us all'.[82] She grappled with the work constructively first in an unpublished manuscript entitled 'The Significance of Phenomenology for a Worldview' (c. 1932),[83] and then in a 50-page précis and appraisal of 'Martin Heidegger's Philosophy of Existence' (1935–37), presented as an appendix to her own *magnum opus*, *Finite and Eternal Being*.[84] In 1931, Heidegger in turn read an early version of *Finite and Eternal Being* – initially composed under the title *Potency and Act* as a qualifying thesis for Freiburg – and invited Stein to what she described as a 'very stimulating and fruitful' discussion about it at his Freiburg home.[85] She was particularly grateful to Heidegger for working through the manuscript despite being aware that any submission as a qualifying thesis would be 'hopeless' in the prevailing political climate (as indeed it turned out to be).[86]

Stein praises the 'richness and force of the often truly illuminating analysis' in Heidegger's 'great fragment', which seems to her the contemporary book that has 'most strongly influenced the philosophical thought of today'.[87] However, Stein also thinks that this vibrancy and depth defies (rather than springs from) the assumption that 'guides and dominates the whole work', namely of the human as at once *solus ipse* and radically temporal.[88] With her friend and colleague Hedwig Conrad-Martius (whom she cites at length), Stein locates the greatest strength of Heidegger's work in his circumvention of 'all subjectivizing, relativizing and idealizing spectres' of modern philosophy towards a renewed, direct access to Being by means of an 'inimitably sharp and energetically developed conception of the human I' as a being that conducts itself vis-à-vis Being.[89] This Heideggerian 'I', as Stein reads it, is capable precisely of grasping 'not only its own Being, but also the Being of the world and the divine Being which grounds all created Being'.[90] Heidegger's own descriptions of human existence as 'thrown', as 'with others', and as 'fallen', in particular, inherently point beyond themselves to an ungrasped and ungraspable origin which, she concludes, is only revealed in Catholic dogma.[91] Heidegger's own refusal of the question of this origin, by contrast, is in Stein's estimation entirely dogmatic, motivated not by unbiased enquiry but rather by the 'axiomatic attempt to prove the temporality of Being', which leads him to 'bar any unfolding perspective on eternity' in his analyses.[92]

This dogmatism is particularly evident, for Stein, in Heidegger's discussion of death. This discussion, though in many ways the most profound aspect of *Being and Time*, must be queried both regarding its self-positioning vis-à-vis religious belief and regarding its own analysis. On the former, Heidegger contends that the ontological analysis of death as the end of human life implies no judgement on the question whether or not there is a life after death – indeed, that the 'ontic' question of life after death can only be asked after the 'full ontological essence' of death has been grasped.[93] But Heidegger's analysis cannot be said to leave open the possibility of life after death (except in an extremely attenuated sense of life) if it is already defined as the end of existence or Dasein. Consequently, Stein points out, the decisive question regarding the meaning of death, and therefore of Dasein, is precisely whether it is indeed the end of existence or merely the transition from one form of being to another. 'If it should turn out to be the case that the analysis of Dasein cannot provide an answer to this question', she concludes, 'then this would show precisely that the analysis of Dasein is not capable of resolving the question of the meaning of death, and therefore also cannot give sufficient information about the meaning of Dasein'.[94]

Such inadequacy is made likelier by the internal problems of Heidegger's analysis of death. One of these – relating to the possibility of a genuine engagement with death in the experience of the death of a loved one – has already been mentioned: In Heidegger's phenomenology, anticipation of death must fulfil a role that even on his own admission elsewhere, only love can fulfil, namely the *valorization* of the life threatened by death.[95] A similar perspective can be brought to bear on Heidegger's analysis of dread (*Angst*). Heidegger describes dread as at once dread *of* and dread *for* one's own being. Stein regards this as a sleight of hand, concealing two very different senses of 'one's own being':

> Is it the same aspect of being *of* which and *for* which one is afraid? That of which one is afraid is the possibility of not being attested by dread: It is the experience of the *nullity of our being*. That for which one is afraid – i.e. that with which man is concerned in his being – is being as *plenitude that one wants to preserve and not let go*. This goes unmentioned in Heidegger's entire analysis, and yet alone would be able to ground it. . . . Dread *of* not-being-able-to-be and dread *for* being-able-to-be [are] possible only because human existence [lit.: being] is participation in a plenitude which always slips through our fingers and is always being gained: life and death at the same time.[96]

Stein's critique is more sensitive than those of Delp or Przywara (discussed above) to Heidegger's method: Rather than faulting him for altering the traditional sense of 'being' or failing to adhere to a dogmatically assumed doctrine of analogy, her criticisms arise from phenomenological observation and conceptual analysis. Stein's conclusion is that Heidegger's analyses, insofar as they are phenomenologically correct, point beyond themselves to realities that exceed the grasp of phenomenology, but must nevertheless be acknowledged as conditions of the possibility of the phenomena at hand. This line of thought is not wholly alien to Heidegger: after all, for him death is just such a reality systematically exceeding the grasp of phenomenology.[97] What Stein seeks to show is that 'death' or 'nothing' can fulfil their function in his analysis only by a systematic ambiguity, which must be exposed.

For Stein, it is at this point that an appeal to revelation or dogma as a supplementary source of knowledge legitimately comes into play. If (Stein reasons) phenomenology requires a grounding it cannot encompass, and if an available set of (religious) teachings both accurately predicts the results of phenomenological enquiry and proffers such grounding, then the theologian is justified in heeding the metaphysical claims of that teaching.[98] This does not render phenomenological analysis superfluous within a theological enterprise. Rather, it tasks phenomenology with providing a 'grammar' of certain things that Christian doctrine asserts but does not describe. Thus, for example, Heidegger offers a grammatical analysis of 'life', and so also delineates what characteristics must be posited of the Christian idea of life after death if that life is to count as 'life' in any recognizably human sense. The most significant of these characteristics, on a Steinian reading, are relationality and orientation towards possibility, to which we will return in the conclusion.

As already indicated, this represents a return to Heidegger's own earliest approach to phenomenology as a method adequate to describing religious experience, and at the same time a contestation of Heidegger's conclusion that a rigorous pursuit of the phenomenological method ultimately does not support but exposes the inadequacy of a dogmatic insistence on the 'basic' nature of specifically *religious* experience. One of the most relevant differences between Stein's Thomist and Heidegger's Lutheran sensibilities in relation to their shared commitment to phenomenology is the Catholic affirmation – rejected or disregarded by most of Lutheran tradition – of God's continual presence within man. Responding to the question whether God is in all things, Aquinas argues that God, who is 'very Being by His own essence', is indeed not only present but 'innermost in each thing'; for to be is nothing other than to be continually preserved in being by God, 'as light is caused in the air by the sun as long as the air remains illuminated'.[99] Thus, whereas the Lutheran tradition has always stressed what Kierkegaard calls the 'infinite qualitative difference' between man and God – the immeasurable rift both between created and uncreated being and between human depravity and divine holiness – the Thomist tradition has tended to emphasize the God who is '*magis intimum cuilibet*'. While this idea remained in the background of late-nineteenth-century neo-Scholasticism, it regained its central position in the Thomist revival of Maritain, Gilson and Stein herself.

But this means that for a Thomist thinker like Stein, a phenomenological analysis of human existence risks not merely incompleteness but incoherence by bracketing the divine. This is the implicit argument running through *Finite and Eternal Being*, in which she seeks to show – beginning from Aquinas' *De ente et essentia* ('Of Being and Essence') and proceeding by way of phenomenological analysis – that 'the "I am" of the person only finds its fullness, its ultimate meaning and grounding, in the "I am" of the Eternal One'.[100] What Heidegger contributes, from this perspective, are certain correctives and emphases latent in the Thomist tradition, but buried by the Vatican I emphasis on a 'perennial philosophy'. In particular, Heidegger can be interpreted as suggesting an eschatological account of the ontological difference postulated by Aquinas. Where in neo-Scholastic thought, the creature is statically poised between 'is' and 'is not' – a middle position correlative with the difference between its being and its essence – in Heidegger, this ontological difference is not a question of being and essence but of eschatological diastasis.

This leads us to the final major strand in the theological reception of Heidegger, namely what may be called post-metaphysical theology.

Post-metaphysical theology

Unlike the other strands of theological reception, the appropriation of Heidegger for the development of a theology that 'overcomes' metaphysics has hardly found a footing in German scholarship, but has its two central loci in American and in French philosophical theology. (A significant exception is Heinrich Ott, discussed above in relation to Barth.[101]) In America, no one has done more than John Caputo and Merold Westphal to advocate the importance of Heidegger for such a theological project.[102] In France, Emanuel Levinas, Jean-Luc Marion, Michel Henry, Jean-Louis Chrétien, Jean-Yves Lacoste and others have all contributed significantly to an indigenous French 'theological' phenomenology that sees in Heideggerian philosophy the potential – stunted by Heidegger's own rejection of a transcendent horizon – for responding to the call of the divine without turning God into an idol by metaphysical speculation.[103] This strand of Heideggerian reception has developed into its own field of study, and in this brief section, I will offer no more than a few basic observations and (in the endnotes) references to further reading.

In a basic sense, Heidegger's later philosophy is a call to a particular attitude to the world – an attitude of responding and letting be, rather than forcefully enframing the world. This shift is linked to an interpretation of being as an elusive but distinct actor, simultaneously revealing and concealing itself to man, and thus both having and creating a history.[104] There is a structural similarity between this account of being (and therefore of thinking and speaking) and the Christian account of God and the Christian life. As Heinrich Ott in particular has shown, the history of salvation is structurally comparable to Heidegger's history of the disclosure of being, and the covenantal call of God, demanding a human response, is structurally comparable to Heidegger's conception of language as call and response. Often, theologians seeking to appropriate Heidegger for a theology centred not on metaphysical claims but on narrative, revelation, or mystical experience do little more than appeal to such structural parallels.[105]

However, although Heidegger's history of being or ascetic philosophy of mindfulness may be useful in recalling theologians to neglected strands within their own tradition, it is by no means news: non-metaphysical approaches to God exhibiting certain analogies to Heidegger's quasi-mystical vision have been present in the Christian tradition since its beginnings, not least in Origen, Gregory of Nyssa, Pseudo-Dionysius, Maximus the Confessor, John Scotus Eriugena and Meister Eckhart. At best, then, an analogical or associative reading of Heidegger's later philosophy can serve the theologian as a focusing lens on internal Christian resources, while at worst, it may be a skewed lens on those resources. The latter is especially true if, as readers such as John Caputo claim, Heidegger's history of being is itself the product of a deliberate 'transference of the categories of Christianity to early Greek texts', and thus the erection of 'a rival *Heilsgeschichte* to the biblical one'.[106] The strength of this aetiological claim will depend in large part on one's estimation of the continuing influence of Heidegger's early readings in mysticism and the New Testament (discussed in Chapters 2 and 3).

But an analogical theological reading of Heidegger's later philosophy faces a further problem, namely Heidegger's own repeated and forceful rejection of the identification of God not merely with a metaphysical or onto-theological *causa prima* or *summum ens*, but also with his own post-metaphysical understanding of being. Any theology that wishes rigorously to engage his teaching, rather than merely to find in it a convenient analogy for theology's own work, therefore has to reconsider not only its identification of God with the *esse subsistens* of traditional metaphysics – a renunciation readily undertaken in Emmanuel Levinas's God 'uncontaminated by being'[107]or Jean-Luc Marion's 'God without being'[108] –, but also its professed response to God as the self-giving being of the late Heidegger. What such a reconsideration would mean is far from clear: and indeed, Jean-Yves Lacoste concludes simply that 'theology has nothing to learn here, except that which it is absolutely not'.[109]

As already noted in Chapter 6, Heidegger insisted on the non-identity of God and being (on any construal of the two terms), but remained largely reticent about their roles or positions relative to each other. He merely specified that 'the experience of God and his revealedness . . . occurs in the dimension of being'[110] – in other words, that any genuine thought of God must be an elaboration of the more basic thought of 'divinity', which in turn arises from the experience of 'holiness', an experience itself rooted in the 'truth [i.e. openness] of being'.[111] A theology wishing to engage with Heidegger's view of God, rather than merely with his understanding of being in its structural parallels to the Christian God, would have to focus on the implications of this (broadly phenomenological) account of the constitution of 'God' for the believer. This requires a renewed consideration both of Heidegger's earliest work on mysticism and of his engagement with the anti-metaphysical tradition of Luther and Kierkegaard in the 1910s and 1920s. The latter is important for two reasons.

The first reason is the surface similarity between Luther's critique of metaphysics and Heidegger's later, 'post-metaphysical' thought. Scholars have long noted the affinity, or even genealogical descent, of the Kantian critique of metaphysics from the Protestant Reformation. Bultmann (here representative of many other theologians) extends this line to Heidegger's critique of metaphysics, noting in 1963 that 'a strange parallel' obtains between Heidegger's critique of onto-theology and the Protestant critique already familiar from Luther and revived and developed by dialectical theology.[112] However, if there are significant parallels, there are also large unresolved tensions. The Kantian critique is rooted entirely in the constitutive finitude of man and his faculties, whereas the Lutheran critique is rooted not primarily in man's finitude (which is a necessary consequence of his creation) but in his sinfulness (which is a contingent result of his free will). Luther never fully resolves the complex relationship between finitude and sinfulness, and modern theology has too often neglected the task of a rigorous engagement with this relationship. An important question for a theological engagement with Heidegger's critique of metaphysics, therefore, is its configuration of the relation of finitude and sinfulness vis-à-vis that of Luther and his tradition.[113]

The second reason, related to the first, is the centrality of revelation for any Lutheran (and more broadly Christian) understanding of God. We have already discussed the debate between the early Heidegger, Brunner and Barth concerning the role of revelation in any human knowledge of God – particularly vis-à-vis the question of an 'existential' or 'ontological' openness of man to God's call. In relation to the later Heidegger, this debate takes on a slightly different meaning. While in his early work, Heidegger regarded a phenomenological description of the 'ontological' constitution of human existence as a necessary prerequisite to any 'scientific' understanding of the possible relations of man to God, he retreated from any prescription of the relationship between philosophy (or thought) and theology (or faith) in his later thought.[114] However, it remains an open question whether this apophaticism vis-à-vis the Christian God is in fact compatible with Heidegger's (differently configured) apophaticism vis-à-vis his own 'last' or 'divine god'. Heidegger's projection of the appearance of the 'last god', on which, as he notes in his 1966 *Spiegel* interview, our 'salvation' depends, is rooted in a present experience of radical god-forsakenness and must (if it is to be authentic) bespeak a radical uncertainty whether or not such an appearance will take place. This apophatic eschatology may gesture towards the importance, for and within theology, of an eschatological attitude: a gesture picked up, for example, by Jean-Yves Lacoste.[115] Yet it is also in direct conflict with a Christian eschatology, which has its roots in nothing other than the revelation of God in Christ that has already taken place. Within Christian theology, the anticipated *parousia* is to be the fulfilment of God's appearance, within past history, as 'firstborn from the dead' (Col. 1.18). Even a resolutely eschatological theological orientation therefore cannot be radically apophatic. Any theological appropriation of Heidegger's post-metaphysical thought must take seriously that abiding conflict between his thought and Christian proclamation.

Conclusion

My aim, in this short book, has been to provide a reliable account of the role and developing understanding of theology in Martin Heidegger's thought, and of the main trajectories that theological engagements with his work have followed, particularly in the German- and English-speaking world. I hope to have shown, in particular, the importance of *eschatology* as an abiding category of Heidegger's thought both in relation to theology and in general. This seems to me a fertile field of both historical and systematic theological and philosophical enquiry, which calls for more work.[116]

As far as reception history is concerned, my aim has been to isolate the main pressure points in Heidegger's own work that have determined, and continue to determine, both critical and constructive theological responses to his thought. A key question within Heideggerian philosophy and, even more so, in theological engagements with Heidegger has always been whether his phenomenological concepts parasitically 'secularize' theological ideas, or whether they uncover the existential ground – itself more basic than the 'existentiell' or life-choice between faith and non-belief – of all human existence, including Christian thought and practice. The secularization critique was advanced in various forms from earliest days by both theologians (including Emil Brunner, Erich Przywara and Edith Stein) and philosophers (including Heidegger's student Löwith and his teacher Husserl). Heidegger consistently repudiated it, most fully in his 1947 '*Letter on Humanism*', and his work has often been hailed by its followers as an 'overcoming' of Christianity.

But such wholesale rhetoric conceals the particularity of Heidegger's theological-philosophical development, as well as of any particular theological image of the world. This book has therefore tried to follow out the complexity and volatility of Heidegger's engagement with Christian sources, as well as the wide variety of theological engagement with him. Doing so, I hope to have made clear both that Heidegger mounts a formidable case against certain basic assumptions of the theologies of his time, and that he cannot sustain his own claim to conceptual priority in its fullness, or not without serious sacrifices. It is considerably more interesting to find and test the pressure points that each exposes in the other than to cover up those pressure points by dismissing opposing claims out of hand. I hope, not least, to have inspired readers to continue this process and creatively harness its results.

Heidegger himself wished for an independent and critical *Mitdenken* (thinking-with) rather than the development of a Heidegger school or 'scholasticism'. His consistent emphasis on the need to *live* philosophically, encapsulated in the motto of his Collected Works – 'Paths, not Works' – are an encouragement to readers to pursue fearlessly the questions he raises, even if this leads to the need for different answers from his own, or indeed a reformulation of the questions. Such pursuit may lead back to Christian origins as well as forward to an unknown future: 'Paths of thought bear in them the mystery that we can walk them forward and backward – indeed, that often the way back alone leads forward.'[117]

Notes

1   Notable primary sources (in English or German) include Jarava Lal Mehta, *The Philosophy of Martin Heidegger* (New York: Harper & Row, 1971); Chung-yuan Chang, 'Taoist Philosophy and Heidegger's Poetic Thinking', *Indian Philosophical Quarterly* 4 (1977), pp. 305–11; Keiji Nishitani, *Religion and Nothingness* (trans. Jan van Bragt; Berkeley: University of California Press, 1982 [1961]), and *Was ist Religion?* (trans. Dora Fischer-Barnicol; Frankfurt a.M.: Insel Verlag, 2nd edn, 1986); Kah Kyung Cho, *Bewußtsein und Natursein: Phänomenologischer West-Ost-Diwan* (Freiburg: Alber, 1987); Koichi Tsujimura, 'Die Wahrheit des Seins und das absolute Nichts', in Ôhashi Ryôsuke (ed.), *Die Philosophie der Kyoto-Schule: Texte und Einführungen* (Freiburg: Alber, 1990), pp. 441–54; as well as the memoirs in Neske (ed.), *Erinnerung an Martin Heidegger*, pp. 65–71, 119–30, 165–72, 216–17, 232–3. Notable secondary sources include Graham Parkes (ed.), *Heidegger and Asian Thought* (Honolulu: University of Hawaii, 1987); Hartmut Buchner (ed.),

Japan und Heidegger (Sigmaringen: Thorbecke, 1989); Gwang-Il Seo, 'Die Heidegger-Rezeption in Korea: mit einem Einblick in die Probleme der Heidegger-Forschung und Interpretation' [Düsseldorf, unpublished doctoral thesis, 1991]; George Pattison, *Agnosis: Theology in the Void* (London: Macmillan, 1996), pp. 108–37; Rolf Elberfeld, 'Heidegger und das ostasiatische Denken: Annäherungen zwischen fremden Welten', in Dieter Thomä (ed.), *Heidegger Handbuch* (Stuttgart: J. B. Metzler, 2003); and particularly the collection *Heidegger und das ostasiatische Denken* (Heidegger-Jahrbuch 7), eds. Alfred Denker, Holger Zaborowski, Georg Stenger, Ryôsuke Ohashi, and Shunsuke Kadowaki (Freiburg: Karl Alber Verlag, 2013).

2 Other Japanese scholars attending Heidegger's seminars in the 1920s and 1930s included Hajime Tanabe, Kiysoshi Miki, Shuzo Kuki, Tetsuro Watsuji, Shin'ichi Hisamatsu and Koichi Tsujimaru (see Elberfeld, 'Heidegger und das ostasiatische Denken', pp. 469–74).

3 See Paul Shih-yi Hsiao, 'Heidegger and our Translation of the *Tao Te Ching*', in Parkes (ed.), *Heidegger and Asian Thought*, pp. 93–103.

4 GA 8, 136.

5 'Aus einem Gespräch von der Sprache: Zwischen einem Japaner und einem Fragenden' (1953/54), in GA 12, 79–145.

6 Quoted in Willfred Hartig, *Die Lehre des Budda und Heidegger* (Constance: University of Constance Research Reports, 1997), p. 269.

7 Kuhlmann, 'Krisis der Theologie', *Zeitschrift für Theologie und Kirche* 12 (1931), pp. 123–46; p. 144. Kuhlmann, a forceful and lucid voice in the debate about theology and philosophy conducted in the late 1920s and early 1930s, is nowadays almost entirely forgotten, and very little can be ascertained about him. He is likely to have been a student of Eberhard Grisebach in Jena, where he earned his doctorate with a thesis on Friedrich Brunstäd and Paul Tillich (*Brunstäd und Tillich: Zum Problem einer Theonomie der Kultur* [Tübingen: Mohr Siebeck, 1928]). He later resided in Berlin, but whether or not he was attached to the university there is not clear. His last extant publications date from 1935.

8 Stephen Mulhall's *Faith and Reason* (London: Duckworth, 1994) remains one of the most incisive accounts of Kierkegaard's problematization of the language of metaphysics in the context of faith.

9 Barth to Brunner, 13 March 1925, in *Barth/Brunner*, pp. 114–18; p. 116.

10 *Sein und Zeit* (1927), GA 2, §62, 306n. 1.

11 Recalled twice by Heidegger's student Hans-Georg Gadamer: in
Philosophische Lehrjahre, p. 37, and in 'Marburger Theologie', p. 29.
Thurneysen commented to Barth about the occasion that Heidegger
had been generally approving of Thurneysen's lecture, but had
questioned 'our relation to Kant, whom he counts with Aristotle,
and whom the young Luther renounced'; Thurneysen to Barth,
21 February 1924, in *Barth/Thurneysen* II. 229. Thurneysen's lecture
was published as 'Schrift und Offenbarung', *Zwischen den Zeiten*
6 (1924), pp. 3–30.

12 *Sein und Zeit* (1927), GA 2, §3, 10 (emphasis removed).

13 Heidegger to Bultmann, 14 November 1931, in *Bultmann/Heidegger*,
pp. 171–3; p. 172.

14 *Sein und Zeit* (1927), GA 2, §62, 306.

15 Ibid., §38, 180.

16 Ibid.,§62, 306n. 1.

17 See e.g. Barth's letter to Brunner dated 13 March 1925, in
Barth/Brunner, pp. 114–18; p. 116 (quoted in Chapter 5 above).

18 See esp. Heinrich Ott, *Denken und Sein: Der Weg Martin Heideggers
und der Weg der Theologie* (Zollikon: Evangelischer Verlag, 1959).

19 See the section 'Post-Metaphysical Theology' below. The most
thorough discussion of Ott in relation to both Heidegger and
theology remains J. Robinson and J. Cobb (eds.), *The Later
Heidegger and Theology* (New York: Harper & Row, 1963).

20 'Podiumsdiskussion in Chicago (25./26.4.1962)', in Barth, *Gespräche
1959–1962*, pp. 231–79; pp. 242–3.

21 See esp. Eberhard Jüngel, 'Der Schritt zurück: Eine
Auseinandersetzung mit der Heidegger-Deutung Heinrich Otts',
Zeitschrift für Theologie und Kirche 58 (1961), pp. 104–22; Jüngel,
*Gottes Sein ist im Werden: Verantwortliche Rede vom Sein Gottes
bei Karl Barth, eine Paraphrase* (Tübingen: Mohr Siebeck, 1965);
Timothy Stanley, *Protestant Metaphysics after Karl Barth and Martin
Heidegger* (London: SCM, 2010).

22 Heidegger's Marburg student Hans-Georg Gadamer notes in his 1977
memoir that a 'newly acquired edition of Thomas' was the 'symbol
of Heidegger's entrance at the Protestant Marburg'; *Philosophische
Lehrjahre*, pp. 19–20. Some notable, more recent interpretations
of the relation of Heidegger's fundamental ontology to Scholastic
philosophy are John D. Caputo, *Heidegger and Aquinas: An Essay*

on *Overcoming Metaphysics* (New York: Fordham University
Press, 1982), and S. J. McGrath, *The Early Heidegger & Medieval
Philosophy: Phenomenology for the Godforsaken* (Washington:
Catholic University of America Press, 2006).

23 Munich: Kösel & Pustet, 1932.

24 Przywara, 'Drei Richtungen der Phänomenologie', *Stimmen der Zeit*
115 (1928), pp. 252–64; p. 252. Hedwig Conrad-Martius offers a
similar analysis in 'Sein und Zeit' (Review), *Philosophischer Anzeiger*
8 (1933), p. 185.

25 Alfred Delp, *Tragische Existenz: Zur Philosophie Martin Heideggers*
(Freiburg: Herder, 1931). 'Tragic existence' became a popular
term and a convenient shortcut in critically describing Heidegger's
philosophy, well beyond the borders of the German language. See e.g.
H. Thielemans SJ, 'Existence tragique: la métaphysique du Nazism',
Nouvelle Revue Théologique 63, 6 (1936), pp. 561–79.

26 Karl Barth, *Church Dogmatics* II/1: *The Doctrine of God* (trans.
G. W. Bromiley and T. F. Torrance; Edinburgh: T&T Clark, 1957),
p. 237, summarizing the presentation of the Thomistic use of *analogia*
in Johannes Andreas Quenstedt, *Theologia didactico-polemica sive
systema theologicum* (Wittenberg: Schumacher, 1685), I.8.2.1; cf.
Thomas Aquinas, *Summa Theologiae* 1.13.3.

27 Similar arguments are reiterated by many contemporaneous critics,
perhaps most famously Karl Löwith; see e.g. his 'Les implications
politiques de la philosophie de l'existence chez Heidegger', *Les Temps
Modernes* 14 (1946), pp. 343–60; p. 345.

28 'Was ist Metaphysik?' (1929), GA 9, 35.

29 Delp, *Tragische Existenz*, p. 114.

30 Note C. S. Lewis' similar, though more appreciative, analysis of the
'cultural myth' (as opposed to the scientific theory) of evolution in
'The Funeral of a Great Myth', *Christian Reflections*, ed. Walter
Hooper (Grand Rapids: Eerdmans, 1967), pp. 82–93.

31 Przywara, 'Drei Richtungen', p. 262. On the unity of being and
essence in God, see e.g. Thomas Aquinas, *Summa Theologiae* 1.2.1.

32 Przywara, 'Drei Richtungen', p. 262.

33 Ibid., p. 264.

34 Heidegger, *Sein und Zeit* (1927), GA 2, §9, 42.

35 L. P. Hemming, in private correspondence with the author.

36 See ESGA 11/12, 483.

37 See, most recently, Peter S. Dillard, *Heidegger and Philosophical Atheology: A Neo-Scholastic Critique* (London: Continuum, 2009).

38 See, for example, John Milbank, 'Only Theology Overcomes Metaphysics', in Milbank (ed.), *The Word Made Strange* (Oxford: Blackwell, 1997), pp. 36–54; John Milbank and Catherine Pickstock, *Truth in Aquinas* (London: Routledge, 2001), ch. 2; Conor Cunningham, *Genealogy of Nihilism: Philosophies of Nothing and the Difference of Theology* (London: Routledge, 2002), ch. 6; S. J. McGrath, *The Early Heidegger & Medieval Philosophy: Phenomenology for the Godforsaken* (Washington: Catholic University of America Press, 2006); S. J. McGrath, *Heidegger: A (Very) Critical Introduction* (Grand Rapids: Eerdmans, 2008). These readings have also met with significant counter-critiques; see esp. L. P. Hemming (ed.), *Radical Orthodoxy? – A Catholic Enquiry* (Farnborough: Ashgate, 2000); L. P. Hemming, *Heidegger's Atheism: The Refusal of a Theological Voice* (Notre Dame, IN: University of Notre Dame Press, 2002).

39 Heidegger, *Being and Time* (trans. John Macquarrie and Edward Robinson; Oxford: Blackwell, 1962).

40 '*Wege – nicht Werke*' is the motto, chosen by Heidegger, that prefaces the *Gesamtausgabe* (complete edition) of his work (see GA 1, unnumbered opening page).

41 Interpreters like Stephen Mulhall go as far as suggesting that its incompleteness is ultimately systematic rather than accidental, enacting the constitutive incompleteness of all phenomenological analysis. See e.g. Mulhall, *Heidegger and Being and Time* (London: Routledge, 2nd edn, 2005), ch. 8; Mulhall, 'Human Mortality: Heidegger on How to Portray the Impossible Possibility of Dasein', in Hubert L. Dreyfus and Mark A. Wrathall (eds.), *A Companion to Heidegger* (Oxford: Blackwell, 2005), pp. 297–310.

42 Tillich, *The Courage to Be* (New Haven: Yale University Press, 2000 [1952]), p. 148. My thanks to Timothy Stanley for drawing my attention to this.

43 See John Macquarrie, *An Existentialist Theology: A Comparison of Heidegger and Bultmann* (London: SCM Press, 1965), p. 30.

44 Macquarrie, *Existentialist Theology*, p. 103.

45 See esp. Tillich, *Systematic Theology* (3 vols; London: Nisbet, 1953–64), vol. 2, pp. 19–43. This is not an exclusively theological view at the time: compare, for example, the very similar analysis in Otto Friedrich Bollnow, 'Existenzphilosophie', in Nicolai Hartmann (ed.), *Systematische Philosophie* (Berlin: Kohlhammer,

1942), pp. 302–430. (Interestingly, Heidegger references this essay – no doubt to some extent polemically – as 'an attack' on existential philosophy; see 'Das Rektorat 1933/34' (1945), GA 16, 394.)

46 Gerhardt Kuhlmann, 'Zum theologischen Problem der Existenz: Fragen an Rudolf Bultmann', *Zeitschrift für Theologie und Kirche* 10 (1929), pp. 28–57; pp. 47–52.

47 See also Robinson and Cobb (eds.), *The Later Heidegger and Theology*, particularly Schubert Ogden's chapter, 'The Understanding of Theology in Ott and Bultmann' (157–76), for a discussion whether later theologians 'go beyond' or 'fall behind' Bultmann in his theological interpretation of Heidegger.

48 'Die Eschatologie des Johannes-Evangeliums', *Zwischen den Zeiten* 6 (1928), pp. 4–22; p. 14. Elements of 'the old dramatic eschatology', as they appear e.g. in Jn 5.28f and 6.54, are ascribed to a later redactor. See 'Eschatologie des Johannes-Evangeliums', pp. 4–5.

49 A representative list of references is given in 'Eschatologie des Johannes-Evangeliums', 5n.

50 Bultmann, 'Eschatologie des Johannes-Evangeliums', p. 6.

51 Ibid., p. 6.

52 Ibid., p. 8.

53 Ibid., pp. 8–9.

54 Ibid., p. 8.

55 Ibid., p. 9.

56 Rudolf Bultmann, 'Die Geschichtlichkeit des Daseins und der Glaube: Antwort an Gerhardt Kuhlmann', *Zeitschrift für Theologie und Kirche* 11 (1930), pp. 229–64.

57 Bultmann, 'Die Geschichtlichkeit des Daseins und der Glaube', p. 346.

58 Ibid., p. 351 (emphasis added).

59 Ibid., p. 351.

60 Ibid., pp. 351–2.

61 See e.g. Søren Kierkegaard, *Eighteen Upbuilding Discourses* (trans. H. and E. Hong Princeton: Princeton University Press, 1990).

62 Stanley Cavell, 'Knowing and Acknowledging', in Idem, *Must We Mean What We Say?* (Cambridge: Cambridge University Press, 1969), pp. 238–66. For a philosophical-theological assessment of Cavell's concepts of acknowledgment and scepticism, see Judith (Tonning) Wolfe, 'Acknowledging a Hidden God: A Theological Critique of Stanley Cavell on Scepticism', *Heythrop Journal* 48, 3 (2007), pp. 384–405.

63 This recognition – or acknowledgement – is salutary when framed in
a Cavellian way, i.e. when the primacy of neighbourliness is assumed,
and the threat is, rather, the denial of separateness and the arrogation
of complete knowledge of the other; see e.g. Cavell, *Disowning
Knowledge*, particularly chapters 2 and 6. But the premises of
Heidegger's analysis are very different.

64 Bultmann, 'Die Geschichtlichkeit des Daseins und der Glaube', p. 358.

65 Ibid., p. 359.

66 Ibid., p. 353.

67 Aquinas, *Summa Theologiae* 1–2.114.2. The identification of
beatitude and communion with God (deification) is most explicitly
made in 1.12.2 and 3.9.3 ad 3.

68 Aquinas, *Summa Theologiae* 1.8.1 (see also 1.4.1 ad 3).

69 See esp. Max Müller, *Existenzphilosophie: Von der Metaphysik zur
Metahistorik* (Freiburg: Karl Alber Verlag, 4th edn, 1986); John Caputo,
Heidegger and Aquinas: An Essay on Overcoming Metaphysics
(New York: Fordham University Press, 1982), esp. 211–88.

70 Karl Rahner, [untitled], in Richard Wisser (ed.), *Martin Heidegger in
Gespräch* (Freiburg: Alber, 1970), pp. 48–9.

71 The Karl Rahner-Archiv Innsbruck holds the manuscripts of Rahner's
student notes on Heidegger's seminars on Hegel's *Phenomenology of
Spirit* (WS 1934/35) and Leibniz' concept of 'world' (WS 1935/36), as
well as his 'Introduction to Metaphysics' (SS 1935).

72 See Ott, *Heidegger*, p. 260.

73 The title of Rahner's theological dissertation was 'Der Ursprung
der Kirche aus der Seitenwunde Jesu Christi nach den Aussagen der
Kirchenväter' ('The Source of the Church in the Side Wound of Jesus
Christ according to the Church Fathers').

74 See e.g. Herbert Vorgrimler, *Understanding Karl Rahner: An
Introduction to his Life and Thought* (London: SCM, 1986 [1985]);
Thomas Sheehan, *Karl Rahner: The Philosophical Foundations*
(Athens: Ohio University Press, 1987), p. 6.

75 Quoted in Vincent Berning, *Martin Honecker: Auf dem Wege von der
Logik zur Metaphysik* (Weilheim: Gustav-Siewerth-Akademie, 2003),
p. 401.

76 Honecker's intellectual stature and generosity, both in this context
and generally, have recently been argued in convincing detail by
Vincent Berning in *Martin Honecker: Auf dem Wege von der Logik
zur Metaphysik* (Weilheim-Bierbronnen: Gustav-Siewerth-Akademie,
2003).

77 Karl Rahner, *Geist in Welt* (Innsbruck: F. Rauch, 1939), p. 17.

78 See e.g. Rahner, 'Antwort (Ein Weg zur Bestimmung des Verhältnisses von Natur und Gnade)', *Orientierung* 14 (1950), pp. 141–5; rpt. in amended form as 'Über das Verhältnis von Natur und Gnade', in Rahner, *Schriften zur Theologie* (16 vols; Einsiedeln: Benziger, 1954–84), vol. 1, pp. 323–45. An earlier, philosophical 'version' of the supernatural existential is already developed in Rahner, *Hörer des Wortes: Zur Grundlegung einer Religionsphilosophie* (Munich: Kösel, 1941).

79 See Hansjürgen Verweyen, 'Wie wird ein Existential übernatürlich?: Zu einem Grundproblem der Anthropologie Karl Rahners', *Trier theologische Zeitschrift* 95 (1986), pp. 115–31; Karen Kilby, *Karl Rahner: Philosophy and Theology* (London: Routledge, 2004).

80 Edith Stein to Roman Ingarden, 8 June 1918, in ESGA 4, 85–6; p. 85.

81 Stein to Ingarden, 9 October 1926, in ESGA 4, 172. See also her letters of 15 October 1921 (ESGA 4, 144), 24 October 1926 (ESGA 4, 174), and 2 October 1927 (ESGA 4, 185). The substance of Stein's analysis, collected as 'Die weltanschauliche Bedeutung der Phänomenologie' (1932), was published posthumously in Stein, *Welt und Person* (Freiburg: Herder, 1962), pp. 1–17.

82 Stein to Ingarden, 2 October 1927, in ESGA 4, 185. See also ESGA 11/12, 7.

83 Stein, 'Die weltanschauliche Bedeutung der Phänomenologie' (1932), in Stein (ed.), *Welt und Person* (Freiburg: Herder, 1962), pp. 1–17.

84 *Endliches und ewiges Sein: Versuch eines Aufstiegs zum Sinn des Seins*, though completed in 1938, could not be published during Stein's lifetime because of National Socialist restrictions on Jewish publications. It was published posthumously, with the Heidegger appendix, as volume 1 of Edith Steins Werke, eds. Lucy Gelber and Romaeus Leuven [Freiburg: Herder, 1951]). The appendix was dropped from subsequent re-prints, and first re-inserted in 2006 as 'Anhang: Martin Heideggers Existenzphilosophie' in ESGA 11/12, 445–99.

85 Stein to Ingarden, 15 December 1931, in ESGA 4, 225–6.

86 Stein made four such applications between 1919 (under Husserl in Göttingen) and 1932 (in Freiburg), but was rejected on account of her sex and, later, her Jewishness, on all occasions. In 1919, Husserl concluded his reference letter with the warm but hopeless sentence: 'Should academic careers be opened to ladies, I would recommend Miss Dr Stein above all others and in warmest terms for a licence to lecture'; Husserl to the Habilitation Committee Göttingen, 6 February 1919; at the Edith Stein-Archiv Cologne.

87   Stein, 'Martin Heideggers Existenzphilosophie', ESGA 11/12, 445.

88   Ibid., 471.

89   Ibid., 481, quoting Hedwig Conrad-Martius, 'Sein und Zeit' (review), *Philosophischer Anzeiger* 8 (1933), p. 185.

90   Stein, 'Martin Heideggers Existenzphilosophie', ESGA 11/12, 481.

91   Ibid., 465–70.

92   Ibid., 482.

93   Heidegger, *Sein und Zeit* (1927), GA 2, §49, 247–8.

94   Stein, 'Martin Heideggers Existenzphilosophie', ESGA 11/12, 472.

95   See Chapter 3 above.

96   Stein, 'Martin Heideggers Existenzphilosophie', ESGA 11/12, 473.

97   See esp. Mulhall, *Heidegger and Being and Time*, ch. 4.

98   There is an interesting similarity between this claim and G. K. Chesterton's description of the church as 'a truth-telling thing' in *Orthodoxy* (London: John Lane, 1909), p. 291 ('Authority and the Adventurer').

99   Thomas Aquinas, *Summa Theologiae* 1.8.1 (see also 1.4.1 ad 3).

100   Stein, *Endliches und ewiges Sein*, ESGA 11/12, xviii.

101   Other possible exceptions among significant theologians of the last generations are Bernhard Welte (1906–83) and Eberhard Jüngel (born 1934). However, Welte did not derive a particular programme from Heidegger, but engaged in a looser and ever-shifting 'thinking-with' the questions raised by the philosopher and their relevance to theology. His reflections on Heidegger, which span a working career that unfolded in parallel with Heidegger's last years in Freiburg and long semi-retirement, are well-represented by the material collected in the second part of *Martin Heidegger/Bernhard Welte: Briefe und Begegnungen*, eds. Alfred Denker and Holger Zaborowski (Stuttgart: Klett-Cotta Verlag, 2003). Jüngel's theology of love, meanwhile, is much more loosely indebted to the late Heidegger (who is only one among many influences); see particularly his *God's Being Is in Becoming: The Trinitarian Being of God in the Theology of Karl Barth: A Paraphrase* (London: T&T Clark, 2004 [1965]) and *God as the Mystery of the World: On the Foundation of the Theology of the Crucified One in the Dispute between Theism and Atheism* (Grand Rapids: Eerdmans, 1983 [1977]).

102   See esp. John Caputo, *The Mystical Element in Heidegger's Thought* (Athens, OH: Ohio University Press, 1978), *Heidegger and Aquinas: An Essay on Overcoming Metaphysics* (New York: Fordham

University Press, 1982), *Radical Hermeneutics* (Bloomington: Indiana University Press, 1987), and 'Who Comes after the God of Metaphysics?', in John Caputo (ed.), *The Religious* (Oxford: Blackwell, 2002), pp. 1–22; Caputo, Mark Dooley, and Michael Scanlon (eds.), *Questioning God* (Bloomington: Indiana University Press, 2001); Merold Westphal, *Overcoming Onto-theology: Toward a Postmodern Christian Faith* (New York: Fordham University Press, 2001), and *Transcendence and Self-Transcendence* (Indianapolis: Indiana University Press, 2004). Other notable authors in English include Jeffrey Bloechl and Richard Kearney; see e.g. Jeffrey Bloechl, *Liturgy of the Neighbor: Emmanuel Levinas and the Religion of Responsibility* (Pittsburgh: Duquesne University Press, 2000), and Bloechl (ed.), *Religious Experience and the End of Metaphysics* (Indianapolis: Indiana University Press, 2003); Richard Kearney, *Anatheism: Returning to God After God* (New York: Columbia University Press, 2009). See also L. P. Hemming, *Heidegger's Atheism: The Refusal of a Theological Voice* (Notre Dame: University of Notre Dame Press, 2002).

103   See e.g. Emanuel Levinas, *Totalité et Infini: Essai sur l'extériorité* (The Hague: Martinus Nijhoff, 1961), and *Autrement qu'êtreou au-delà de l'essence* (The Hague: Martinus Nijhoff, 1974); Jean-Luc Marion, *Dieu sans l'être* (Paris: PUF, 1982), and *Étant donné: Essai d'une phénoménologie de la donation* (Paris: PUF, 1997); Michel Henry, *C'est moi la Vérité: Pour une philosophie du christianisme* (Paris: Éditions du Seuil, 1996), *Incarnation: Une philosophie de la chair* (Paris: Éditions du Seuil, 2000), and *Paroles du Christ* (Paris: Éditions du Seuil, 2002); Jean-Louis Chrétien, *L'appel et la réponse* (Paris: Éditions de Minuit, 1992); Jean-Yves Lacoste, *Expérience et absolu: Questions disputés sur l'humanité de l'homme* (Paris: PUF, 1994) and *La phénoménalité de Dieu: Neuf etudes* (Paris: Éditions du Cerf, 2008). The classic discussion of the 'theological turn' in French phenomenology is Dominique Janicaud (ed.), *Phenomenology and the Theological Turn: The French Debate* (New York: Fordham University Press, 2001).

104   This shift is marked by Heidegger's preference (from the mid-1930s) for the Hölderlinian spelling *Seyn*, often rendered in English by the Middle English spelling 'beyng'.

105   See, among many other examples, William J. Richardson, 'Heidegger and Theology', *Theological Studies* 26, 1 (1965), pp. 86–100; Thomas O'Meara, 'Heidegger and His Origins: Theological Perspectives', *Theological Studies* 47 (1986), pp. 205–26. John Caputo, in *The Mystical Element in Heidegger's Thought*,

Chapters 4 and 5, concludes that the similarities between Heidegger and Meister Eckhart are structural rather than substantial: an 'analogy of proportionality' obtains between the relation of being and thought (or Dasein) on the one hand, and God and the soul on the other (see p. 144). Unlike many other theologians, Caputo reads this analogy critically rather than purely positively.

106   John Caputo, 'Heidegger and Theology', *Cambridge Companion to Heidegger*, p. 336. See also Caputo, *The Mystical Element in Heidegger's Thought* (1978) and Caputo, 'Demythologizing Heidegger: *Aletheia* and the History of Being', *Review of Metaphysics* 41 (1988), pp. 519–46.

107   Emmanuel Levinas, *Autrement qu'êtreou au-delà de l'essence* (The Hague: Martinus Nijhoff, 1974), preface.

108   Jean-Luc Marion, *Dieu sans l'être* (Paris: PUF, 1982).

109   Jean-Yves Lacoste, 'Martin Heidegger', in Lacoste (ed.), *Encyclopedia of Christian Theology* (3 vols; London: Routledge, 2005), vol. 2, pp. 677–80; p. 679.

110   'Gespräch mit Martin Heidegger' (1951), GA 15, 436.

111   Heidegger, 'Brief über den Humanismus' (1946), GA 9, 351.

112   'Reflexionen zum Denkweg Martin Heideggers nach der Darstellung von Otto Pöggeler' (1963), published in *Bultmann/Heidegger*, pp. 305–17; pp. 314–15.

113   Indirect preliminary guidance may be found in Stephen Mulhall's *Philosophical Myths of the Fall* (Princeton: Princeton University Press, 2007), esp. ch. 2.

114   See e.g. Heidegger's 1970 preface to his 1927 lecture 'Phenomenology and Theology' (in GA 9, 45–6).

115   See esp. Lacoste, *Note sur le temps: Essai sur les raisons de la mémoire et de l'espérance* (Paris: PUF, 1990). See also J. P. Manoussakis and Neal DeRoo (eds.), *Phenomenology & Eschatology* (Aldershot: Ashgate, 2009), esp. the essays by Jeffrey Bloechl, Kevin Hart, Richard Kearney, Jean-Yves Lacoste, and Claude Romano; as well as Wolfhart Pannenberg, *Theology and the Kingdom of God* (trans. R. J. Neuhaus; Philadelphia: Westminster Press, 1969).

116   My *Heidegger's Eschatology*, particularly its concluding chapter, begin this task, which I will continue to pursue in future work.

117   Heidegger, 'Aus einem Gespräch von der Sprache' (1959), GA 12, 94.

BIBLIOGRAPHY

Works by Heidegger

Volumes of the Gesamtausgabe:

GA 1   *Frühe Schriften* (1912–1916), ed. Friedrich-Wilhelm von Herrmann (Frankfurt: Klostermann, 1978).
English translation:
'The Problem of Reality in Modern Philosophy' (1912), trans. Philip Bossert and John van Buren, in John van Buren (ed.), *Supplements: From the Earliest Essays to Being and Time and Beyond* (Albany: SUNY Press, 2002), pp. 39–48.
'[Conclusion to] The Theory of Categories and Meaning in Duns Scotus' (1916), trans. John van Buren, in *Supplements*, pp. 61–8.

GA 4   *Erläuterungen zu Hölderlins Dichtung* (1936–1968), ed. Friedrich-Wilhelm von Herrmann (Frankfurt: Klostermann, 2nd edn, 1996).
ET: *Elucidations of Hölderlin's Poetry* (trans. Keith Hoeller; New York: Humanity Books, 2000).

GA 5   *Holzwege* (1935–1946), ed. Friedrich-Wilhelm von Herrmann (Frankfurt: Klostermann, 2nd edn, 2003).
ET: *Off the Beaten Track* (trans. Julian Young; Cambridge: Cambridge University Press, 2002).

GA 6.1 *Nietzsche I* (1936–1939), ed. Brigitte Schillbach (Frankfurt: Klostermann, 1996).
ET: *Nietzsche: Volumes I and II* (trans. David Farrell Krell; San Francisco: Harper & Row, 1979).

GA 6.2 *Nietzsche II* (1939–1946), ed. Brigitte Schillbach (Frankfurt: Klostermann, 1997).
ET: *Nietzsche: Volumes I and II* (trans. David Farrell Krell; San Francisco: Harper & Row, 1979).

GA 7 *Vorträge und Aufsätze* (1936–1953), ed. Friedrich-Wilhelm von
      Herrmann (Frankfurt: Klostermann, 2000).
      In English:
      'Overcoming Metaphysics' (1936), in *The End of Philosophy*
      (trans. Joan Stambaugh; Chicago: University of Chicago Press,
      2003), pp. 84–110.
      'The Thing' (1950), in *Poetry, Language, Thought* (trans. and ed.
      Albert Hofstadter; New York: HarperCollins, 1971), pp. 161–84.
      'Building Dwelling Thinking' (1951), in *Poetry, Language,
      Thought*, pp. 141–60.
      '. . . Poetically Man Dwells . . .' (1951), in *Poetry, Language,
      Thought*, pp. 209–27.
      'The Question Concerning Technology' (1953), in *The Question
      Concerning Technology, and other Essays* (trans. and ed. William
      Lovitt; New York: Harper & Row, 1977), pp. 3–35.
      'Science and Reflection' (1953), in *The Question Concerning
      Technology*, pp. 155–78.

GA 8 *Was heißt Denken?* (1951–1952), ed. Paola-Ludovika Coriando
      (Frankfurt: Klostermann, 2002).
      ET: *What is Called Thinking?* (trans. John Glenn Gray;
      New York: Harper & Row, 1968).

GA 9 *Wegmarken* (1919–1961), ed. Friedrich-Wilhelm von Herrmann
      (Frankfurt: Klostermann, 2nd edn, 1996).
      ET: *Pathmarks* (trans. William McNeill; Cambridge: Cambridge
      University Press, 1998).

GA 10 *Der Satz vom Grund* (1955–1956), ed. Petra Jaeger (Frankfurt:
      Klostermann, 1997).
      ET: *The Principle of Reason* (trans. Reginal Lilly; Bloomington:
      Indiana University Press, 1996).

GA 11 *Identität und Differenz* (1955–1957), ed. Friedrich-Wilhelm von
      Herrmann (Frankfurt: Klostermann, 2nd edn, 2006).
      ET: *Identity and Difference* (trans. Joan Stambaugh; Chicago:
      University of Chicago Press, 2002).

GA 12 *Unterwegs zur Sprache* (1950–1959), ed. Friedrich-Wilhelm von
      Herrmann (Frankfurt: Klostermann, 1985).
      ET: *On the Way to Language* (trans. Peter Hertz; New York:
      Harper & Row, 1971).

GA 13 *Aus der Erfahrung des Denkens* (1910–1976), ed. Hermann
      Heidegger (Frankfurt: Klostermann, 2nd edn, 2002).

GA 14 *Zur Sache des Denkens* (1962–64), ed. Friedrich-Wilhelm von
      Herrmann (Frankfurt: Klostermann, 2007).

ET: *On Time and Being* (trans. Joan Stambaugh; Chicago: University of Chicago Press, 2002).

GA 15 *Seminare* (1951–1973), ed. Curd Ochwadt (Frankfurt: Klostermann, 2nd edn, 2005).

GA 16 *Reden und andere Zeugnisse eines Lebensweges* (1910–1976), ed. Hermann Heidegger (Frankfurt: Klostermann, 2000).
In English:
'Per mortem ad vitam: Thoughts on Johannes Jörgensen's *Lies of Life and Truth of Life*' (1910), trans. John Protevi and John van Buren. *Supplements.*
'The Self-Assertion of the German University' (1933). *The Heidegger Controversy: A Critical Reader* (trans. Maria Alter and John Caputo, ed. Richard Wolin; Cambridge, MA: MIT Press, 1993), pp. 29–39.
'[Appeal to] German Students' (1933), in *The Heidegger Controversy*, pp. 46–7.

GA 18 *Grundbegriffe der aristotelischen Philosophie* (SS 1924), ed. Mark Michalski (Frankfurt: Klostermann, 2002).
ET: *Basic Concepts of Aristotelian Philosophy* (trans. Robert Metcalf and Mark Tanzer; Bloomington: Indiana University Press, 2009).

GA 20 *Prolegomena zur Geschichte des Zeitbegriffs* (SS 1925), ed. Petra Jaeger (Frankfurt: Klostermann, 2nd edn, 1988).
ET: *History of the Concept of Time* (trans. Theodore Kisiel; Bloomington: Indiana University Press, 2009).

GA 21 *Logik: Die Frage nach der Wahrheit* (WS 1925/26), ed. Walter Biemel (Frankfurt: Klostermann, 2nd edn, 1995).
ET: *Logic: The Question of Truth* (trans. Thomas Sheehan; Bloomington: Indiana University Press, 2010).

GA 29/30 *Die Grundbegriffe der Metaphysik: Welt–Endlichkeit–Einsamkeit* (WS 1929/30), ed. Friedrich-Wilhelm von Herrmann (Frankfurt: Klostermann, 3rd edn, 2004).
ET: *The Fundamental Concepts of Metaphysics: World, Finitude, Solitude* (trans. William McNeill and Nicholas Walker; Bloomington: Indiana University Press, 1995).

GA 39 *Hölderlins Hymnen 'Germanien' und 'Der Rhein'* (WS 1934/35), ed. Susanne Ziegler (Frankfurt: Klostermann, 3rd edn, 1999).

GA 40 *Einführung in die Metaphysik* (SS 1935), ed. Petra Jaeger (Frankfurt: Klostermann, 1983).
ET: *Introduction to Metaphysics*, trans. Gregory Fried and Richard Polt (New Haven: Yale University Press, 2000).

GA 42 *Schelling: Vom Wesen der menschlichen Freiheit (1809)* (SS
       1936), ed. Ingrid Schüssler (Frankfurt: Klostermann, 1988).
       ET: *Schelling's Treatise on the Essence of Human Freedom*
       (trans. Joan Stambaugh; Athens, OH: Ohio University Press,
       1985).

GA 43 *Nietzsche: Der Wille zur Macht als Kunst* (WS 1936/37), ed.
       Bernd Heimbüchel (Frankfurt: Klostermann, 1985).

GA 44 *Nietzsche metaphysische Grundstellung im abendländischen
       Denken: Die ewige Wiederkehr des Gleichen* (SS 1937), ed.
       Marion Heinz (Frankfurt: Klostermann, 1986).

GA 46 *Zur Auslegung von Nietzsches Zweiter Unzeitgemäßer
       Betrachtung* (WS 1938/39), ed. Hans-Joachim Friedrich
       (Frankfurt: Klostermann, 2003).

GA 47 *Nietzsches Lehre vom Willen zur Macht als Erkenntnis* (SS 1939),
       ed. Eberhard Hanser (Frankfurt: Klostermann, 1989).

GA 48 *Nietzsche: Der europäische Nihilismus* (1940), ed. Petra Jaeger
       (Frankfurt: Klostermann, 1986).

GA 49 *Die Metaphysik des deutschen Idealismus* (1941), ed. Günter
       Seubold (Frankfurt: Klostermann, 2nd edn, 2006).

GA 50 *Nietzsches Metaphysik* (1941/42), ed. Petra Jaeger (Frankfurt:
       Klostermann, 1990).

GA 56/7 *Zur Bestimmung der Philosophie* (KNS 1919 and SS 1919), ed.
       Bernd Heimbüchel (Frankfurt: Klostermann, 2nd edn, 1999).

GA 58 *Grundprobleme der Phänomenologie* (WS 1919/20), ed. Hans-
       Helmuth Gander (Frankfurt: Klostermann, 1992).

GA 60 *Phänomenologie des religiösen Lebens* (1918/19, WS 1920/21
       and SS 1921), ed. Matthias Jung, Thomas Regehly, and Claudius
       Strube (Frankfurt: Klostermann, 1995).
       ET: *The Phenomenology of Religious Life* (trans. Matthias
       Fritsch and Jennifer Anna Gosetti-Ferencei; Bloomington: Indiana
       University Press, 2004).

GA 61 *Phänomenologische Interpretationen zu Aristoteles: Einführung
       in die phänomenologische Forschung* (WS 1921/22), ed. Walter
       Bröcker and Käte Bröcker-Oltmanns (Frankfurt: Klostermann,
       2nd edn, 1994).
       ET: *Phenomenological Interpretations of Aristotle* (trans. Richard
       Rojcewicz; Bloomington: Indiana University Press, 2001).

GA 62 *Phänomenologische Interpretationen ausgewählter Abhandlungen
       des Aristoteles zu Ontologie und Logik* (1922 and SS 1922), ed.
       Günther Neumann (Frankfurt: Klostermann, 2005).

In English:
'Phenomenological Interpretations in Connection with Aristotle:
An Indication of the Hermeneutical Situation' (1922), trans. John
van Buren. *Supplements*, pp. 111–45.

GA 63 *Ontologie. Hermeneutik der Faktizität* (SS 1923), ed. Käte
Bröcker-Oltmanns (Frankfurt: Klostermann, 2nd edn, 1995).
ET: *Ontology: The Hermeneutics of Facticity* (trans. John van
Buren; Bloomington: Indiana University Press, 1999).

GA 64 *Der Begriff der Zeit* (1924), ed. Friedrich-Wilhelm von Herrmann
(Frankfurt: Klostermann, 2004).
ET: *The Concept of Time* (trans. William McNeill; Oxford:
Blackwell, 1992).

GA 65 *Beiträge zur Philosophie (Vom Ereignis)* (1936–1938), ed.
Friedrich-Wilhelm von Herrmann (Frankfurt: Klostermann, 2nd
edn, 1994).
ET: *Contributions to Philosophy (From Enowning)* (trans. Parvis
Emad and Kenneth Maly; Bloomington: Indiana University Press,
1999).

GA 66 *Besinnung* (1938–1939), ed. Friedrich-Wilhelm von Herrmann
(Frankfurt: Klostermann, 1997).
ET: *Mindfulness* (trans. Parvis Emad; London: Continuum, 2006).

GA 75 *Zu Hölderlin – Griechenlandreisen,* ed. Curd Ochwaldt
(Frankfurt: Klostermann, 2000).

GA 79 *Bremer und Freiburger Vorträge* (1949/1957), ed. Petra Jaeger
(Frankfurt: Klostermann, 2005).

GA 87 *Nietzsche: Seminare 1937 und 1944,* ed. Peter von Ruckteschell
(Frankfurt: Klostermann, 2004).

Single works:

'Das Problem der Sünde bei Martin Luther' (1924), in Jaspert, Bernd
(ed.), *Sachgemäße Exegese: Die Protokolle aus Rudolf Bultmanns
Neutestamentlichen Seminaren 1921–1951* (Marburg: Elwert, 1996),
pp. 28–33.
ET: 'The Problem of Sin in Luther' (1924), trans. John van Buren.
Supplements, pp. 105–10.
Sein und Zeit (Tübingen: Max Niemeyer Verlag, 18th edn, 2001 [1927]).
ET: *Being and Time* (trans. John Macquarrie and Edward Robinson;
Oxford: Blackwell, 1962).
Being and Time (trans. Joan Stambaugh; Albany: State University of
New York Press, 1996).

'"Nur noch ein Gott kann uns retten"': *Spiegel*-Gespräch mit Martin
   Heidegger am 23. September 1966', *Der Spiegel* 30, 23 (31 May
   1976), pp. 193–219.
   ET: '"Only a God Can Save Us"': *Der Spiegel*'s Interview with Martin
   Heidegger' (1966). *The Heidegger Controversy*, pp. 91–115.

Correspondences:

Martin Heidegger/Elisabeth Blochmann: Briefwechsel 1918–1969, ed.
   Joachim Storck (Marbach: Deutsches Literaturarchiv, 2nd edn, 1990).
'Drei Briefe Martin Heideggers an Karl Löwith', in Hartmut Tietjen (ed.),
   Zur philosophischen Aktualität Heideggers, eds. Dietrich Papenfuss
   and Otto Pöggeler (vol. 2; Frankfurt: Klostermann, 1990), pp. 27–38.
Martin Heidegger/Karl Jaspers: Briefwechsel 1920–1963, eds. Walter
   Biemel and Hans Saner (Frankfurt: Klostermann, 1990).
   ET: *The Heidegger – Jaspers Correspondence (1920–1963)*, eds.
   Walter Biemel and Hans Saner (trans. Gary Aylesworth; Amherst, NY:
   Humanity Books, 2003).
Hannah Arendt/Martin Heidegger: Briefe 1925–1975, ed. Ursula Ludz
   (Frankfurt: Klostermann, 2nd edn, 1999).
Martin Heidegger/Heinrich Rickert: Briefe 1912–1933, ed. Alfred Denker
   (Frankfurt: Klostermann, 2002).
Martin Heidegger/Bernhard Welte: Briefe und Begegnungen, eds. Alfred
   Denker and Holger Zaborowski (Stuttgart: Klett-Cotta Verlag, 2003).
Martin Heidegger/Max Müller: Briefe und andere Dokumente, eds.
   Holger Zaborowski and A. Bösl (Freiburg: Karl Alber Verlag, 2004).
'Mein liebes Seelchen!': *Briefe Martin Heideggers an seine Frau Elfride,
   1915–1970*, ed. Gertrud Heidegger (Munich: Deutsche Verlags-Anstalt,
   2005).
Rudolf Bultmann/Martin Heidegger: Briefwechsel 1925–1975,
   eds. Andreas Großmann and Christof Landmesser (Frankfurt:
   Klostermann, 2009).

Heidegger Jahrbücher (Heidegger yearbooks):

I: *Heidegger und die Anfänge seines Denkens*, eds. Alfred Denker,
      Hans-Helmuth Gander and Holger Zaborowski (Freiburg: Karl Alber
      Verlag, 2004).
      In English:
      'Letter to Father Engelbert Krebs' (1919), trans. John van Buren.
      Supplements, pp. 69–70.

IV: *Heidegger und der Nationalsozialismus I: Dokumente*, eds. Alfred
     Denker and Holger Zaborowski (Freiburg: Karl Alber Verlag, 2010).
V: *Heidegger und der Nationalsozialismus II: Interpretationen*, eds.
     Alfred Denker and Holger Zaborowski (Freiburg: Karl Alber Verlag,
     2010).
VII: *Heidegger und das ostasiatische Denken*, eds. Alfred Denker,
     Holger Zaborowski, Georg Stenger, Ryôsuke Ohashi, and Shunsuke
     Kadowaki (Freiburg: Karl Alber Verlag, 2013).

Other primary works

Acta Apostolicae Sedis (Vatican City: Typis Polyglottis Vaticanis, 1909–).
Althaus, Paul. *Die letzten Dinge: Lehrbuch der Eschatologie* (Gütersloh:
     Mohn, 9th edn, 1964 [1922]).
Aquinas, Thomas. *Summa Theologiae: Latin text and English translation,*
     introductions, notes, appendices, and glossaries, ed. Thomas Gilby
     et al (61 vols; London: Blackfriars in conjunction with Eyre &
     Spottiswoode, 1964–81).
Arendt, Hannah. *Der Liebesbegriff bei Augustin: Versuch einer*
     philosophischen Interpretation (Berlin: Springer, 1929).
     ET: *Love and Saint Augustine*, eds. Joanna Vecchiarelli Scott and
     Judith Chelius Stark (Chicago: University of Chicago Press, 1996).
Arndt, Ernst Moritz. *Sämtliche Werke*, ed. E. Schirmer (10 vols;
     Magdeburg: Anst, 1908).
—. *Werke. Auswahl in zwölf Teilen*, eds. August Leffson and Wilhelm
     Steffens (Berlin: Bong, n.d).
Augustine, Bishop of Hippo. *Confessions* (trans. and ed. Henry
     Chadwick; Oxford: Oxford University Press, 1991).
Aulén, Gustaf. *Christus Victor: An Historical Study of the Three Main*
     Types of the Idea of Atonement (trans. A. G. Herber; London: SPCK,
     1931).
Balthasar, Hans Urs von. *Apokalypse der deutschen Seele* (3 vols;
     Salzburg: Pustet, 1937–39).
—. *Eschatologie in unserer Zeit: Die letzten Dinge des Menschen und*
     das Christentum (1954/5), ed. Jan-Heiner Tück (Einsiedeln: Johannes
     Verlag, 2005).
—. 'Eschatologie', in Johannes Feiner, Josef Trütsch and Franz Böckle
     (eds.), *Fragen der Theologie heute* (Einsiedeln: Benziger Verlag, 2nd
     edn., 1957), pp. 403–21.
Barth, Heinrich. 'Ontologie und Idealismus: Eine Auseinandersetzung von
     Heinrich Barth mit Martin Heidegger', *Zwischen den Zeiten* 7 (1929),
     pp. 511–40.

Barth, Karl. *Der Römerbrief* (Munich: Chr. Kaiser, 1919 [2nd fully revised edn, 1922]).
ET: *The Epistle to the Romans* (trans. Edwyn C. Hoskyns; London: Oxford University Press, 1968).
—. 'Unerledigte Anfragen an die heutige Theologie', in Barth, Karl and Eduard Thurneysen (eds.), *Zur inneren Lage des Christentums* (Munich: Chr. Kaiser, 1920), pp. 1–14.
—. 'Das Wort Gottes als Aufgabe der Theologie', *Christliche Welt* 36 (1922), pp. 858–73.
ET: 'The Word of God and the Task of Theology', in Karl Barth (ed.), *The Word of God and Theology* (ed. and trans. Amy Marga; London: Continuum, 2011), pp. 171–98.
—. 'Verheißung, Zeit – Erfüllung', *Zwischen den Zeiten* 9 (1931), pp. 457–63.
—. *Kirchliche Dogmatik* (4 vols; Zürich: Evangelischer Verlag, 1932–70).
ET: *Church Dogmatics*, eds. G. W. Bromiley and T. F. Torrance (trans. H. Knight, G. W. Bromiley, J. K. S. Reid, and R. H. Fuller; Edinburgh: T&T Clark, 1936–77).
—. 'Philosophie und Theologie', in Huber, Gerhard (ed.), *Philosophie und christliche Existenz* (Basle: Helbing & Lichtenhahn, 1960), pp. 93–105.
—. *Church Dogmatics* III/2: *The Doctrine of Creation* (eds. G. W. Bromiley and T. F. Torrance; trans. H. Knight, G. W. Bromiley, J. K. S. Reid, and R. H. Fuller; Edinburgh: T&T Clark, 1960).
Barth, Karl and Eduard Thurneysen. *Briefwechsel 1913–1935* (3 vols; Zürich: Theologischer Verlag, 1973–2000).
Barth, Karl and Emil Brunner. *Briefwechsel 1911–1966*, ed. Eberhard Busch (Zürich: Theologischer Verlag, 2000).
Barth, Karl and Rudolf Bultmann. *Briefwechsel 1911–1966*, ed. Bernd Jaspert (Zürich: Theologischer Verlag, 2nd revised and expanded edn, 1994).
Bloechl, Jeffrey. *Liturgy of the Neighbor: Emmanuel Levinas and the Religion of Responsibility* (Pittsburgh: Duquesne University Press, 2000).
—(ed.), *The Face of the Other and the Trace of God. Essays on the Thought of Emmanuel Levinas* (New York: Fordham University Press, 2000).
—. *Religious Experience and the End of Metaphysics* (Indianapolis: Indiana University Press, 2003).
Boehme, Herbert. *Bekenntnisse eines jungen Deutschen* (Munich: Franz Eher, 1935).
—. *Das deutsche Gebet* (Munich: Franz Eher, 1936).
Bollnow, Otto Friedrich. 'Existenzphilosophie', in Nicolai Hartmann (ed.), *Systematische Philosophie* (Berlin: Kohlhammer, 1942), pp. 302–430.

Bousset, Wilhelm. *Der Antichrist in der Überlieferung des Judentums, des Neuen Testaments und der alten Kirche* (Göttingen: Vandenhoeck & Ruprecht, 1895).

Braig, Carl. *Vom Sein: Abriß der Ontologie* (Freiburg: Herder, 1896).

—. *Vom Denken: Abriß der Logik* (Freiburg: Herder, 1896).

—. *Vom Erkennen: Abriß der Noetik* (Freiburg: Herder, 1897).

Brunner, Emil. 'Theologie und Ontologie, oder: Die Theologie am Scheidewege', *Zeitschrift für Theologie und Kirche* 12 (1931), pp. 111–22.

Bultmann, Rudolf. 'Die Frage der "dialektischen" Theologie: Eine Auseinandersetzung mit Erik Peterson', *Zwischen den Zeiten* 4 (1926), pp. 40–59.

—. 'Martin Heidegger', in Hermann Gunkel und Leopold Zscharnack (eds.), *Religion in Geschichte und Gegenwart* (Tübingen: Mohr Siebeck, 2nd edn, 1927–31. Vol. II (1928), cols. 1687–88).

—. 'Die Eschatologie des Johannes-Evangeliums', *Zwischen den Zeiten* 6 (1928), pp. 4–22.

—. 'Die Geschichtlichkeit des Daseins und der Glaube: Antwort an Gerhardt Kuhlmann', *Zeitschrift für Theologie und Kirche* 11 (1930), pp. 339–64.

—. *Theologie des Neuen Testaments* (2 vols; Tübingen: Mohr Siebeck, 1948–53).

ET: *Theology of the New Testament* (2 vols; London: SCM Press, 1952–55).

—. *History and Eschatology* (Edinburgh: Edinburgh University Press, 1957).

Bultmann, Rudolf and Friedrich Gogarten. *Briefwechsel 1921–1967*, ed. Hermann Götz Göckeritz (Tübingen: Mohr Siebeck, 2002).

Bultmann Lemke, Antje. 'Der unveröffentlichte Nachlaß von Rudolf Bultmann – Ausschnitte aus dem biographischen Quellenmaterial', in Bernd Jaspert (ed.), *Rudolf Bultmanns Werk und Wirkung* (Darmstadt: Wissenschaftliche Buchgesellschaft, 1984), pp. 194–210.

Caputo, John D. *The Mystical Element in Heidegger's Thought* (Athens, OH: Ohio University Press, 1978).

—. *Heidegger and Aquinas: An Essay on Overcoming Metaphysics* (New York: Fordham University Press, 1982).

—. *Radical Hermeneutics* (Bloomington: Indiana University Press, 1987).

—. 'Who Comes after the God of Metaphysics?', in John Caputo (ed.), *The Religious* (Oxford: Blackwell, 2002).

—. 'Heidegger and Theology', *The Cambridge Companion to Heidegger*, ed. Charles Guignon (Cambridge: Cambridge University Press, 2nd edn, 2006), pp. 326–44.

Caputo, John D., Mark Dooley, and Michael Scanlon (eds.), *Questioning God* (Bloomington: Indiana University Press, 2001).

Cavell, Stanley. *Must We Mean What We Say?* (Cambridge: Cambridge University Press, 1976).
—. *The Claim of Reason* (Oxford: Oxford University Press, 1979).
—. *Conditions Handsome and Unhandsome: The Constitution of Emersonian Perfectionism* (Chicago: University of Chicago Press, 1990).
—. *Disowning Knowledge: In Seven Plays of Shakespeare* (Cambridge: Cambridge University Press, 2nd expanded edn, 2003).
—. *Cities of Words: Pedagogical Letters on a Register of the Moral Life* (Cambridge, MA: Harvard University Press, 2004).
Cho, Kah Kyung. *Bewußtsein und Natursein: Phänomenologischer West-Ost-Diwan* (Freiburg: Alber, 1987).
Chrétien, Jean-Louis. *L'appel et la réponse* (Paris: Éditions de Minuit, 1992). ET: *The Call and the Response* (trans. Anne Davenport; New York: Fordham University Press, 2004).
Conrad-Martius, Hedwig. 'Sein und Zeit', Review. *Philosophischer Anzeiger* 8 (1933), p. 185.
—. 'Sein und Zeit', Review. *Deutsche Kunstwissenschaft* 46 (1933), pp. 246–51.
Delp, Alfred. *Tragische Existenz: Zur Philosophie Martin Heideggers* (Freiburg: Herder, 1931).
Deutsche Reden in schwerer Zeit (24 vols; Berlin: Carl Heymanns Verlag, 1914–15).
Dilthey, Wilhelm. *Leben Schleiermachers* (1870). 2 vols, in Martin Redeker (ed.), *Gesammelte Schriften* (Stuttgart: B. G. Teubner, 1966 and 1985), pp. 13–14.
Dr. –b. 'Tragische Existenz. Auseinandersetzung mit der Philosophie Martin Heideggers', *Germania: Zeitung für das deutsche Volk* 65, 361 (29 December 1935).
Echternach, Helmut. 'Die Auferstehungshoffnung als Voraussetzung der Todeswirklichkeit: Zur Auseinandersetzung über das Todesproblem mit Heidegger, Nietzsche und anderen', *Christentum und Wissenschaft* 6 (1930), pp. 241–9.
Eucken, Rudolf. *Die weltgeschichtliche Bedeutung des deutschen Geistes* (Stuttgart: Deutsche Verlags-Anstalt, 1914).
Fichte, Johann Gottlieb. *Reden an die deutsche Nation* (1808), in Fritz Medicus (ed.), *Werke: Auswahl in sechs Bänden* (Leipzig: Felix Meiner, 1911–22). ET: *Addresses to the German Nation* (trans. Gregory Moore; Cambridge: Cambridge University Press, 2008).
Fondane, Benjamin. 'Sur la route de Dostoyewski: Martin Heidegger', *Cahiers du Sud* 19 (1932), pp. 378–92.
Förster, Friedrich Wilhelm. *Autorität und Freiheit: Betrachtungen zum Kulturproblem der Kirche* (Kempten-Munich: Kösel, 1910).

Gadamer, Hans-Georg. *Philosophische Lehrjahre: eine Rückschau* (Frankfurt: Klostermann, 1977).
—. *Heideggers Wege: Studien zum Spätwerk* (Tübingen: Mohr Siebeck, 1983).
—. 'Selbstdarstellung 1975', in Jean Grondin (ed.), *Gadamer Lesebuch* (Tübingen: Mohr Siebeck, 1997), pp. 1–30.
George, Stefan. *Das neue Reich* (Berlin: George Bondi, 1928).
Goebbels, Joseph. *Das Tagebuch von Joseph Goebbels, 1925/26*, ed. Helmut Heiber (Stuttgart: Deutsche Verlags-Anstalt, n.d.).
—. *Michael. Ein deutsches Schicksal in Tagebuchblättern* (Munich: Franz Eher, 1928).
Gogarten, Friedrich. *Gehören und Verstehen: Ausgewählte Aufsätze (1928–1966)*, ed. Hermann Götz Göckeritz (Tübingen: Mohr Siebeck, 1988).
Gunkel, Hermann. *Schöpfung und Chaos in Urzeit und Endzeit: Eine religionsgeschichtliche Untersuchung über Gen 1 und Apk Joh 21* (Göttingen: Vandenhoeck & Ruprecht, 1895).
Hegel, G. W. F. *Grundlinien der Philosophie des Rechts* (1820), in Eva Moldenhauer and Karl Markus Michel (eds.), *Werke in 20 Bänden* (Frankfurt: Suhrkamp, 3rd edn, 2001).
    ET: *Philosophy of Right* (trans. T. M. Knox; Oxford: Oxford University Press, 1942).
Heim, Karl. 'Ontologie und Theologie', *Zeitschrift für Theologie und Kirche* 11 (1930), pp. 325–38.
Henry, Michel. *C'est moi la Vérité: Pour une philosophie du christianisme* (Paris: Éditions du Seuil, 1996).
    ET: *I am the Truth: Towards a Philosophy of Christianity* (trans. Susan Emanuel; Stanford: Stanford University Press, 2003).
—. *Incarnation: Une philosophie de la chair* (Paris: Éditions du Seuil, 2000).
—. *Paroles du Christ* (Paris: Éditions du Seuil, 2002).
    ET: *Words of Christ* (trans. Christina Gschwandter; Grand Rapids: Eerdmans, 2012).
Hitler, Adolf. *Mein Kampf* (Munich: Franz Eher, 855th edn, 1943) [vol. 1: 1925, vol. 2: 1927].
    ET: *Mein Kampf* (trans. James Vincent Murphy; London: Hutchinson, 1939).
Hölderlin, Friedrich. *Sämtliche Werke und Briefe*, ed. Jochen Schmidt (3 vols; Frankfurt: Deutsche Klassiker Verlag, 1992–94).
    ET: *Friedrich Hölderlin: Poems & Fragments* (trans. Michael Hamburger; London: Anvil Press, 4th edn, 2004).
Husserl, Edmund. *Logische Untersuchungen* (2 vols; Halle: Max Niemeyer, 1907).
    ET: *Logical Investigations* (trans. J. N. Findlay; 2 vols; London: Routledge, 2001).

—. *Briefwechsel*, ed. Karl Schuhmann (10 vols; The Hague: Kluwer Academic Publishers, 1994).

Jaspers, Karl. *Psychologie der Weltanschauungen* (Berlin: Springer, 1919).

Jüngel, Eberhard. 'Der Schritt zurück: Eine Auseinandersetzung mit der Heidegger-Deutung Heinrich Otts', *Zeitschrift für Theologie und Kirche* 58 (1961), pp. 104–22.

—. *Gottes Sein ist im Werden: Verantwortliche Rede vom Sein Gottes bei Karl Barth, eine Paraphrase* (Tübingen: Mohr Siebeck, 1965). ET: *God's Being is in Becoming: The Trinitarian Being of God in the Theology of Karl Barth, a Paraphrase* (trans. John Webster; Edinburgh: T&T Clark, 2nd edn, 2001).

—. *Gott als Geheimnis der Welt* (Tübingen: Paul Siebeck Verlag, 1977). ET: *God as the Mystery of the World* (trans. Darrell L. Guder; Edinburgh: T&T Clark, 1983).

—. *Barth-Studien* (Gütersloh: Mohn, 1982). ET: (selections): *Karl Barth: A Theological Legacy* (trans. Garrett E. Paul; Philadelphia: Westminster Press, 1986).

Kearney, Richard. *The God Who May Be: A Hermeneutic of Religion* (Bloomington: University of Indiana Press, 2001).

—. *Anatheism: Returning to God After God* (New York: Columbia University Press, 2009).

Kearney, Richard and Joseph Stephen O'Leary (eds.), *Heidegger et la question de Dieu* (Paris: B. Grasset, 1980).

Kierkegaard, Søren. *Begrebet Angest: En simpel psychologisk-paapegende Overveielse i Retning af det dogmatiske*. Attributed to Vigilius Haufniensis. Copenhagen, 1843. ET: *The Concept of Anxiety* (trans. and ed. Reidar Thomte; Princeton: Princeton University Press, 1980).

—. *Sygdommen til Døden: En christelig psychologisk Udvikling til Opbyggelse og Opvækkelse*. Attributed to Anti-Climacus. Copenhagen, 1849. ET: *The Sickness unto Death* (trans. and ed. Edna H. Hong and Howard V. Hong; Princeton: Princeton University Press, 1983).

—. *Gesammelte Werke* (trans. H. Gottsched and C. Schrempf; 12 vols; Jena: Eugen Diederichs, 1909–22. [Heidegger's edition]).

—. *Eighteen Upbuilding Discourses* (trans. H. and E. Hong; Princeton: Princeton University Press, 1990).

König, Karl. *Neue Kriegspredigten* (Jena: Diederichs, 1914).

Kraus, Karl. *Die letzten Tage der Menschheit*, ed. E. Früh (Frankfurt: Suhrkamp, 1992).

Kuhlmann, Gerhardt. 'Zum theologischen Problem der Existenz: Fragen an Rudolf Bultmann', *Zeitschrift für Theologie und Kirche* 10 (1929), pp. 28–57.

—. 'Krisis der Theologie', *Zeitschrift für Theologie und Kirche* 12 (1931), pp. 123–46.

—. *Theologische Anthropologie im Abriß* (Tübingen: Mohr, 1935).

—. *Die Theologie am Scheidewege* (Tübingen: Mohr, 1935).

Lacoste, Jean-Yves. *Note sur le temps: Essai sur les raisons de la mémoire et de l'espérance* (Paris: Presses Universitaires de France, 1990).

—. *Expérience et absolu: Questions disputés sur l'humanité de l'homme* (Paris: Presses Universitaires de France, 1994).
   ET: *Experience and the Absolute: Disputed Questions on the Humanity of Man* (trans. M. Raftery; New York: Fordham University Press, 2004).

—. 'Martin Heidegger', in Lacoste, Jean-Yves (ed.), *Encyclopedia of Christian Theology*, vol. 2 (3 vols; London: Routledge, 2005), pp. 677–80.

—. *La phénoménalité de Dieu: Neuf etudes* (Paris: Éditions du Cerf, 2008).

Lagarde, Paul de. 'Die Religion der Zukunft', *Deutsche Schriften*, vol. 1 (Göttingen: Dieterich, 1878), pp. 217–55.

Leibniz, G. W. *Die philosophischen Schriften von Gottfried Wilhelm Leibniz*, ed. C. I. Gerhardt (Hildesheim: Georg Olms, 1960–78).

Levinas, Emmanuel. *Totalité et Infini: Essai sur l'extériorité* (The Hague: Martinus Nijhoff, 1961).
   ET: *Totality and Infinity: An Essay on Exteriority* (trans. A. Lingis; Pittsburgh: Duquesne University Press, 1969).

—. *Autrement qu'êtreou au-delà de l'essence* (The Hague: Martinus Nijhoff, 1974).
   ET: *Otherwise than Being: or, Beyond Essence* (trans. A. Lingis; The Hague: Martinus Nijhoff, 1981).

Lewis, C. S. *The Pilgrim's Regress* (London: J. M. Dent, 3rd edn, 1943).

—. *Mere Christianity* (New York: Macmillan, 1943).

—. *Till We Have Faces: A Myth Retold* (London: Geoffrey Bles, 1956).

—. *Essay Collection*. ed. Lesley Walmsley (2 vols; London: HarperCollins, 2000).

Löwith, Karl. *Das Individuum in der Rolle des Mitmenschen* (München: Drei Masken-Verlag, 1928).

—. 'Grundzüge der Entwicklung der Phänomenologie zur Philosophie und ihr Verhältnis zur protestantischen Theologie', *Theologische Rundschau* 2 (1930), pp. 26–64 and 333–61.

—. 'Phänomenologische Ontologie und protestantische Theologie', *Zeitschrift für Theologie und Kirche* 11 (1930), pp. 365–99.

—. 'Les implications politiques de la philosophie de l'existence chez Heidegger,' *Les Temps Modernes* 2 (1946), pp. 343–60.

—. *Weltgeschichte und Heilsgeschehen: Die theologischen Voraussetzungen der Geschichtsphilosophie* (Stuttgart: W. Kohlhammer Verlag, 1953).

—. *Mein Leben in Deutschland vor und nach 1933. Ein Bericht* (Stuttgart: J. B. Metzler, 1986.

Luther, Martin. D. *Martin Luthers Werke: kritische Gesammtausgabe* (120 vols; Weimar: Hermann Böhlaus, 1883–2009).
ET: *Luther's Works*, ed. Jaroslav Pelikan (56 vols; St Louis: Concordia Publishing House, 1955–86).

Marion, Jean-Luc. *Dieu sans l'être* (Paris: Presses Universitaires de France, 1982).
ET: *God without Being* (trans. T. A. Carlson; Chicago: University of Chicago Press, 1995).

—. *Étant donné: Essai d'une phénoménologie de la donation* (Paris: Presses Universitaires de France, 1997).
ET: *Being Given: Towards a Phenomenology of Givenness* (trans. J. L. Kosky; Stanford: Stanford University Press, 2002).

Meinong, Alexius. *Untersuchungen zur Gegenstandstheorie und Psychologie* (Leipzig: Barth, 1904).

Moeller van den Bruck, Arthur. *Das dritte Reich* (Hamburg: Hanseatische Verlagsanstalt, 1923).
ET: *Germany's Third Empire* (trans. and ed. E. O. Lorimer; London: Allen & Unwin, 1934).

Möhler, Johann Adam. *Symbolik*, ed. Josef Rupert Geiselmann (2 vols; Cologne: Jakob Hegner, 1960).

Müller, Max. *Existenzphilosophie: Von der Metaphysik zur Metahistorik* (Freiburg: Karl Alber Verlag, 4th edn, 1986).

Nietzsche, Friedrich. *Unzeitgemäße Betrachtungen*, ed. Peter Pütz (Munich: Goldmann, 1999).
ET: *Unfashionable Observations* (trans. Richard T. Grey; Stanford: Stanford, 1995).

Nishitani, Keiji. *Religion and Nothingness* (trans. Jan van Bragt; Berkeley: University of California Press, 1982 [1961]).

Ott, Heinrich. *Denken und Sein: Der Weg Martin Heideggers und der Weg der Theologie* (Zollikon: Evangelischer Verlag, 1959).

Overbeck, Franz. *Über die Christlichkeit unserer heutigen Theologie* (Leipzig: C. G. Naumann, 1873).
ET: *How Christian is our Present-Day Theology?* (trans. Martin Henry; London: T&T Clark, 2005).

—. *Über die Anfänge der patristischen Literatur* (Basle: Benno Schwabe & Co., 2nd edn, n.d. [first published 1882]).

—. *Das Johannes-Evangelium*, ed. C. A. Bernoulli (Tübingen: Mohr, 1911).

—. *Christentum und Kultur: Gedanken und Anmerkungen zur modernen Theologie*, ed. C. A. Bernoulli (Darmstadt: Wissenschaftliche Buchgesellschaft, 1919).

Pannenberg, Wolfhart. *Theology and the Kingdom of God* (trans. Richard John Neuhaus; Philadelphia: Westminster Press, 1969).

Peterson, Erik. *Theologische Traktate* (Würzburg: Echter, 1994 [1951]).
—. *Theologie und Theologen: Briefwechsel mit Karl Barth u.a.,*
    Reflexionen und Erinnerungen, ed. Barbara Nichtweiß (Würzburg:
    Echter, 2009).
Przywara, Erich. 'Drei Richtungen der Phänomenologie', *Stimmen der*
    Zeit 115 (1928), pp. 252–64.
—. *Analogia entis* (Munich: Kösel & Pustet, 1932).
Rahner, Karl. *Geist in Welt: Zur Metaphysik der endlichen Erkenntnis bei*
    Thomas von Aquin (Innsbruck: F. Rauch, 1939).
    ET: *Spirit in the World* (trans. William Dych; New York: Herder &
    Herder, 1968).
—. 'Introduction au concept de philosophie existentiale chez Heidegger',
    Recherches de science religieuse 30 (1940), pp. 152–71.
    ET: 'The Concept of Existential Philosophy in Heidegger', trans.
    A. Tallon. *Philosophy Today* 13 (1969), pp. 126–37.
—. *Hörer des Wortes: Zur Grundlegung einer Religionsphilosophie*
    (Munich: Kösel, 1941).
    ET: *Hearers of the Word* (trans. Joseph Donceel; New York:
    Continuum, 1994).
—. 'Antwort (Ein Weg zur Bestimmung des Verhältnisses von Natur und
    Gnade)', *Orientierung* 14 (1950), pp. 141–5.
—. *Schriften zur Theologie* (16 vols; Einsiedeln: Benziger, 1954–84).
    ET: *Theological Investigations* (trans. Cornelius Ernst; 23 vols;
    London: Darton, Longman and Todd, 1961–92).
—. *Zur Theologie des Todes* (Freiburg: Herder, 1958).
    ET: *On the Theology of Death* (New York: Seabury Press, 1971).
Reinach, Adolf. *Sämtliche Werke,* ed. Karl Schuhmann (Munich:
    Philosophia, 1989).
Rosenberg, Alfred. *Der Mythus des 20. Jahrhunderts: Eine Wertung*
    der seelisch-geistigen Gestaltenkämpfe unserer Zeit (Munich:
    Hoheneichen-Verlag, 33rd edn, 1934 [1930]).
—. *Der entscheidende Weltkampf: Rede des Reichsleiters Alfred*
    Rosenberg auf dem Parteikongreß in Nürnberg 1936 (Munich:
    M. Müller & Sohn, 1936).
Sartre, Jean Paul. *L' Être et le néant: essai d'ontologie phénoménologique*
    (1943), ed. Arlette Elkaïm-Sartre (Paris: Gallimard, 1996).
    ET: *Being and Nothingness: An Essay on Phenomenological Ontology*
    (trans. Hazel E. Barnes; London: Methuen, 1957).
Scheler, Max. *Vom Ewigen im Menschen* (Leipzig: Der Neue Geist-Verlag,
    1921).
    ET: *On the Eternal in Man* (trans. Bernard Noble; London: SCM
    Press, 1960).
Schell, Herman. *Apologie des Christentums.* Vol 1: *Religion und*
    Offenbarung (Paderborn: Schöningh, 1902).

—. *Katholische Dogmatik,* eds. Josef Hasenfuss and Paul-Werner Scheele (3 vols; Munich: Schöningh, 1994).

Schleiermacher, Friedrich. *Reden über die Religion: an die Gebildeten unter ihren Verächtern* (Gotha: Friedrich Andreas Perthes, 2nd edn, 1888 [1799]).
ET: *On Religion: Speeches to its Cultured Despisers* (trans. Richard Crouter; Cambridge: Cambridge University Press, 1996).

—. *Der christliche Glaube nach den Grundsätzen der evangelischen Kirche im Zusammenhang dargestellt,* ed. Rolf Schäfer (Berlin: Walter de Gruyter, 2008 [1830/1]).
ET: *The Christian Faith,* ed. H. R. Mackintosh and James S. Stewart (Edinburgh: T&T Clark, 1928).

Schumann, Gerhard. *Die Lieder vom Reich* (Munich: Albert Langen and Georg Mueller, 1936).

Schweitzer, Albert. *Von Reimarus zu Wrede, eine Geschichte der Leben-Jesu-Forschung* (Tübingen: Mohr Siebeck, 1906).
ET: *The Quest of the Historical Jesus* (trans. William Montgomery; London: A. & C. Black, 1910).

Siewerth, Gustav. *Gott in der Geschichte: Zur Gottesfrage bei Hegel und Heidegger,* ed. Alma von Stockhausen (Düsseldorf: Patmos Verlag, 1971).

—. *Das Schicksal der Metaphysik: Von Thomas zu Heidegger* (Freiburg: Johannes Verlag, new edn, 1987 [1959]).

Stein, Edith. 'Husserls Phänomenologie und die Philosophie des Hl. Thomas von Aquino', in Martin Heidegger (ed.), *Festschrift, Edmund Husserl zum 70. Geburtstag gewidmet* (Halle: Niemeyer, 1929), pp. 315–38.

—. *Welt und Person* (Freiburg: Herder, 1962).

—. *Selbstbildnis in Briefen III: Briefe an Roman Ingarden,* ed. Maria Amata Neyer (Freiburg: Herder, 2nd edn, 2005). (Edith Stein Gesamtausgabe 4.)
ET: *Self-Portrait in Letters: 1916–1942,* trans. Josephine Koeppel (Washington, DC: ICS Publications, 1993).

—. *Endliches und Ewiges Sein: Versuch eines Aufstiegs zum Sinn des Seins,* ed. Andreas Uwe Müller (Freiburg: Herder, 2006). (Edith Stein Gesamtausgabe 11/12.)
ET: *Finite and Eternal Being: An Attempt at an Ascent to the Meaning of Being* (trans. Kurt Reinhardt; Washington, DC: ICS Publications, 2002).

Thielemans, H. 'Existence tragique: La metaphysique du nazisme', *Nouvelle revue théologique* 63 (1936), pp. 561–79.

Thurneysen, Eduard. *Dostojewski* (Munich: Chr. Kaiser, 1921).
ET: *Dostoevsky: A Theological Study* (trans. Keith R. Crim; London: Epworth, 1964).

—. 'Christus und seine Zukunft: Ein Beitrag zur Eschatologie', *Zwischen den Zeiten* 9 (1931), pp. 187–211.

Tillich, Paul. *Systematic Theology* (3 vols; London: Nisbet, 1953–64).

—. *Theology of Culture* (New York: Oxford University Press, 1959).

—. *The Courage to Be* (New Haven: Yale University Press, 2000 [1952]).

Tsujimura, Koichi. 'Die Wahrheit des Seins und das absolute Nichts', in Ôhashi Ryôsuke (ed.), *Die Philosophie der Kyoto-Schule: Texte und Einführungen* (Freiburg: Alber, 1990), pp. 441–54.

Walther, Gerda. *Phänomenologie der Mystik* (Freiburg: Otto Walter, 2nd edn, 1955).

Westphal, Merold. *Overcoming Onto-Theology: Toward a Postmodern Christian Faith* (New York: Fordham, 2001).

—. *Transcendence and Self-Transcendence* (Indianapolis: Indiana University Press, 2004).

Williams, Charles. *Descent into Hell* (London: Faber & Faber, 1937).

Secondary works

Albert, Claudia. *Deutsche Klassiker im Nationalsozialismus: Schiller, Kleist, Hölderlin* (Stuttgart: J. B. Metzler, 1994).

Badisches Statistisches Landesamt. *Die Religionszugehörigkeit in Baden in den letzten 100 Jahren aufgrund amtlichen Materials* (Freiburg: Badisches Statistisches Landesamt, 1928).

Bärsch, Claus-Ekkehard. *Erlösung und Vernichtung. Dr. phil. Joseph Goebbels. Zur Psyche und Ideologie eines jungen Nationalsozialisten (1923–1927)* (Munich: Klaus Boer Verlag, 1987).

—. *Die politische Religion des Nationalsozialismus* (Munich: Wilhelm Fink, 2nd edn, 2002 [1998]).

Bartscher, Werner. *Hölderlin und die Deutsche Nation* (Berlin: Junker und Dünnhaupt, 1942).

Bautz, Wilhelm Friedrich (ed.), *Biographisch-Bibliographisches Kirchenlexikon* (18 vols; Hamm: Traugott Bautz Verlag, 1970–).

Beniston, Judith. *Welttheater: Hofmannsthal, Richard von Kralik, and the Revival of Catholic Drama in Austria, 1890–1934* (London: Maney & Son, 1998).

Benson, Bruce Ellis and Norman Wirzba (eds.), *Words of Life: New Theological Turns in French Phenomenology* (New York: Fordham University Press, 2009).

Berning, Vincent. *Martin Honecker: Auf dem Wege von der Logik zur Metaphysik* (Weilheim: Gustav-Siewerth-Akademie, 2003).

Böckmann, Paul. *Hölderlin und seine Götter* (Munich: C. H. Beck, 1935).

Bollmus, Reinhard. *Das Amt Rosenberg und seine Gegner. Studies zum Machtkampf im nationalsozialistischen Herrschaftssystem* (Stuttgart: Oldenbourg, 1970).

Bühler, Pierre, Ingolf Dalferth, and Andreas Hunziker (eds.), *Hermeneutische Theologie – heute?* (Tübingen: Mohr Siebeck, 2013).

Buren, John van. *The Young Heidegger: Rumour of the Hidden King* (Bloomington: Indiana University Press, 1994).

Cairns, Dorion. *Conversations with Husserl and Fink* (The Hague: Martinus Nijhoff, 1976).

Camilleri, Sylvain. *Phénoménologie de la religion et herméneutique théologique dans la pensée du jeune Heidegger: commentaire analytique des Fondements philosophiques de la mystique médiévale (1916–1919)* (Dordrecht: Springer, 2008).

Capelle, Philippe. *Philosophie et théologie dans la pensée de M. Heidegger* (Paris: Éditions du Cerf, 2nd edn, 2001).

—. '"Katholizismus," "Protestantismus," "Christentum" und "Religion" im Denken Martin Heideggers: Tragweite und Abgrenzungen', in Denker, Alfred, Hans-Helmuth Gander and Holger Zaborowski (eds.), *Heidegger und die Anfänge seines Denkens* (Freiburg: Karl Alber Verlag, 2004), pp. 346–71.

Carman, Taylor. *Heidegger's Analytic* (Cambridge: Cambridge University Press, 2003).

Casper, Bernhard. 'Martin Heidegger und die Katholische Fakultät Freiburg 1909–1923', *Freiburger Diözesan-Archiv* 100 (1980), pp. 534–41.

Chang, Chung-yuan. 'Taoist Philosophy and Heidegger's Poetic Thinking', *Indian Philosophical Quarterly* 4 (1977), pp. 305–11.

Ciocan, Cristian (ed.), *Philosophical Concepts and Religious Metaphors: New Perspectives on Phenomenology and Theology* (Bucharest: Zeta Books, 2009).

Cohn, Norman. *The Pursuit of the Millennium* (Oxford: Oxford University Press, 2nd edn, 1970).

Coriando, Paola-Ludovica (ed.), *'Herkunft aber bleibt stets Zukunft': Martin Heidegger und die Gottesfrage* (Frankfurt: Klostermann, 1998).

Corvez, Maurice. *L'être et la conscience morale* (Louvain: Editions Nauwelaerts, 1968).

Critchley, Simon and Reiner Schürmann. *On Heidegger's Being and Time* (London: Routledge, 2008).

Crowe, Benjamin. *Heidegger's Religious Origins* (Indianapolis: Indiana University Press, 2006).

—. *Heidegger's Religious Origins* and *Heidegger's Phenomenology of Religion: Realism and Cultural Criticism* (Indianapolis: Indiana University Press, 2007).

Cunningham, Conor. *Genealogy of Nihilism: Philosophies of Nothing and the Difference of Theology* (London: Routledge, 2002).

Daly, Gabriel. *Immanence and Transcendence: A Study in Catholic Modernism and Integralism* (Oxford: Clarendon, 1980).

Dell, August. 'Ontologische Daseinsanalyse und theologisches Daseinsverständnis', in Bornkamm, Heinrich (ed.), *Imago Dei: Beiträge zur theologischen Anthropologie* (Giessen: Töpelmann, 1932), pp. 215–32.

Denker, Alfred. 'Heideggers Lebens- und Denkweg 1909–1919', in Denker, Alfred, Hans-Helmuth Gander and Holger Zaborowski (eds.), *Heidegger und die Anfänge seines Denkens* (Freiburg: Karl Alber Verlag, 2004), pp. 97–122.

Denker, Alfred and Elsbeth Büchin. *Martin Heidegger und seine Heimat* (Stuttgart: Klett-Cotta, 2005).

Dierker, Wolfgang. *Himmlers Glaubenskrieger: Der Sicherheitsdienst der SS und seine Religionspolitik 1933–1941* (Paderborn: Schöningh, 2002).

Dillard, Peter S. *Heidegger and Philosophical Atheology: A Neo-scholastic Critique* (London: Continuum, 2009).

Dunker, Axel. *'Den Pessimismus organisieren': Eschatologische Kategorien in der Literatur zum Dritten Reich* (Bielefeld: Aisthesis, 1994).

Ebbinghaus, Julius. 'Julius Ebbinghaus', in Ludwig Pongratz (ed.), *Philosophie in Selbstdarstellungen*, vol. 3 (Hamburg: Felix Meiner, 1977).

Elberfeld, Rolf. 'Heidegger und das ostasiatische Denken: Annäherungen zwischen fremden Welten', in Dieter Thomä (ed.), *Heidegger Handbuch* (Stuttgart: J. B. Metzler, 2003), pp. 469–74.

Emad, Parvis. *On the Way to Heidegger's Contributions to Philosophy* (Madison, WI: University of Wisconsin Press, 2007).

Ennen, Edith. 'Ernst Moritz Arndt: 1769–1860', in *Bonner Gelehrte: Beiträge zur Geschichte der Wissenschaften in Bonn* (Bonn: H. Bouvrier & Co Verlag, 1968), pp. 9–35.

Farías, Víctor. *Heidegger and Nazism* (Philadelphia: Temple University Press, 1989 [1987]).

Faye, Emmanuel. *Heidegger: l'introduction du nazisme dans la philosophie* (Paris: Albin Michel, 2005).

Feick, Hildegard and Susanne Ziegler (eds), *Index zu Heideggers Sein und Zeit* (Tübingen: Max Niemeyer Verlag, 4th edn, 1991).

Fleteren, Frederick van. *Martin Heidegger's Interpretations of Saint Augustine* (Lewiston: Edwin Mellen Press, 2005).

Fritsche, Johannes. *Historical Destiny and National Socialism in Heidegger's Being and Time* (Berkeley: University of California Press, 1999).

Garstka, Christoph. *Arthur Moeller van den Bruck und die erste deutsche Gesamtausgabe der Werke Dostojewskijs im Piper-Verlag 1906–1919* (Frankfurt: Peter Lang, 1998).

Glendinning, Simon. *On Being With Others: Heidegger–Wittgenstein–Derrida*. (London: Routledge, 1998).

Greisch, Jean. *Herméneutique et Grammatologie* (Paris: Éditions du CNRS, 1977).

—. *Hermeneutik und Metaphysik: Eine Problemgeschichte* (Munich: Wilhelm Fink, 1993).

—. 'The Eschatology of Being and the God of Time in Heidegger', *International Journal of Philosophical Studies* 4, 1 (1996), pp. 17–43.

Grimm, Gunter, Werner Faulstich und Peter Kuon (eds.), *Apokalypse: Weltuntergangsvisionen in der Literatur des 20. Jahrhunderts* (Frankfurt am Main: Suhrkamp, 1986).

Grimm, Jacob and Wilhelm. *Deutsches Wörterbuch*.(33 vols; Leipzig: S. Hirzel, 1854–1971).

Hartig, Willfred. *Die Lehre des Budda und Heidegger* (Constance: University of Constance Research Reports, 1997).

Haugeland, John. 'Truth and Finitude: Heidegger's Transcendental Existentialism', in Mark Wrathall and Jeff Malpas (eds.), *Heidegger, Authenticity, and Modernity: Essays in Honor of Hubert L. Dreyfus* (Cambridge, MA: MIT Press, 2000), pp. 43–77.

Hayens, K. C. 'Gerhard Schumann: Poet of the Third Reich', *German Life and Letters* 2, 1 (1937), pp. 62–70.

Hemming, Laurence Paul (ed.), *Radical Orthodoxy? – A Catholic Enquiry* (Farnborough: Ashgate, 2000).

Hemming, Laurence Paul. *Heidegger's Atheism: The Refusal of a Theological Voice* (Notre Dame, IN: University of Notre Dame Press, 2002).

—. 'Are We Still in Time to Know God? Apocalyptic, Sempiternity, and the Purposes of Experience', in L. Boeve, Y. de Maeseneer, and S. van den Bossche (eds.), *Religious Experience and Contemporary Theological Epistemology* (Leuven: Leuven University Press, 2003), pp. 159–76.

Herbermann, C. G., gen. (ed.), *The Catholic Encyclopedia* (15 vols; New York: Robert Appleton, 1907–14).

Herrmann, Friedrich-Wilhelm von. 'Gottsuche und Selbstauslegung. Das 10. Buch der Confessiones des heiligen Augustinus im Horizont von Heideggers hermeneutischer Phänomenologie des faktischen Lebens', *Studia Phænomenologica* 1, 3–4 (2001), pp. 201–20.

Herrmann, Friedrich-Wilhelm von and Norbert Fischer (eds.), *Heidegger und die christliche Tradition* (Hamburg: Felix Meiner, 2007).

—. *Die Gottesfrage im Denken Martin Heideggers* (Hamburg: Felix Meiner, 2011).

Hildebrandt, Kurt. *Hölderlin, Philosophie und Dichtung* (Berlin: W. Kohlhammer, 1939).

Hoffmeister, Donna. 'Hölderlin-Biography, 1924–1982: Transformations of a Literary Life', *Seminar* 21, 3 (1983), pp. 207–31.

Hölscher, Lucian. *Weltgericht oder Revolution: protestantische und sozialistische Zukunftsvorstellungen im deutschen Kaiserreich* (Stuttgart: Klett-Cotta, 1989).

Horner, Robyn. *Jean-Luc Marion: A Theo-Logical Introduction* (London: Ashgate, 2005).

Irlenborn, Bernd. *Der Ingrimm des Aufruhrs: Heidegger und das Problem des Bösen* (Vienna: Passagen Verlag, 2000).

Janicaud, Dominique. *La Phénoménologie éclatée* (Paris: Éditions de l'Eclat, 1998).

—. *Heidegger en France* (2 vols; Paris: A. Michel, 2001).

— (ed.), *Le Tournant théologique de la phénoménologie française* (Combas: Éditions de l'Éclat, 1991).
ET: *Phenomenology and the Theological Turn: The French Debate* (New York: Fordham University Press, 2001).

Jonkers, Peter and Ruud Welten (eds.), *God in France: Eight Contemporary French Thinkers on God* (Leuven: Peeters, 2005).

Kerr, Fergus. *Immortal Longings: Versions of Transcending Humanity* (London: SPCK, 1997).

Kilby, Karen. *Karl Rahner: Theology and Philosophy* (London: Routledge, 2004).

Kisiel, Theodore. *The Genesis of Heidegger'sBeing and Time* (Berkeley: University of California Press, 1995).

—. 'Why Students of Heidegger Will Have to Read Emil Lask', in Alfred Denker and Marion Heinz (eds.), *Heidegger's Way of Thought: Critical and Interpretative Signposts* (London: Continuum, 2nd edn, 2002), pp. 101–36.

Kisiel, Theodore and John van Buren (eds.), *Reading Heidegger from the Start: Essays in His Earliest Thought* (Albany: State University of New York Press, 1994).

Kommerell, Max. *Der Dichter als Führer in der Deutschen Klassik: Klopstock, Herder, Goethe, Schiller, Jean Paul, Hölderlin* (Berlin: Georg Bondi, 1928).

Kralik, Richard von. *Die katholische Literaturbewegung der Gegenwart: Ein Beitrag zu ihrer Geschichte* (Regensburg: Habbel, 1909).

—. *Ein Jahr katholischer Literaturbewegung* (Regensburg: Habbel, 1910).

Kümmel, W. G. *Das Neue Testament: Geschichte der Erforschung seiner Probleme* (Freiburg: Karl Alber Verlag, 1958).
ET: *The New Testament: The History of the Investigation of its Problems*, trans. S. McClean Gilmour and Howard Clark Kee; London: SCM Press, 1973).

Kurz, Gerhard. 'Braune Apokalypse', in Jürgen Brokoff and Joachim Jacob (eds.), *Apokalypse und Erinnerung in der deutsch-jüdischen Kultur des frühen 20. Jahrhunderts* (Göttingen: Vandenhoeck & Ruprecht, 2002), pp. 131–46.

Löffler, Klemens. 'Periodical Literature (Germany)', trans. Douglas J.
    Potter, in Charles George Herbermann (eds.), *Catholic Encyclopedia*,
    vol. 11 (New York: Robert Appleton, 1911), pp. 677–80.
MacIntyre, Alasdair. *Edith Stein: A Philosophical Prologue* (London:
    Continuum, 2006).
Macquarrie, John. *An Existentialist Theology: A Comparison of
    Heidegger and Bultmann* (London: SCM Press, 1965).
—. *Heidegger and Christianity* (London: SCM Press, 1994).
McCormack, Bruce. *Karl Barth's Critically Realistic Dialectical Theology:
    Its Genesis and Development, 1909–1936* (Oxford: Oxford University
    Press, 1997).
McGrath, S. J. 'The Facticity of Being God-Forsaken: The Young
    Heidegger and Luther's Theology of the Cross', *American Catholic
    Philosophical Quarterly* 79, 2 (2005), pp. 273–90.
—. *The Early Heidegger & Medieval Philosophy: Phenomenology for
    the Godforsaken* (Washington: Catholic University of America Press,
    2006).
—. *Heidegger: A (Very) Critical Introduction* (Grand Rapids: Eerdmans,
    2008).
McGrath, S. J. and Andrzej Wiercinski (eds.), *A Companion to
    Heidegger's Phenomenology of Religious Life* (Amsterdam: Rodopi,
    2010).
Manoussakis, J. P. and Neal DeRoo (eds.), *Phenomenology &
    Eschatology: Not Yet in the Now* (Aldershot: Ashgate, 2009).
Martin, Bernd (ed.), *Martin Heidegger und das 'Dritte Reich': Ein
    Kompendium* (Darmstadt: Wissenschaftliche Buchgesellschaft, 1989).
Mehta, Jarava Lal. *The Philosophy of Martin Heidegger* (New York:
    Harper & Row, 1971).
Meuffels, Otmar and Rainer Dvorak (eds.), *Wahrheit Gottes – Freiheit
    des Denkens: Herman Schell als Impulsgeber für Theologie und Kirche*
    (Würzburg: Schöningh, 2001).
Meyer, Hans. *Martin Heidegger und Thomas von Aquin* (Munich:
    Schöningh, 1964).
Milbank, John. *The Word Made Strange* (Oxford: Blackwell, 1997).
Milbank, John and Catherine Pickstock. *Truth in Aquinas* (London:
    Routledge, 2001).
Morgan, Ben. 'Heidegger and the Mysticism of Everyday Life', in George
    Pattison (ed.), *Heidegger and Religion 1: Heidegger and the Theology
    of Crisis* (Oxford: Oxford Research Archive, 2008), pp. 10–24.
Mulhall, Stephen. *Faith and Reason* (London: Duckworth, 1994).
—. *Philosophical Myths of the Fall* (Princeton: Princeton University Press,
    2005).
—. *Heidegger and Being and Time* (London: Routledge, 2nd edn, 2005).

Neske, Günther (ed.), *Erinnerung an Martin Heidegger* (Pfullingen: Neske, 1977).

Neske, Günther and Emil Kettering (eds.), *Antwort: Martin Heidegger im Gespräch* (Pfullingen: Neske, 1988).
ET: *Martin Heidegger and National Socialism* (New York: Paragon House, 1990).

Neumaier, Anna. *Apokalyptik als Redeform des Nationalsozialismus: eine Diskursanalyse früher Reden Hitlers* (Bremen: Institut für Kulturwissenschaftliche Deutschlandstudien. 2010).

Noller, Gerhard (ed.), *Heidegger und die Theologie: Beginn und Fortgang der Diskussion* (Munich: Chr. Kaiser, 1967).

Ochwadt, Curd and Erwin Tecklenborg (eds.), *Das Maß des Verborgenen: Heinrich Ochsner zum Gedächtnis* (Hannover: Charis-Verlag, 1981).

O'Meara, Thomas. 'Tillich and Heidegger: A Structural Relationship', *Harvard Theological Review* 61, 2 (April 1968), pp. 249–61.

—. 'Heidegger and His Origins: Theological Perspectives', *Theological Studies* 47 (1986), pp. 205–26.

Ott, Hugo. *Martin Heidegger: Unterwegs zu seiner Biographie* (Frankfurt: Campus, 1988).
ET: *Martin Heidegger: A Political Life* (trans. Allan Blunden; London: HarperCollins, 1993).

—. 'Martin Heidegger's Catholic Origins', *American Catholic Philosophical Quarterly* 69, 2 (Spring 1995), pp. 137–56.

Paletschek, Sylvia. 'Entwicklungslinien aus der Perspektive der Fakultätssitzungen', in Wirbelauer, Eckhard (ed.), *Die Freiburger Philosophische Fakultät 1920–1960: Mitglieder, Strukturen, Vernetzungen* (Freiburg: Karl Alber, 2006), pp. 58–107.

Parkes, Graham (ed.), *Heidegger and Asian Thought* (Honolulu: University of Hawaii Press, 1987).

Pattison, George. *Agnosis: Theology in the Void* (Basingstoke: Macmillan, 1996).

—. *Anxious Angels: A Retrospective View of Religious Existentialism* (Basingstoke: Macmillan, 1999).

—. *The Later Heidegger* (London: Routledge, 2000).

Paulo, Craig J. N. de (ed.), *The Influence of Augustine on Heidegger: The Emergence of an Augustinian Phenomenology* (Lewiston: Edwin Mellen Press, 2006).

Pettigrew, David and François Raffoul (eds.), *French Interpretations of Heidegger* (New York: SUNY Press, 2008).

Pfeiffer, Arnold. *Franz Overbecks Kritik des Christentums* (Göttingen: Vandenhoeck & Ruprecht, 1975).

Philipse, Herman. *Heidegger's Philosophy of Being: A Critical Interpretation* (Princeton: Princeton University Press, 1998).

Piepmeier, Rainer. 'Erziehung des Menschengeschlechts', in Joachim Ritter and Karlfried Gründer (eds.), *Historisches Wörterbuch der Philosophie*, vol. 2 (Basel: Schwabe, 2005), pp. 735–9.

Pöggeler, Otto. 'Heideggers Begegnung mit Hölderlin', *Man and World* 10, 1 (1977), pp. 13–61.

—. 'Heidegger und Bultmann: Philosophie und Theologie', in Markus Happel (ed.), *Heidegger–neu gelesen* (Würzburg: Königshausen & Neumann, 1997), pp. 41–53.

—. 'Heideggers Luther-Lektüre im Freiburger Theologenkonvikt', in Denker, Alfred, Hans-Helmuth Gander and Holger Zaborowski (eds.), *Heidegger und die Anfänge seines Denkens* (Freiburg: Karl Alber Verlag, 2004), pp. 185–96.

—. *Philosophie und hermeneutische Theologie: Heidegger, Bultmann und die Folgen* (Paderborn: Wilhelm Fink, 2009).

Redles, David. *Hitler's Millennial Reich* (New York: New York University Press, 2005).

Reynolds, Stephen. 'Heidegger's *Introduction to the Phenomenology of Religion*'. [Unpublished DPhil dissertation. University of Oxford, 2008.]

Richardson, William J. *Heidegger: Through Phenomenology to Thought* (New York: Fordham University Press, 1963).

—. 'Heidegger and Theology', *Theological Studies* 26, 1 (1965), pp. 86–100.

Richter, Oskar. *Die Lieblingsvorstellungen der Dichter des deutschen Befreiungskrieges* (Leipzig: Seele, 1909).

Robinson, James and John Cobb (eds.), *The Later Heidegger and Theology* (New York: Harper & Row, 1963).

Safranski, Rüdiger. *Ein Meister aus Deutschland: Heidegger und seine Zeit* (Frankfurt am Main: Fischer Verlag, 2001).
ET: *Martin Heidegger: Between Good and Evil* (trans. Ewald Osers; Cambridge, MA: Harvard University Press, 1998).

Schaber, Johannes. 'Te lucis ante terminum: Martin Heidegger und das benediktinische Mönchtum', in Sánchez de Murillo (ed.), *Edith Stein Jahrbuch 8: Das Mönchtum* (Würzburg: Echter Verlag, 2002), pp. 281–94.

—. 'Martin Heideggers "Herkunft" im Spiegel der Theologie- und Kirchengeschichte des 19. und beginnenden 20. Jahrhunderts', in Denker, Alfred, Hans-Helmuth Gander and Holger Zaborowski (eds.), *Heidegger und die Anfänge seines Denkens* (Freiburg: Karl Alber Verlag, 2004), pp. 159–84.

—. 'Der Theologiestudent Martin Heidegger und sein Dogmatikprofessor Carl Braig', *Freiburger Diözesanarchiv* 125 (2005), pp. 332–47.

Schaeffler, Richard. *Frömmigkeit des Denkens?: Martin Heidegger und die katholische Theologie* (Darmstadt: Wissenschaftliche Buchgesellschaft, 1978).

Schindler, Hans. *Barth und Overbeck* (Gotha: Leopold Klotz Verlag, 1936).

Scholder, Klaus and Gerhard Besier. *Die Kirchen und das Dritte Reich* (3 vols; Berlin: Propyläen, 1985 and 2001).

Schreiner, Klaus. 'Messianism in the Political Culture of the Weimar Republic', in Peter Schäfer and Mark Cohen (eds.), *Towards the Millennium* (Leiden: Brill, 1998), pp. 311–62.

Schrift, Alan. *Twentieth-Century French Philosophy: Key Themes and Thinkers* (Oxford: Blackwell, 2005).

Schrijvers, Joeri. 'On Doing Theology "after" Onto-Theology: Notes on a French Debate', *New Blackfriars* 87, 1009 (2006), pp. 302–14.

—. *Ontotheological Turnings?: The Decentering of the Modern Subject in Recent French Phenomenology* (New York: SUNY, 2011).

—. *An Introduction to Jean-Yves Lacoste* (London: Ashgate, 2012).

Sheehan, Thomas. *Karl Rahner: The Philosophical Foundations* (Athens, OH: Ohio University Press, 1987).

—. 'Heidegger's *Lehrjahre*', in John Sallis et al. (eds.), *The Collegium Phaenomenologicum* (Dordrecht: Kluwer, 1988), pp. 77–137.

—. 'Husserl and Heidegger: The Making and Unmaking of a Relationship', in *Edmund Husserl: Psychological and Transcendental Phenomenology and the Confrontation with Heidegger (1927–1931)* (ed. and trans. Thomas Sheehan and R. E. Palmer; The Hague: Kluwer Academic Publishers, 1997), pp. 1–40.

Simpson, John and Edmund Weiner (eds.), *The Oxford English Dictionary* (Oxford: Oxford University Press, 2nd edn, 1989).

Stanley, Timothy. *Protestant Metaphysics after Karl Barth and Martin Heidegger* (London: SCM Press, 2010).

Steigmann-Gall, Richard. *The Holy Reich: Nazi Conceptions of Christianity, 1919–1945* (Cambridge: Cambridge University Press, 2003).

Thurnher, Rainer. 'Heideggers Distanzierung von der metaphysisch geprägten Theologie und Gottesvorstellung', in Norbert Fischer and Friedrich-Wilhelm von Herrmann (eds.), *Die Gottesfrage im Denken Martin Heideggers* (Hamburg: Felix Meiner, 2011), pp. 175–93.

Unger, Richard. *Friedrich Hölderlin* (Boston: Twayne, 1984).

Verweyen, Hansjürgen. 'Wie wird ein Existential übernatürlich?: Zu einem Grundproblem der Anthropologie Karl Rahners', *Trier theologische Zeitschrift* 95 (1986), pp. 115–31.

Vetter, Helmuth. 'Hermeneutische Phänomenologie und Dialektische Theologie: Heidegger und Bultmann', in Großmann, Andreas and Christoph Jamme (eds.), *Metaphysik der praktischen Welt: Perspektiven im Anschluß an Hegel und Heidegger* (Amsterdam: Atlanta, 2000), pp. 268–86.

Vigliotti, Robert. 'The Young Heidegger's Ambitions for the Chair of Catholic Philosophy and Hugo Ott's Charge of Opportunism', *Studia Phænomenologica* 1, 3–4 (2001), pp. 323–50.

Voegelin, Eric. *Die politischen Religionen*, ed. Peter J. Opitz (Munich: Fink, 1993 [1938]).

Vonberg, Markus. 'Der Meßkircher Zeitungskrieg: "Oberbadischer Grenzbote" und "Heuberger Volksblatt" im liberal-ultramontanen Streit', in Edwin Ernst Weber (ed.), *Renitenz und Genie: Meßkirch und der badische Seekreis zwischen 1848/49 und dem Kulturkampf* (Konstanz: Gesellschaft Oberschwaben, 2003), pp. 153–87.

Vondung, Klaus. *Die Apokalypse in Deutschland* (München: Deutscher Taschenbuch-Verlag, 1988).

ET: *The Apocalypse in Germany* (Columbia, MO: University of Missouri Press, 2000).

—. 'Die Apokalypse des Nationalsozialismus', in Michael Ley and Julius H. Schoeps (eds.), *Der Nationalsozialismus als politische Religion* (Bodenheim b. Mainz: Philo Verlagsgesellschaft, 1997), pp. 33–52.

—. 'National Socialism as a Political Religion: Potentials and Limits of an Analytical Concept', *Totalitarian Movements and Political Religions* 6, 1 (2005), pp. 87–95.

Vorgrimler, Herbert. *Understanding Karl Rahner: An Introduction to his Life and Thought* (London: SCM Press, 1986).

Walther, Gerda. *Zum anderen Ufer: Vom Marxismus und Atheismus zum Christentum* (Remagen: Der Leuchter/Otto Reichl Verlag, 1960).

Wehrli, Rudolf. *Alter und Tod des Christentums bei Franz Overbeck* (Zürich: Theologischer Verlag, 1977).

Weiß, Otto. *Der Modernismus in Deutschland: Ein Beitrag zur Theologiegeschichte* (Regensburg: Pustet, 2001).

White, Carol. *Time and Death: Heidegger's Analysis of Finitude* (London: Ashgate, 2005).

Wirbelauer, Eckhard (ed.), *Die Freiburger Philosophische Fakultät 1920–1960* (Freiburg: Karl Alber, 2007).

Wisser, Richard (ed.), *Martin Heidegger in Gespräch* (Freiburg: Alber, 1970).

Wolf, Hubert (ed.), *Antimodernismus und Modernismus in der katholischen Kirche: Beiträge zum theologiegeschichtlichen Vorfeld des II. Vatikanums* (Paderborn: Schöningh, 1998).

Wolfe, Judith. 'Acknowledging a Hidden God: A Theological Critique of Stanley Cavell on Scepticism', *Heythrop Journal* 48, 3 (2007), pp. 384–405.

—. 'Messianism', in Nick Adams, George Pattison and Graham Ward (eds.), *Oxford Handbook of Theology and Modern European Thought* (Oxford: Oxford University Press, 2013), pp. 301–23.

—. *Heidegger's Eschatology: Theological Horizons in Martin Heidegger's Early Thought* (Oxford: Oxford University Press, 2013).

Wright, Kathleen. 'Heidegger and the Authorization of Hölderlin's Poetry', in Harries, Karsten and Christoph Jamme (eds.), *Martin

Heidegger: Politics, Art, Technology (New York: Holmes and Meier, 1994), pp. 164–74.

Zaborowski, Holger. '"Herkunft aber bleibt stets Zukunft." Anmerkungen zur religiösen und theologischen Dimension des Denkweges Martin Heideggers bis 1919', in Denker, Alfred, Hans-Helmuth Gander and Holger Zaborowski (eds.), *Heidegger und die Anfänge seines Denkens* (Freiburg: Karl Alber Verlag, 2004), pp. 123–58.

—. 'Die "ungeheure Schwierigkeit des christlichen Lebens" und die "Todfeindschaft"zwischen Philosophie und Glauben – Anmerkungen zu Martin Heideggers Denkweg von 1919 bis 1928', in Nissing, Hanns-Georg (ed.), *Vernunft und Glaube: Perspektiven gegenwärtiger Philosophie* (Munich: Institut zur Förderung der Glaubenslehre, 2008), pp. 165–83.

—. *Eine Frage von Irre und Schuld?: Martin Heidegger und der Nationalsozialismus* (Frankfurt: Fischer Verlag, 2010).

Zaborowski, Holger and Stephan Loos (eds.), *Leben, Tod und Entscheidung: Studien zur Geistesgeschichte der Weimarer Republik* (Berlin: Duncker und Humblot, 2003).

Zupko, Jack. 'Thomas of Erfurt', in Edward N. Zalta (ed.), *The Stanford Encyclopedia of Philosophy*. Autumn 2008 edition. <http://plato.stanford.edu/archives/fall2008/entries/erfurt/> .

INDEX